KT-151-541

Stephen Chambers

1987

SPORT AND RECREATION
IN ANCIENT GREECE

SPORT AND RECREATION IN ANCIENT GREECE

A Sourcebook with Translations

WALDO E. SWEET

Foreword by Erich Segal

New York   Oxford
OXFORD UNIVERSITY PRESS
1987

Oxford University Press

Oxford   New York   Toronto
Delhi   Bombay   Calcutta   Madras   Karachi
Petaling Jaya   Singapore   Hong Kong   Tokyo
Nairobi   Dar es Salaam   Cape Town
Melbourne   Auckland

and associated companies in
Beirut   Berlin   Ibadan   Nicosia

Copyright © 1987 by Oxford University Press, Inc.

Published by Oxford University Press, Inc.,
200 Madison Avenue, New York, New York 10016

Oxford is a registered trademark of Oxford University Press

All rights reserved. No part of this publication may be reproduced,
stored in a retrieval system, or transmitted, in any form or by any means,
electronic, mechanical, photocopying, recording, or otherwise,
without the prior permission of Oxford University Press.

Library of Congress Cataloging-in-Publication Data
Sweet, Waldo E.
Sport and recreation in ancient Greece.
Bibliography: p.
Includes index.
1. Games, Greek—History—Sources.
2. Sports—Greece—History—Sources. 3. Recreation—
Greece—History—Sources. 4. Women in sports—
Greece—History—Sources. I. Title.
GV21.S94   1987   796'.0938   86-18209
ISBN 0-19-504126-7
ISBN 0-19-504127-5 (pbk.)

2 4 6 8 9 7 5 3 1

Printed in the United States of America
on acid-free paper

Foreword
by Erich Segal

I first discovered the true character of ancient Greece in a modern helicopter.

In 1972, I was flying from Athens to cover the lighting of the sacred flame at Olympia for a U.S. television network. Not far from Corinth we passed over the ruins of the city of Sicyon. And viewing them from a height of 500 feet gave me a sudden, unexpected insight.

All that remained of this kingdom, whose heyday had been in the sixth century BC, were the clear outlines of its theater and its stadium, the gathering places for the Greeks' two greatest passions: drama and sport. And from my lofty perspective the two structures looked like contiguous circles, forming a symmetry that was also a symbol of the entire Greek mentality. For, both consciously and unconsciously, they equated these two seemingly disparate activities, which together formed a unity that epitomized Hellenic culture.

But if they were equally important to the Greeks, why do scholars always focus so intensely on the theater and all but ignore the stadium? A facile answer might be that there is so little extant athletic material compared to our abundance of dramatic texts. But this volume is a splendid rejoinder to that argument. It has also been claimed—even by noted sports historians—that for the Greeks athletics were "not very important in the great sum of things."[1] This is quite wrong. If anything, sport was even more vital to them than the theater. The latter was restricted to a few festival days each year; the former was an integral part of their daily lives.

Of course, to allude to what the Greeks practiced in the stadium and the arena as "sport" is itself misleading. Our English word carries the connotation of levity. They took it far more seriously. Their word for competition is *agon,* the source of the English "agony." And *agon* could refer to encounters ranging from duels to debates. To the ancient Hellenes, life was a perpetual contest. As the philosopher Heraclitus put it, "Strife is the father of everything."

[1]H.A. Harris, *Greek Athletes and Athletics* (Bloomington and London 1966), p 187

Indeed, to some historians—notably the Swiss Jakob Burckhardt (1818–1897)—this "agonal drive" was the key to understanding an entire mentality. In his unequivocal words, "All Greek life was animated by this principle." His view still has strong support even in our own day.[2]

Stories about athletes permeate Greek mythology: Pelops, Herakles, Atalanta (best known for her running, but a champion at other sports as well), and dozens more. There is even a legend told by Pausanias (late second century AD) that Odysseus had to outsprint his rivals to win Penelope's hand.

The Greeks literally worshiped their real athletes. Mothers would take their sick children to touch the statue of an Olympic victor in the belief that his "magic" would cure them. While today's sports heroes may be able to gain a fortune, in antiquity they could even win a kingdom. Herodotus reports a contest held in Sicyon in which first prize was the king's daughter and the succession to his throne.[3]

We find further evidence of the gravity with which the Greeks regarded their "games" in the etymology of our words "athlete" and "athletics." They stem from the Greek *athlos*, which could mean a contest taking place in a stadium or on a battlefield. The poet Pindar uses *athlos* to describe both the Olympic Games and the labors of Herakles.

An awareness of how deeply sports were ingrained in the Greeks' mentality enables us to understand other facets of their culture. Their drama, for example, is replete with athletic images, both literal and metaphorical. Aeschylus' *Oresteia* is dominated by references to the *pankration*.[4] Euripides uses the imagery of sport throughout his plays, but the dramatic impact is perhaps most important in *Hippolytus*. At a climactic moment, Theseus accuses Hippolytus of trying to seduce Phaedra. The young man vehemently denies it, disclaiming interest in all women. This is not, as some interpreters have argued, because he is emotionally unstable, but because, as he explicitly says, he is totally preoccupied with a single lofty goal in life: "My only desire is to triumph in the Greek games *(agonas)*." Euripides' audience would have found this a very persuasive defense.

If we appreciate how important such victories were to the Greeks, we can see that *Hippolytus* presents a true tragic conflict in Hegel's famous definition: "The supreme collision of two opposing forces of equal strength." In this case, it is a clash between Phaedra—and Olympia.

The adjective *athlios* (literally, "like an athlete") is found often in Greek tragedy and well illustrates the dual reverberation we have been discussing. *Oedipus Rex* provides a ready example. To begin with, the king is described as *wrestling* for the salvation of Thebes. Then, as he begins to piece together his identity, he considers the possible implications of his having killed King Laius: "What man

[2] See, for example, Victor Ehrenberg, *Ost und West*. For a discussion of differing philosophies of sport in other cultures, see Erich Segal, " 'To Win or Die': A Taxonomy of Sporting Attitudes," *Journal of Sport History* 11, no 2 (Summer 1984), pp 25–31.

[3] Herodotus VI, 126 ff. Of further interest is the fact that the athletic contests were followed in the evening by contests in music and "wit."

[4] See A. Lebeck, *The Oresteia: A Study in Language and Structure* (Cambridge, Mass. 1971). Also, Michael Poliakoff, *Studies in the Terminology of the Greek Combat Sports* (Königstein 1982).

would be more athletic *(athlioteros)* than I?'' When Oedipus at last learns the awful truth of his identity, the chorus comments that he who was once the greatest of all archers is now the ''most athletic'' man on earth.

Clearly, in these contexts, *athlios* implies a kind of existential struggle against fate on the part of the hero—or heroine—of tragedy. Indeed, the final line of *Oedipus Rex* warns us that we should judge no man to be happy ''till he cross the finish line of life.''

In this light it is not surprising that early Christian writers use the term ''athlete'' as a synonym for ''martyr.'' The Apostle Paul's language is alive with enthusiasm for sport. This can be clearly seen in an overly literal version of his famous ''I have fought the good fight'' statement in Corinthians II. ''I have *agonized* the *agon* well, I have completed the run. I have kept the faith. What finally awaits me is the victor's wreath for righteousness.'' One scholar has actually used this passage to argue that Paul himself was a long-distance runner. In any case, this language must have appealed to his audience. For there was surely a stadium in every city Paul visited.

The Greeks, of course, did not ''invent'' sports, any more than the Romans destroyed them. They have existed in one form or another since the dawn of time. The Greeks are distinguished, however, for their fervent attitude toward *competition*. In fact, despite pious platitudes, ''good losers'' are no more admired today than they were in Pindar's time. (One of his poems describes the homecoming of an unvictorious athlete: ''Even his mother will not smile on him.'') What American coach does not preach the ''Vince Lombardi philosophy?'' The late mentor of the Green Bay Packers has been immortalized for his words: ''Winning isn't everything—it's the *only* thing.'' The crowds at ancient Olympia would have roared approval.

Sport is the most immutable and modern aspect of our heritage from the Greeks and, therefore, the stadium door is perhaps the most accessible means of entering the ancient world. Baron de Coubertin, father of the modern Olympic movement, knew this when he remarked in a lecture that, although contemporary students might grow weary of reading about the exploits of Alexander and Caesar, their interest in the classics would always be aroused by ''the dust of the stadium.''

We still smell that dust. And hear the trumpets. And feel the glory.

Preface

The words "sport" and "recreation" cover the content of this book, although it is not always possible to distinguish between the two. In a recent survey, Kyle defines them thus:[1]

> "Sport" is a non-ancient and vague term at best. "Athletics" usually suggests serious competition, training, prizes, and the goal of victory. "Physical education" implies instruction and exercise of the body. "Recreation" or "leisure" applies to non-work, relaxation and rejuvenation with pleasure or fun as goal. "Sport" is used as a general rubric for all these areas as well as hunting, dance, and even board games. Herein "sport" generally will refer to public, physical activities, especially those with competitive elements, pursued for victory, pleasure, or the demonstration of excellence.

In this book we will follow Kyle's definitions, stressing that sport is competitive and recreation is not.

The subtitle of this book might well have been "How to Evaluate the Evidence." Many students go to college without having learned a healthy scepticism for the "facts." The forthcoming chapters will demonstrate the often contradictory aspects of evidence on which "facts" are established. Another objective of this book is to furnish more understanding of an amazing people, the ancient Greeks. Perhaps our most important aim, however, is to increase students' ability to evaluate different points of view, both in the study of ancient Greek sport and recreation and in their daily lives.

A word about the organization of this book: The chapters do not need to be read seriatim. However, most people will want to begin with the first two chapters. Chapters 3–28 cover a variety of topics and may be read in any order. Chapters 29–33 present sizable excerpts from ancient authors.

The books and articles listed at the end of each chapter under Further Readings have been carefully selected for their interest and readability. Students who would like an overview of what they will study should read Kyle's article referred to

[1] Don Kyle, "Directions in Ancient Sport History," *Journal of Sport History* 10, no 1 (1983).

above. Those who wish to explore some field further should use Thomas F. Scanlon's *Greek and Roman Athletics: A Bibliography,* Nigel B. Crowther's "Studies in Greek Athletics, Parts I and II," and *West Coast Newsletter of Ancient Athletics* (published quarterly by Dr. Brian Legakis, 219 Poplar St., Aptos CA 95003).

Deciding how to spell Greek names in English is an almost impossible task. We have used the spelling with which we feel comfortable; in dubious cases we have often followed the encyclopedia *Der Kleine Pauly.* In general, unusual names like those of the Olympic victors are given their Greek form. Common names are usually given their English form—for example, Corinth not Korinthos. Roman numerals are given with BC or AD to indicate the century. Thus, V BC is to be read "fifth century BC."

Ann Arbor   W.E.S.

Acknowledgments

Particular thanks are due to the Department of Classical Studies and the College of Literature, Science, and the Arts at The University of Michigan for support and encouragement while I was developing the teaching materials which ultimately became this book.

I am grateful especially to Professor John H. D'Arms, department chairman, for assistance in inaugurating this undergraduate course, and to subsequent chairmen for continuing support.

I am indebted to those colleagues who used the materials in student discussion groups: Professor John H. Humphrey, and teaching assistants Vincent P. McCarren, Timothy J. McNiven, T. Keith Dix, Martin Gassler, Rebecca Miller, Nicholas Stavrinides, Mark J. Petrini, and Michael Poliakoff.

In the early stages of writing this book, I was also indebted to Petrini and Poliakoff for many hours of editorial assistance.

In the difficult field of Greek music, Professor Orsamus M. Pearl gave valuable guidance.

In searching for answers to several questions about nudity in ancient athletics, I am indebted to Professors Steven J. Galetti and Phyllis M. Ocker of our School of Education for supervising a questionnaire, to Dr. Robert E. Anderson, senior physician in our Department of Athletics, for directing me to medical specialists in physiology, and to John Fredericks and Stuart Krebs of the Forest Hills Club, Saranac, Michigan, for insight into the experience of physical activity without clothing.

Over the ten years of teaching the course, I benefited immeasurably from talking with scholars on various aspects of ancient athletics, and I would like to mention a few: Harry W. Pleket and Willem den Boer at the University of Leiden; David C. Young at the University of California at Santa Barbara; Eleanor G. Huzar at Michigan State University; Erich Segal at Yale University; Daniel P. Harmon, Jack W. Berryman, and Steven H. Hardy at the University of Washington.

Special thanks are due to Steve Adams, Latin student and Big 10 champion in discus and shot put, whose keen interest in ancient athletics spurred me into completing plans for the course.

During several research trips abroad, I was grateful for the help and hospitality at the American School of Classical Studies at Athens, the American Academy in Rome, and the Joint Library of the Hellenic and Roman Societies in London.

I would also like to acknowledge the many courtesies of curators at the various art museums, and to thank them and the Trustees of the British Museum for permission to reproduce their photographs.

Above and beyond all those mentioned comes the one person without whom this book would never have been written, my loving and beloved wife Betty.

Contents

Abbreviations

The following abbreviations are used for sources that are frequently cited in the text and in the lists of Further Readings following each chapter. References to IAG, IG, and Syll³ are included for the use of the teacher who wishes to examine the Greek original.

CIG	*Corpus Inscriptionum Graecarum*
Drees	L. Drees, *Olympia: Gods, Artists, and Athletes*
Finley-Pleket	M.I. Finley and H.W. Pleket, *The Olympic Games: The First Thousand Years*
Gardiner AAW	E.N. Gardiner, *Athletes of the Ancient World*
Gardiner GASF	E.N. Gardiner, *Greek Athletic Sports and Festivals.*
Harper's	*Harper's Dictionary of Classical Literature and Antiquities.*
Harris GAA	H.A. Harris, *Greek Athletes and Athletics*
Harris SpGR	H.A. Harris, *Sport in Greece and Rome*
IAG	*Iscrizioni Agonistiche Greche*, Luigi Moretti
IG	*Inscriptiones Graecae*
Miller *Arete*	Stephen G. Miller, *Arete*
OCD	*Oxford Classical Dictionary*
Robinson	R.S. Robinson, *Sources for the History of Greek Athletics*
Syll³	*Sylloge Inscriptionum Graecarum*, W. Dittenberger
Whibley	L. Whibley, editor, *A Companion to Greek Studies*
Yalouris	Nicolaos Yalouris, editor, *The Eternal Olympics*

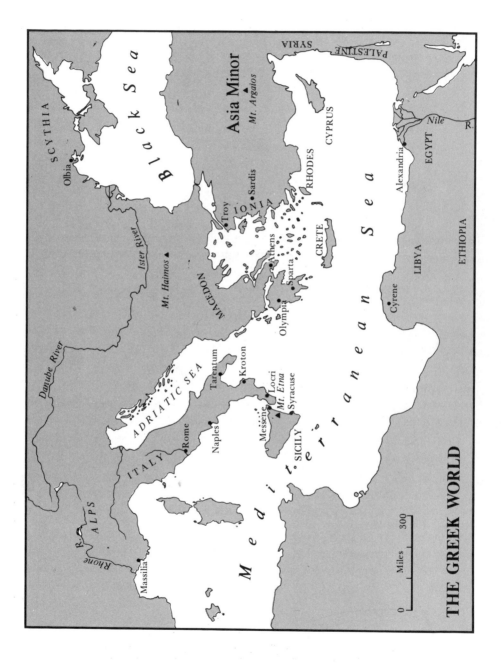

THE GREEK WORLD

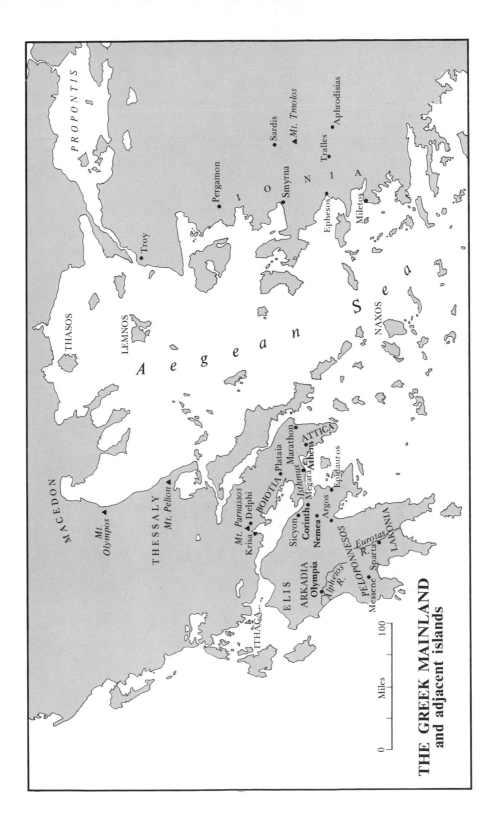

THE GREEK MAINLAND
and adjacent islands

PROPONTIS

Sardis
▲ Mt. Tmolos
Aphrodisias

Pergamon
IONIA
Smyrna
Tralles

Troy
Ephesos
Miletos

THASOS
LEMNOS

A e g e a n   S e a

NAXOS

MACEDON
THESSALY
▲ Mt. Pelion

Mt.
Olympos ▲

Mt. Parnassos
Krisa ▲ Delphi

Plataia
Marathon
ATTICA
BOIOTIA
Isthmus Athens
Megara
Sicyon
Corinth
Nemea
Argos
Epidauros

Eurotas
R.

LAKONIA

ELIS
ARKADIA
Olympia
Alpheios
R.
PELOPONNESOS
Messene
Sparta

ITHACA

100

Miles

0

SPORT AND RECREATION
IN ANCIENT GREECE

1

Introduction to Greek Athletics

The ancient people we call Greeks, from the Latin word *Graecus,* called themselves Hellenes and their country Hellas. But Hellas was not a political entity. It was a group of independent city-states that shared many attributes. The Hellenes had a common language divided into several dialects. They had a belief in a common origin and in a tradition of migrations from the North. They had a common religion and a colorful mythology. They inhabited not only the area called Greece today but also most of the islands of the Aegean, Egypt, Cyrene on the coast of Africa, the lower half of Italy, Sicily, and the coast of the Black Sea. They all stressed athletics, and their cities sent their best athletes to Olympia and other religious festivals. Despite all these similarities, the city-states never coalesced into a single political entity. A person who lived in Athens would not say that he was a Hellene; he was an Athenian. The period covered in this book extends from about 1200 BC, the legendary date of the Trojan War,[1] to perhaps 393 AD, when the Emperor Theodosius ordered all pagan sites destroyed in the name of Christianity, and Olympia and the Olympic Games were abandoned. The last known Olympic victor was Varazadates, prince of Armenia, who won the boxing in 385 AD.

Although the modern Olympics resemble the ancient games in many ways, the ancient Olympic Games and other athletic festivals were primarily a religious activity. Any cheating or other irregularity such as bribery was almost unthinkable; the Greeks regarded such misconduct as sacrilegious (see Pausanias on "The Zanes" in chapter 31). Athletics were more important to the Greeks than to us today: victory in important games usually meant not only enormous financial rewards but also preference in positions of power like political or military office.

In 500 BC, just before the wars against Persia, there were about 50 sets of games held at regular intervals. Six centuries later, in 93 AD, the number of games had increased to over 300 (see Finley-Pleket, p 68). Among these many sets of games, 4 were preeminent: Olympic Games, Pythian Games, Isthmian Games, and Nemean Games. The sites for all 4 were religious shrines. Although valuable

3

prizes were given at many lesser games, the prize at these 4 was a crown of leaves. They became known as Crown Games and were also called Sacred Games, Circuit Games, or Period Games. The home cities of the victors however usually rewarded their heroes with large prizes.

The events in each of the four Crown Games were similar. There were four running events: *stade* (= 200 meters); *diaulos* (= 400 meters); *dolichos* (= long distance), which varied in length at different games but was probably 24 stades (= 3 miles); and *hoplitodromos* (= race in armor), which also varied in length but at Olympia was 2 stades. There were three combat sports: wrestling, boxing, and *pankration* (= a combination of wrestling and boxing). There was a contest called the *pentathlon* (= *pent,* five; *athlon,* contest), which consisted of five events: long jump, diskos, javelin, run (probably the stade), and wrestling. The method of determining the winner has long been a subject of controversy. There was also horse racing, bareback or with chariots, at different distances with various animals (horses, colts, and mules). In some but not all of these events separate contests were held for boys. This was the custom at Olympia. At other games there were three classes: boys, men, and beardless males. At Delphi, Isthmia, and Nemea there were contests in singing and in playing the lyre and the flute. At Olympia, orators gave speeches, and poets sang poems, but these were not officially part of the Games.

The most prestigious of all the athletic festivals of ancient Greece were the Olympic Games, which were sacred to Zeus. They were held every 4 years at Olympia, a religious precinct in Elis in the northwestern part of the Peloponnesos. The stadium in classical times held 40,000 spectators (Pl 1). The prize for victory was a wreath of wild olive leaves.

The commonly accepted view of the origin of the Olympic Games is that they were first held in 776 BC, that the only event was the stade, and that the winner was Koroibos of Elis. Most scholars, however, believe that the games in 776 BC were not the innovation of a new ceremony but rather the reorganization of older games. It may well be that the officials for the earliest games did not keep accurate records of the victors. In V BC a Greek scholar named Hippias collected what information he could find. The records were still unsatisfactory, so in IV BC the great philosopher Aristotle revised this list of victors, and from that time on the records are good. The most complete list was drawn up many centuries later by Sextus Julius Africanus, whose last entry was 217 AD. These lists had a practical use: they provided a common system of calculating dates by the winner of the Olympic stade, as in "This event happened in the third year after so-and-so won the stade at Olympia." Although doubt has been cast on the accuracy of these lists for the earliest years, for the most part they seem to be historical and accurate. Where we can check against other lists, for example, the Oxyrhynchus Papyrus II.222 (quoted by Miller, *Arete* 31), we find agreement along with a few minor differences.

But when we try to figure out what happened at Olympia *before* 776 BC, we move into the realm of mythology. Some ancient authorities believed that the Greek demigod Herakles was the founder of the games. According to mythology, however, Herakles lived before the Trojan War (ie, before 1200 BC), so how could

Plate 1 Olympia: here is where it all began—or did it?

he have set up the games in 776 BC? The Greek author Pausanias mentions in Book 5 of his guidebook (see Chapter 31) the names of nearly a dozen people who staged the games before 776 BC, including some in which gods competed. For more information about this difficult subject, see Robinson in the list of Further Readings at the end of this chapter.

Here are two entries from the *Victor List* of Africanus (the angular brackets indicate words not in the original text):

Testimonium 1
The first ⟨Olympic Games⟩, in which Koroibos of Elis won the stade. Through the 13th ⟨Olympic Games⟩ this was the only event in the competition.

Testimonium 2
In the 14th ⟨Olympic Games⟩, Desmon of Corinth ⟨won⟩ the stade. The diaulos was added, and Hypenos of Elis won.

Pindar, who composed poems for the victors in many of the Crown Games, followed a different tradition, in which Herakles established the games at some undisclosed date with winners not found in the Africanus list:

Testimonium 3
Tell me, O Muse, who won the first crown with his hands or feet or chariot, thinking of the glory of the games and achieving it by his effort? Best in the stade was Oionos, son of Likymnios, running a straight course, and he came from Midea with his troops. In wrestling, Echemos won glory for his country Tegea. Doryklos, living in the city of Tiryns, won the prize in boxing. Samos of Mantinea, son of Halirhothios, won in the four-horse chariot. Phrastor hit

the mark with his javelin. Nikeus, whirling his arm, threw the weight farther than any other.

Pindar, Olympian Odes 10.60–74

(a) What discrepancies are there between Pindar's accounts and the *Victor List* of Africanus?

Plutarch casts doubt upon the accuracy of the historical records:

Testimonium 4

"We should not be overly impressed with the Olympic Games," I said, "and regard them as a kind of competition which is unchanged and unchangeable. Take the Pythian Games: there were three or four contests in music added to the athletic events, which were established at the beginning pretty much as they are now. But in the Olympic Games everything has been added after the running. Many events were first added and then abolished, like the *kalpē* [= race for mares or race in which driver dismounted or perhaps a combination] and the four-wheeled cart race. The officials ceased to award a crown in the boys' pentathlon. All in all, many changes were made in the games. I am afraid to come out and say that in former times the combat events were continued to the point of death and slaughter of those who fell in defeat, because I am concerned that you will ask me for proof of what I say and that if the name of my authority slips my mind because of the wine I have drunk, you will laugh at me."

Plutarch, Table-talk 5.2–3 (Moralia 675 B–D)

(a) This passage is sometimes taken to show that in early Olympic Games there were duels between armed combatants. Comment.
(b) Does Plutarch seem serious in his criticism?
(c) How certain does Plutarch seem about fatalities in the combat sports in the early Olympic Games?

The introduction of events in the Olympic Games is given in the *Victor List* of Sextus Julius Africanus as follows:

Olympic Games	Year BC	Event
1	776	Stade
14	724	Diaulos
15	720	Dolichos
18	708	Pentathlon and wrestling
23	688	Boxing
25	680	Four-horse chariots
33	648	Pankration and horse race
37	632	Boys' stade and boys' wrestling
38	628	Boys' pentathlon (discontinued immediately)
41	616	Boys' boxing
65	520	Hoplitodromos
70	500	Race for mule carts (discontinued in 444)
71	496	Race for mares (discontinued in 444)
93	408	Two-horse chariots

Olympic Games	Year BC	Event
96	396	Heralds and trumpeters
99	384	Four-colt chariots
128	268	Two-colt chariots
131	256	Colt race
145	200	Boys' pankration

Next to the Olympic Games in reputation were the Pythian Games, held at the sacred oracle in Delphi, in central Greece. Founded (or reorganized) in 582 BC, they were held in the third year after each Olympics. The games were in memory of the Python, a snake deity killed by the god Apollo, to whom the games were consecrated. The crown was made of laurel leaves. The stadium, in a dramatic site, is well preserved, but because it was built on a mountainside it could hold only 7000 spectators (Pl 2).

The Isthmian Games, honoring the memory of the hero Palaimon, were held at a precinct sacred to Poseidon on the Isthmus of Corinth, which connects northern and southern Greece. The games were biennial, held in the second and fourth year

Plate 2 Delphi, dramatic setting for Pythian Games.

of each Olympiad (the 4-year period between two Olympic festivals), The date of founding, or reorganization, was 581 BC, and the crown was wild celery, later changed to pine. The stadium has not been completely excavated, and therefore its capacity is not known.

The Nemean Games, founded, or reorganized, in 573 BC, were held in honor of the hero Adrastos at the sacred precinct of Zeus in the northeastern part of the Peloponnesos. They were held in the second and fourth year of each Olympiad, in a stadium that held 40,000 spectators. One legend has it that these games were founded by Herakles. A team from the University of California at Berkeley began excavating Nemea in 1974. The results of each season's dig have been reported in the periodical *Hesperia*. One important find was a vaulted tunnel leading to the stadium, much like the tunnel at Olympia. This is one of the earliest, if not the earliest, occurrence of the vault in Greece. Of human interest are inscriptions scratched on the walls, including one that reads *"Akrotatos kalos"* (= "Akrotatos is beautiful"), a standard love message. A tomb was found which contained a diskos, javelin tips, and a jumping weight. The diskos was made of iron and is the heaviest ever discovered, weighing 8.5 kilograms (18.7 pounds). Evidence of a square turning post for running was also discovered.

Here is the summary of the four Crown Games:

Games	Site	Prize	Interval	Founding Date
Olympic	Olympia	Wild olive	4 years	776 BC
Pythian	Delphi	Laurel	4 years	582 BC (third year of each Olympiad)
Isthmian	Corinth	Wild celery	2 years	581 BC (second and fourth year of each Olympiad)
Nemean	Nemea	Wild celery (then pine, after destruction of Corinth in 146 BC)	2 years	573 BC (second and fourth year of each Olympiad)

(a) What were the names of the four Crown Games?
(b) What was the traditional date of the founding of the Olympic Games?
(c) What caused the Olympic Games to be discontinued?
(d) To what god were the Pythian Games sacred?
(e) How often were the Pythian Games held?
(f) How often were the Isthmian Games held?
(g) How often were the Nemean Games held?
(h) What were the three combat sports?
(i) What were the events of the pentathlon?

Among the many local games held at regular intervals throughout the Greek world, the Panathenaic Games in Athens are of special interest because of the prizes that were awarded. Victors received vases, or *amphorae,* that stood 2 feet tall and held 9 gallons of olive oil; the winner of one chariot race, for example (IG II, 965), received 100 such vases. Amphorae were painted with scenes and figures that reveal much information about athletics in ancient Greece (Pl 3). The

Plate 3 Black figure Panathenaic amphora. Black figure vases have black figures on a red background. The artist has used half a dozen conventions, the most noticeable of which is to show the arm and leg advancing on the same side at the same time.

Panathenaic Games were founded (or reorganized) in 566 BC and held yearly; those in every fourth year were particularly splendid. In addition to Olympic events, the Panathenaic Games included boat races, throwing the javelin at a target from horseback, dancing, singing, playing musical instruments, and relay races with torches.

As explained earlier, the ancient Olympics came to an end in the late fourth century AD. In the late nineteenth century there was a resurgence of interest in reviving the Olympics. The beginning of the modern Olympics in 1896 in Athens was largely attributable to the Baron Pierre de Coubertin.[2]

Some of the most prominent features of the modern Olympics were not part of the ancient games. The Olympic flame was first used at the 1928 games in Amsterdam; the torch relay form Olympia was introduced in 1936 at the Berlin games.

The release of the white doves began in 1920 in Antwerp. The Olympic symbol of five interlocked rings was designed in 1913 by Coubertin and was first displayed in the Antwerp games in 1920. The motto *"Citius, Altius, Fortius"* (= faster, higher, stronger) was the contribution of Father Henri Didon and first appeared at Antwerp in 1920. The Olympic hymn was written for the 1896 Olympic Games by Spyros Samaras, but was not officially adopted until 1958. The marathon race was not held in any of the ancient Greek games; how it came to be part of the modern Olympics will be explained in Chapter 3 on running events.

It is not well known that there were earlier revivals of the Olympic Games before 1896. According to *The Olympic Games* (Killanin and Rodda, 1976, p 27), Robert Dover instituted the Cotswold Olympic Games in 1636 in England; they were said to have been held for over 200 years. In 1859 a modern Olympic Games was put on by Greeks, but the police disrupted them and they were not a success. The Greeks also attempted a revival in 1870 in the partially excavated stadium in Athens. These games were a great improvement on the previous games. In 1875 a less successful program was put on, again in Athens. A final attempt before Coubertin's were the games of 1889, restricted to the socially elite of Greece; these games were marked by riots. The story of the early struggles to open athletics of the nineteenth and early twentieth centuries to all social classes makes interesting reading.

Further Readings

See Abbreviations page for full titles of abbreviated works.

Religion and Athletics
Drees, pp 11–38.
Finley-Pleket, pp 14–25.
Gardiner AAW, pp 28–52.
Whibley, pp 407–413.
Yalouris, pp 36–37.

Differing Traditions on Origins of Olympic Games
Gardiner GASF, pp. 27–61.
Robinson, pp. 32–46.

Ancient and Modern Olympic Games
Finley-Pleket, pp 1–13.
Greenberg, S., *The Guinness Book of Olympics, Facts and Feats* (Enfield, Middlesex 1983).
Killanin, M., and Rodda, J., *The Olympic Games* (New York 1976).
Young, D.C., *The Myth of Greek Amateur Athletics* (Chicago 1984).

Other Festivals
Gardiner GASF, pp 62–76.

The Stadium
Miller, S.G., "Tunnel Vision: The Nemean Games," *Archaeology* 33 (1980), pp 54–56.
Romano, D.G., "The Ancient Stadium: Athletes and Arete," *Ancient World* 7 (1983), pp 9–16.

2

Athletics in Homer

The earliest Greek literary works, Homer's *Iliad* and *Odyssey,* written around 750 BC, describe athletic games at the time of the Trojan War, traditionally dated around 1200 BC. For each of the other authors discussed in this book we can list certain facts such as their name, dates, and kind of writing. About "Homer," the author (or authors) of the *Iliad* and the *Odyssey,* we know almost nothing. Who Homer was, when he wrote (if he did commit his poems to writing), how he wrote, and other matters are collectively called the "Homeric Question," which we will discuss briefly.

The *Iliad* and the *Odyssey* are the earliest literary works in the Western world, and among the greatest. The *Iliad,* containing 15,693 lines in twenty-four books, is the story of an incident in the Trojan War: the wrath of the Greek hero Achilleus. Book 23 of the *Iliad* describes the funeral games Achilleus held to honor his friend Patroklos, killed in battle.

People with experience in a foreign language realize that exact translation from one language to another is impossible. Nowhere is this more noticeable than in translating poetry. In our prose translations much of the beauty of the Greek poetry is lost. The bare narrative, however, is enough to make reading Homer interesting.

In Homer, most of the characters have two names, one of which is a patronymic, that is, a name taken from the father. Thus Achilleus is called "son of Peleus." To make it easier for you to follow, we have explained each patronymic by giving the other name in square brackets, like this: "son of Peleus [= Achilleus]."

Most of the ancient Greeks believed that the author of the *Iliad* and the *Odyssey* was a blind poet who composed these two works in essentially the form in which we now have them. His birthplace was in dispute, as this ancient Greek couplet shows:

11

Testimonium 1

Seven wealthy towns contend for Homer dead,
Through which the living Homer begged his bread.

Anonymous

There were many theories in antiquity on Homer's dates. Some thought he wrote soon after the Trojan War, whose traditional date was 1184 BC; others put him 500 years later. There were several "Lives of Homer" in ancient times, but none of them contain anything that seems factual.

There have been those in modern times who believe that one man (whom we may call "Homer") wrote the two poems in essentially their present form. At the other extreme, we have scholars who believe that the poems were a collection of ballads by various poets patched together in their present order from different sources. Others believe that the poems were composed before works of literature were written down. This view was attacked when it first appeared, on the grounds that it would be impossible to compose a poem of 15,000 lines without writing, although it was readily granted that one could memorize a poem of that length. Investigation of modern illiterate poets in the Balkans have shown that long ballads actually are composed without the aid of writing. One argument for assuming more than one author is that there are numerous internal contradictions. Opponents of this theory point out that we can find internal contradictions in modern authors where there is no suggestion of multiple authorship. Those who favor a single author point to the elaborate construction of the poems, which argues a single genius.

The following answer to the Homeric Question contains views that many scholars would support, at least in part. It assumes that each of the two poems was composed in writing in about 750 BC by a single author who relied heavily on earlier oral poems. It is not clear whether the same poet wrote both poems. These poems were frequently changed by singers, resulting in several versions. Since the poems were so well known and were sometimes cited in disputes as evidence of the sovereignty of cities, there was pressure to have an official version. Peisistratos, ruler of Athens in VI BC, set up a committee of scholars to produce a revised, authoritative edition of the poems. In III BC a group of scholars in Alexandria in Egypt did further work, and the text they produced is the one we have today.

The events "Homer" describes are supposed to have occurred during the Trojan War and its sequel, about 1200 BC. A serious difficulty in using these poems as evidence (eg, for early athletic games) is that we do not know whether the poet was describing life and customs of his own times (about 750 BC), whether he preserved information about a civilization that flourished 500 years before his time, or whether he was relying on his imagination.

Book 23 of the *Iliad* describes the funeral games held in honor of Achilleus' friend Patroklos.

Testimonium 2

Iliad, Book 23
Funeral Games in Honor of Patroklos

The Prizes (lines 256–270)

And when they had built up the funeral mound on the ground, those who   256
built the memorial started to return [to camp]. But Achilleus stopped the
people and seated them in a broad assembly and had prizes brought from
the ships, large kettles and tripods and horses and mules and heads of
powerful oxen and beautifully dressed women and gray iron.

First he ordered noble prizes to be set aside for the swift charioteers. The   262
first prize was a woman skilled in graceful handicraft and a tripod with two
handles holding twenty-two measures. And for second he designated an
unbroken mare, six years old, carrying in her womb a mule foal. And for
third he set aside a handsome kettle that had never been put over the fire,
holding four measures, still as bright as it was on the day it was made; and
for fourth he set aside two talents[1] of gold; and for fifth he put up a double
cup[2] which had never been put over the fire.

[In lines 271–286 Achilleus invites all to participate but explains that he will not compete because he is mourning for his friend Patroklos.]

The Chariot Race (lines 287–650)

So spoke Achilleus son of Peleus, and the swift charioteers drew near.   287
First of all stood up Eumelos, leader of men, the dear son of Admetos,
much skilled in driving. Then up stood the mighty son of Tydeus [= Diomedes],
and he drove a pair of horses bred from the lines established by Tros,
which he had earlier seized from Aeneas, but Apollo saved the owner. Next
stood up fair-haired Menelaos son of Atreus, a descendant of the gods, and
brought forward his yoked pair of swift horses, Aithe, the mare of Agamemnon, and his own stallion Podagros; Echepolos son of Anchises had given
her to Agamemnon as a gift, so that he might not have to follow him to
windy Ilion [= Troy] but might relax in pleasure at home. For Zeus had given
him great possessions, and he lived in Sicyon with its spacious dancing
grounds. This mare Menelaos had yoked, and greatly did she desire to run.

Antilochos, the fourth driver, the glorious son of Nestor, that king of lofty   301
heart, the son of Neleus, got ready his horses with gleaming coats. Swift

horses born in the land of Pylos drew his chariot. And his father, standing by his side, giving good advice to one who was himself naturally prudent spoke wisely thus:

306   "Antilochos, although you are very young, Zeus and Poseidon have both loved you and taught you all kinds of skills at driving a chariot; therefore we need not teach you, for you know how to turn skillfully around the post. But your horses are the slowest. I therefore think that the race will be sorrowful to you. True, their horses are swifter, but the drivers do not know more than you. And so, dear son, contrive a plan in your heart, so that the prize will not elude you. By plan does a woodcutter accomplish more than by strength; by plan, moreover, the captain on the wine-dark sea steers his swift ship tossed by the winds; and by plan does one driver defeat another. But one person, trusting in his horses and chariot, carelessly swings wide around the post and veers from side to side, and his horses wander over the racecourse and he does not control them. But he who understands the tactics of racing, even though he may be driving inferior horses, always keeps his eye upon the post, passes it close, nor does he fail to consider how much he should urge his horses with their ox hide reins, but he holds them in safety and watches the leading driver.

326   "I am going to give you an unmistakable landmark, and you cannot miss it: a hollow stump sticks up six feet from the ground, either oak or pine. It does not rot in the rain, and on each side two white stones are set firm where the tracks join, and on both sides the driving room is smooth. It is either a monument for some mortal who died long before or was selected as a racing turning point in the days of men of old, and now swift, godlike Achilleus has set this as a mark.

334   "Drive chariot and horses so close to this as to graze it, and in the well-wrought car lean slightly to the left horse, and calling upon the right horse by name, prick him with your goad and let out his reins from your hand. Let your left horse graze the post so that the hub of the well-fashioned wheel will seem to touch it. But avoid making contact with the stone, so that you will not injure your horses and wreck your chariot, which would be a joy to your opponents and a distress to you. But, dear son, be alert and watchful. For if at the post you move into the lead, there will be no one who can sprint to overhaul you or pass you, not even if he were trying to overtake you with divine Arion, the swift horse of Adrastos, whose origin is from the gods, or the horses of Laomedon, who are the best of all the breed in this land."

349   So speaking, Nestor son of Neleus sat down in his seat, once he had covered all the chief points in the matter. And Meriones was the fifth to harness his horses with the flowing manes. And they all climbed into their chariots and threw their lots into a helmet. Achilleus shook the helmet, and out jumped the lot of Antilochos son of Nestor. And after him mighty Eumelos won the next draw, and next to him the son of Atreus, Menelaos, known for his skill with the spear; and after him Meriones got the right to drive, and finally last of all, the son of Tydeus [= Diomedes], by far the best,

got the right to drive his horses. They stood side by side, and Achilleus showed them the turning point, far off on the level plain. And beside it he placed a judge, godlike Phoenix, who was his father's weapon bearer, to note the course of the chariots and to give a true report.

And they all at the same time lifted their whips over their horses and struck them with the lash and called out rapid words. And they quickly rode over the plain, swiftly away from the ships. And under the horses' chests rose the dust like a cloud or storm, and their manes streamed in the flowing breeze. And sometimes the chariots came down hard on the earth which nourishes so many mortals and sometimes they leapt into the air. And the drivers stood in their chariots, and the heart of each man beat with the urge for victory, and each one urged on his horses, who were raising the dust as they flew over the plain. 362

But when the fleet horses were completing the last part of the course toward the gray sea, then the courage of each became clear, and straightway the horses all began to strain. And the swift-footed mares of the grandson of Pheres [=Eumelos] shot ahead, and after them ran the stallions of Diomedes, Trojan horses, and they were not far behind, but very close. For always they seemed about to climb up on the chariot ahead, and their breath heated the back and broad shoulders of Eumelos; and as they flew along, their heads hung over him. And now Diomedes would either have passed his rival or drawn abreast of him if Phoibos Apollo had not been angry with him, and therefore he knocked from his hands his glistening whip. Then tears ran from his angry eyes when they saw the mares of Eumelos increasing their lead, while his own horses were thrown into confusion, running without a goad. But the act of Apollo in cheating the son of Tydeus [=Diomedes] did not escape Athene, but she quickly hurried after Diomedes, the shepherd of the people, and gave him back his whip and put heart into his horses. 373

And in the anger the goddess went after the son of Admetos [=Eumelos]; she broke his horses' yoke, his mares ran off the course, and the pole was dragged in curves along the ground. And he was thrown from the chariot over the wheel and ripped the skin from his elbows and mouth and nose and crushed his forehead above the eyebrows. And his eyes filled with tears and his mighty voice was silent. The son of Tydeus [=Diomedes] pulled his solid-hoofed horses[3] over to one side to pass the wreckage and spurted far ahead of the others. For Athene put heart into his horses and put glory upon him. And then after him came fair-haired Menelaos son of Atreus. And Antilochos called out to his father's horses, "Go, both of you! Run your fastest! I do not command you to contend with those, the horses of the brave son of Tydeus [=Diomedes] since Athene has now increased their speed and on him has she put glory. But catch the horses of Menelaos and do not be left behind, quickly! Do not let Aithe, who is a mare, disgrace you. Oh why, champions, are you being left behind? For this I will tell you and it will surely come to pass: no attention will Nestor, shepherd of the people, give to you, but he will kill you at once with sharp bronze if through 391 your lack of desire we win a lesser prize. But after them, and speed your fastest! I for my part will devise and consider a plan to slip past them in a narrow part of the course, and I will not fail to act."

417   So he spoke, and fearing the loud call of their master they ran faster for a short time, and soon steadfast Antilochos saw a narrow stretch in the sunken racecourse. In the ground was a gully, where water from storms had accumulated and washed the road, and it had hollowed out the entire section. Into this gully went Menelaos, trying to avoid running abreast of Antilochos. But Antilochos turned his solid-hoofed horses off the main track and swung out a little to one side. The son of Atreus [=Menelaos] was alarmed and called out to Antilochos, "Antilochos, you are driving too reck- lessly! Rein in your horses! For the course is too narrow; soon it will be wide enough for you to pass. Do not injure us both by crashing your chariot into mine." So he spoke, but Antilochos pressed on even more, urging with his goad like one who heard not. And they raced on in this position as far as a diskos can be thrown by a strong man raising his arm above his shoul- der, making trial of his strength. The mares of the son of Atreus [=Mene- laos] slackened, for he willingly ceased pressing, fearing that the solid-hoofed horses might somehow crash into each other in the single track and over- turn the well-made cars, and that the drivers, driven by desire for victory, should fall in the dust. And in reproof fair-haired Menelaos addressed him as follows:

439   "Antilochos, no mortal man is more destructive than you. Away! We Achaians [=Greeks] have wrongly said that you had wisdom. But you will not carry off the prize without answering my protest under oath." Saying these words he then called on his horses and spoke thus: "Do not hold back nor cease to run because of any grief in your hearts. Your competitors' feet and knees will fail before yours, for they are both lacking the strength of youth."

446   So he spoke, and fearing the voice of their master they increased their speed and quickly drew near their competitors. And the Argives sitting in a crowd were watching the horses flying dust covered over the plain. And Idomeneus, leader of the Cretans, was the first to see the horses, for he sat outside the crowd, high in a vantage point. And hearing a driver shout- ing, even though he was far off, he recognized him, and he spotted one conspicuous horse, standing out from the others, one which was otherwise bay colored, except that the forehead was marked with a white spot, round like a full moon. And he stood up and said these words to the Argives:

457   "Dear friends, leaders and advisers of the Argives, do I alone see the horses or do you see them too? Another pair of horses seems to me to be in the lead, and another charioteer comes into view. The mares of Eumelos who were first earlier, have somehow faltered, out in the plain. For I cer- tainly saw them turning around the post first, but now I cannot see them anywhere although my eyes are searching carefully everywhere over the Trojan plain. Did the reins slip from the charioteer and could he not hold the horses properly around the mark and did he not make the turn? I think

that he fell there and his chariot broke too, and the mares ran away, when wildness seized their hearts. But you too stand up and look, for I do not distinguish them clearly, but it seems to me that the leading man is Aitolian by race but lord of the Argives, mighty Diomedes son of Tydeus the tamer of horses."

But swift Aias son of Oïleus reproved him harshly: "Idomeneus, why do 473 you always talk so wildly before you are sure? The high-stepping mares are still speeding far away over the broad plain. You are not so much younger than the other Argives and your eyes in your head do not see more keenly. But in your speech you are always talking boastfully. And it is not right for you to talk boastfully, for there are other men here better than you. The mares who are in front are those who were leading before, the mares of Eumelos, and he himself rides holding the reins."

In anger the chief of the Cretans [=Idomeneus] answered him, "Aias, 482 master of abuse, foolish in counsel, you are inferior to the Argives in all other respects, because your heart is unfriendly. Come, let us now wager a tripod or a cauldron, and make Agamemnon son of Atreus our witness, which of the two teams is leading, so that you may get wisdom by losing your wager."

So he [=Idomeneus] spoke, and at once swift Aias son of Oïleus rose 488 up in anger to answer in harsh words, and the quarrel between the two would certainly have gone further, if Achilleus himself had not stood up and spoken these words:

"Reply to each other in harsh and evil words no more, Aias and Idome- 490 neus, because it is not seemly. You would be angry with any one else who tried this. But sit down in the crowd and watch the horses. And they will soon be here contending for victory, and then you will each know which of the horses of the Argives are second and which are in the lead."

Thus he [=Achilleus] spoke, and the son of Tydeus [=Diomedes] came 498 on to the finish in a rush, and constantly he struck his horses with his whip from the shoulder, and they swiftly lifted their hoofs as they came toward the finish of the racecourse, and without ceasing, particles of dust beat against the driver; and his chariot decorated with gold and tin followed after the swift-footed horses, and it left behind in the light dust only a shallow track made by the wheels. And they flew on in their haste. And he stopped in the middle of the crowd and copious sweat streamed to the ground from the horses' heads and breasts. And he [=Diomedes] leapt to the ground from the gleaming car and leaned his whip against the yoke. And stout-hearted Sthenelos did not delay but quickly took the prize and gave the rejoicing companions of Diomedes the woman to lead away and the two-handled tripod to carry. And he [=Diomedes] unharnessed his horses.

And after him Antilochos grandson of Neleus drove his horses, having 514 passed Menelaos by skill, not by speed. But Menelaos had his horses as close to him as a horse is to the wheel which together with the chariot strains over the plain and draws its master; and the tips of the hairs of his tail touch the wheel. And the wheel runs close, nor is there much space between them as the horse races over the broad plain. So close was Menelaos to blameless Antilochos. But earlier he was as much as a diskos throw behind, but he was rapidly overtaking Antilochos. For the noble spirit of Agamemnon's mare, sleek Aithe, increased. And if the race between the two had been any longer, he would have passed Antilochos and would have clearly beaten him. But Meriones, noble weapon bearer of Idomeneus, was a spear's throw behind glorious Menelaos. For his sleek horses were the slowest, and the slowest was he at driving in a race. The son of Admetos [= Eumelos] came in last of all, towing his handsome chariot, driving his horses before him.

534   Seeing him, swift-footed divine Achilleus felt compassion, and standing up he spoke these winged words among the Argives, "The best man brought his solid-footed horses in last. Come, let us give him the second prize at least, as seems right. But let the son of Tydeus [= Diomedes] carry off the first."

539   So he spoke, and all approved of his commands. And now he would have given Eumelos the mare, for all the Achaians [= Greeks] approved, if Antilochos son of greathearted Nestor had not stood up and addressed Achilleus son of Peleus with a protest for his rights.

543   "O Achilleus, I will be much angered with you, if you carry out your word. For you are about to deprive me of my prize, because you are thinking of the fact that his chariot and swift horses came to grief, and he himself, although he is a good man. But he should have prayed to the immortal gods; then he would not have finished last. But if you feel sorry for him and he is dear to your heart, there is much gold in your quarters, bronze there is and flocks; there are female slaves and solid-hoofed horses. So, take some of this wealth and after the awards give him an even more valuable prize or give it now on the spot, so that the Achaians may praise you. But I will not give up this mare. Let whatever man wants her do hand-to-hand battle with me."

555   So he [= Antilochos] spoke, and swift-footed divine Achilleus smiled, happy with Antilochos, for he was his dear friend, and answering him he spoke winged words.

558   "Antilochos, if you do in fact ask me to give Eumelos some other gift from my possessions, I will do exactly that. I will give him a breastplate, which I stripped from Asteropaios, bronze it is, around which there is a plating set in circles of shining tin. And this will be a most fitting award."

563   Such was his answer, and he ordered his dear friend Automedon to bring it from his quarters. And he went and brought it to him, and he put it in the hands of Eumelos, and he received it gladly.

566   Up rose Menelaos among them, grieving in his heart, much angered with Antilochos. And the herald put in his hand the scepter and ordered the Argives to be silent. Then Menelaos, equal to a god, spoke.

570   "Antilochos, formerly so prudent, what have you done? You have brought shame to my reputation and brought disaster on my horses, pushing yours to the front which were so much inferior. But come, chieftains and advisors

of the Argives, give impartial judgment to us both without favor, so that no one of the bronze-clad Achaians may say at another time, 'By attacking Antilochos with false words Menelaos carried off the mare because although his horses were slower, he was superior in reputation and influence.' I say that if I make the claim myself no Danaans [= Greeks] will reprove me, for the claim will be just. Antilochos, favored by Zeus, step forward, this is the law, and standing before your horses and chariot, take in your hands the slender lash with which you drove, and touching your horses swear by him [= Poseidon] who surrounds the earth and shakes it that you did not deliberately commit a foul, interfering with my chariot."

And to him in answer spoke prudent Antilochos, "Bear with me on this 586 occasion. For I am much younger than you, King Menelaos, and you are my elder and my better. You know how the mistakes of a young man come about, for his temperament is rasher and his plans are thoughtless. Therefore let your heart be patient, and I will myself give you the mare which I won. And if you should now ask some greater gift from my possessions, I would prefer to give it instantly on the spot rather than forever fall from my place in your heart, O favored by Zeus, and be an offender against the gods."

Such was his answer, and taking the mare, the son of greathearted Nes- 596 tor put her in the hands of Menelaos. And his heart became happy, as does the dew on the ears of wheat [gladden men's hearts] when the crops are growing at the time the ploughed land bristles with growth. So, Menelaos, your heart in your breast became happy. And addressing him [= Antilochos] he spoke winged words.

"Antilochos, now will I cease to be angry with you, since formerly you 602 were not irresponsible or thoughtless; youthfulness just now overcame your prudence. Another time, avoid deceiving your betters. For another man of the Achaians would not soon have persuaded me. But surely you have endured much and labored much, and so has your father, a good man, and your brother, all for my sake.[4] Therefore will I listen to your appeal, and in fact I will give you the mare, although she is mine, so that these people here may know that my spirit is never arrogant and unfriendly."

Such were his words, and he gave Noëmon, the companion of Antilo- 612 chos, the mare to take away, and then took the shining cauldron. And in fourth place, Meriones took the two talents of gold, just as he had finished in the race. And the fifth prize, the double cup, was unclaimed. This Achilleus gave to Nestor, carrying it through the crowd of the Argives, and stopping by him said,

"May this be a treasured possession for you, revered elder, to be a re- 618 membrance of the funeral of Patroklos. For never again will you see him among the Argives. And therefore I give you this prize with no conditions attached, for you will not have to compete in boxing nor wrestle nor take part in throwing the javelin nor run in the footrace. For harsh old age weighs you down."

With these words he set the cup into the old man's hands. And Nestor 624 addressing him spoke winged words, "Truly, my child, you have said all this suitably, for my limbs and legs are no longer steady, dear friend, nor do my arms move gracefully from my shoulders. Would that I were young and my strength as great as when the Epeians buried their ruler Amaryngkeus at Bouprasios, and his sons conducted the king's funeral games. At that time there was no man my equal, neither among the Epeians nor the Pylians themselves nor the greathearted Aitolians. In boxing I defeated Klytomedes son of Enops; in wrestling Angkaios of Pleuron, who entered the contest against me; in the footrace, I defeated Iphiklos, a worthy opponent, and in the javelin, I threw past both Phyleus and Polydoros. In the horse racing alone was I defeated, by the two sons of Aktor, who overcame me by numerical advantage, keyed up to win because the greatest prize still remained. They were twins; one held the reins firmly, and the other directed the horses with the whip.

643 "That is the way it was once, but now let younger men contest such events. I must yield to pitiable old age, but in those days I excelled among heroes. But go and bury your companion with games. I am happy to receive this gift, and my heart rejoices that you remember me as being kind to you and recall the honor which is due to me from the Achaians, nor will I forget you."

(a) The "talent" of gold in Homer (lines 262–270) is an unknown weight. What seems to be its approximate value here?

(b) Nestor is a well-known figure in the *Iliad,* typical of the elderly advisor. Can you characterize him from these speeches (lines 306–348 and 625–648)? What does his advice consist of? What concrete information does he have? Does his son Antilochos follow his advice?

(c) Describe the racecourse. What pains were taken to prepare it? What condition was it in?

(d) Intervention by the gods is a common device in Homer to explain what we call "luck." What good and bad luck did Diomedes and Eumelos have (lines 373–416)?

(e) Epithets (descriptive adjectives) are common in Homer. They are not always appropriate to the actual situation; for example, the fact that Menelaos is good at the spear (line 355) has no bearing on the race. Find other examples of such epithets in the text.

(f) Discuss the speech of Antilochos to his horses (lines 391–416). Do normal people today converse with animals and tell them their plans?

(g) Explain the tactics of Antilochos (lines 417–492). Did he commit a foul?

(h) Looking at lines 417–492, would you conclude that in the time of Homer there was a standard-size diskos?

(i) In lines 417–492 we have the first mention of what actually happened at the turning post, about which Nestor was so emphatic. Comment.

(j) How could Idomeneus tell the nationality of the leading driver in lines 417–492?

(k) Who is right about the position of the chariots, Idomeneus or Aias (lines 457–513)?

(l) What seems to be the use of tin in Homeric times, to judge from lines 498–513?

(m) Can you explain how the chariot of Diomedes can be described as gleaming (lines 498–513) after all the dust?

(n) What do you conclude about athletic events from the decision of Achilleus concerning a prize for Eumelos? Who had placed second in the race? Was the race open to all members of the Greek army (lines 534–623)?

The Boxing (lines 651–699)

So he spoke, and the son of Peleus [=Achilleus] went down into the full 651 meeting of the Achaians, once he had heard this praise from the son of Neleus [=Nestor]. Then he set forth the prizes for the painful boxing match. He brought forth a mule, a tireless worker, an untrained animal and hardest to train, and tied it up in the assembly. And for the one who lost he offered a two-handled cup. He stood erect and said these words to the Argives:

"Son of Atreus [=Menelaos] and you other well-greaved [greaves= 658 shinguards] Achaians, we summon two men from these here, the two best of those that raise their arms to box. The one to whom Apollo gives victory through endurance and the one whom all the Achaians recognize as superior, let him take away the mule, the tireless worker, to its quarters. But he who loses shall bear off the two-handled cup."

So he spoke, and straightway arose a man, broad and tall and skilled at 664 boxing, Epeios son of Panopeus; and he put his hand on the mule, the tireless worker, and said,

"Let anybody come near to carry off the two-handled cup; I say that no 667 other Achaian will take the mule by victory in boxing, for I assert that I am the best. Is it not enough that I am inferior in warfare? It is not possible for any mortal to excel in all activities. And so thus do I announce and this will come to pass. Standing face to face with him I will burst his skin and break his bones. And let his supporters remain here in groups to carry him forth when he has suffered defeat at my hands."

So he spoke, and everyone was silent, without a word. And Euryalos 676 alone, a mortal similar to the gods, stood up against him, son of King Mekisteus, who was the son of Talaos, who once came to Thebes for the burial of Oidipus when he had died. And there at those funeral games he overcame all the descendants of Kadmos [legendary founder of Thebes]. And the son of Tydeus [=Diomedes], famous with the spear, prepared him for the fight, encouraging him with words, and greatly did he wish for Euryalos to win.

And first he put on him a loincloth, and then he gave him thongs skillfully 683 cut from an ox reared in the fields. And the pair, in their loincloths, stepped forward into the center of the assembly. And holding up their sturdy hands they closed in on one another, and their powerful arms joined in battle. And fearful was the grinding of their jaws, and everywhere sweat poured from their limbs. And divine Epeios pressed on and struck the cheek of his opponent as he looked out from his guard. And Euryalos could no longer stand, but his gleaming limbs collapsed where he stood. And just as when the north wind riffles the water and a fish leaps upon the beach covered with seaweed and the dark wave conceals it, so Euryalos was lifted off his feet by the blow. But greathearted Epeios took him up in his arms and stood him on his feet. And his dear friends gathered around him and led him through the crowd, with his feet trailing, spitting out thick blood, with his head lolling to one side. And they brought him in, with his mind wandering, set him among them and went out to get the two-handled cup.

The Wrestling (lines 700–739)

700   And Achilleus son of Peleus at once set prizes for the third event, displaying them to the Danaans for the painful wrestling match, for the victor a large tripod, designed to be set over the fire, which the Achaians agreed was valued at twelve oxen. And for the vanquished he put forward into the middle a woman, and many skills she possessed, and they valued her at four oxen. He stood up straight and spoke these words in the presence of the Argives: "Stand up, those of you who strive for this prize."

707   So he spoke, and then mighty Aias son of Telamon arose, and against him stood up Odysseus of many resources, experienced in all tricks. When they had both put on their loincloths they went into the middle of the assembly, and held each other's arms with sturdy hands, like rafters which a famous builder has raised in a lofty dwelling to meet the force of the winds. And then their backs cracked as they locked with one another, hooking their heavy arms, and rivers of sweat poured down and weals in great number appeared on their ribs and shoulders, swollen red with blood. And always they fought for victory for possession of the well-built tripod.

719   Neither could Odysseus throw his opponent or force him to the ground nor could Aias, but the strength of Odysseus held firm. But when they began to try the patience of the well-greaved Achaians, then mighty Aias son of Telamon addressed him, "God-descended son of Laertes, Odysseus of many devices, either throw me or I shall throw you; all these things will be in the hands of Zeus."

725   With these words he lifted him up. But Odysseus did not forget his skills. He struck him behind the knee and collapsed his legs, and cast him backwards. And Odysseus fell upon Aias' chest, and the people watched and were amazed. Next much-tried divine Odysseus tried to lift him, and he moved him from the ground a little, but he did not lift him, and he then hooked Aias' knee, and they both fell to the ground together, and they were soiled with dust. And now springing up suddenly they would both have started to wrestle a third time, if Achilleus had not stood up and restrained them: "Fight no longer, do not exhaust yourselves with these troubles. You both have won victory. Go, taking equal prizes, so that the other Achaians may

compete." So he spoke, and they listened and obeyed, and wiping off the dust, put on their tunics.

The Running (lines 740–797)

The son of Peleus [=Achilleus] at once assigned other prizes for swift-ness in running. For first, an engraved silver mixing bowl; it held six mea-sures, and in beauty it far surpassed everything upon the whole earth, since the skillful Sidonians [=people of Palestine] made it well, and Phoenician men brought it ashore in a harbor and gave it as a gift to Thoas. And Eu-neos son of Iason gave it to the hero Patroklos as a ransom for Lykaon son of Priamos. And Achilleus set forth this prize in honor of his companion for the one who should be the fastest with his swift feet. Then for second he set forth a great ox, heavy and fat, and for last a half talent of gold. And he stood straight and said these words among the Argives, "Stand up, you who will compete for this prize." 740

So he spoke, and straightway stood up swift Aias son of Oïleus, and up stood Odysseus of many wiles, and then Antilochos son of Nestor. For he surpassed all the young men in running. And they stood abreast. And Achil-leus pointed out the goal. 754

And the running was at full speed from the start. Then quickly Aias son of Oïleus seized the lead. And divine Odysseus came close behind, as close as the shuttle of a fair-dressed woman is to her breast when she stretches it with her hands, drawing the woof thread up from the warp and holds it close to her breast. So close ran Odysseus, and stepped in Aias' footprints before dust could start to rise. And always as Odysseus ran swiftly on, he breathed upon the neck of Aias. And all the Achaians cheered him as he labored for victory and called on him as he struggled. But when they were completing the last part of the race, straightway Odysseus prayed in his heart to bright-eyed Athene, 758

"Listen, O goddess, and as a good helper give swiftness to my feet." So he spoke in prayer. And Pallas Athene heard him and made his limbs light, both legs and arms as he lifted them up. But when they were about to lunge for the finish, at that point Aias slipped as he ran—for Athene tripped him—where the dung had fallen in the sacrifice of deep-lowing oxen which swift-footed Achilleus slew in honor of Patroklos. And his mouth and nose were filled with the dung of those oxen. Then much-tried Odysseus carried away the mixing bowl, since he finished ahead, and gleaming Aias got the ox. 770

And he holding by the horn the ox reared in the fields, spitting out the dung, spoke thus among the Argives: "Alas, surely the goddess tripped me by the feet, who like a mother has always stood by Odysseus and given him aid." 780

So he spoke and they all laughed good-naturedly at him. And then Antil-ochos with a smile received the prize for last place and said these words among the Argives; "I say to you all, dear friends, who are men of knowl-edge, that even in this day and age the immortals honor men who are older. 784

For Aias is a little older than I am, but Odysseus belongs to an earlier generation of older men. They say that he is in vigorous old age, and it would be hard for any Achaian to contend with him in racing, except Achilleus."

793   So he spoke and honored Achilleus the son of Peleus. And answering him with these words Achilleus said, "Antilochos, your praise shall not be said without reward, but I will give you in addition a half talent of gold." So speaking he put it in his hands, and he received it gladly.

Fighting in Armor (lines 798–825)

798   Then the son of Peleus [= Achilleus] brought into the assembly a spear which cast a long shadow and put it down, and a shield and helmet, the armor of Sarpedon, which Patroklos took from him. And he [= Achilleus] stood up straight and spoke these words among the Argives, "We ask two men to contend for this, two of the very best, to put on their armor and take their sharp-cutting bronze to contend with one another before the crowd. Whichever first strikes his opponent's fair skin and grazes the flesh within through armor and dark blood and reaches the vital organs, to him will I give this fair Thracian sword, studded with silver, which I took from Asteropaios. And the armor of Sarpedon they may carry off as common property, and we will give them a fair feast in our quarters."

811   So he spoke, and straightway rose mighty Aias son of Telamon and so rose mighty Diomedes son of Tydeus. And when they had armed themselves on opposite sides of the assembly, they both came together in the middle to fight, both glaring fiercely. And amazement seized all the Achaians. But when they came near to each other, three times they rushed together, three times did they close in. Then Aias pierced the other's shield, symmetrical on all sides, but he did not reach the flesh. For the breastplate behind the shield stopped the blow. Then the son of Tydeus [= Diomedes], aiming over the great shield of Aias with the blade of his shining spear, constantly attacked the neck. And then the Achaians fearing for Aias ordered them to stop and take equal prizes. But to the son of Tydeus [= Diomedes] Achilleus gave the great sword of the hero, bringing it to him with its scabbard and well-made belt.

Throwing the Weight (lines 826–849)

826   Now the son of Peleus [= Achilleus] brought out a *solos,* a formless mass of iron[5] which Eëtion of mighty strength used to throw, but swift godlike Achilleus slew him and brought this mass of iron in his ship with his other possessions. And he stood up straight and spoke these words among the Argives.

831   "Stand up, you who will compete for this prize. If anyone has fertile fields far away from towns, this iron will last him for five rolling years as he uses it. For if his shepherd or plowman are without other iron, they will not have to go to the city but this will furnish it."

836   So he spoke, and up stood Polypoites, steadfast in battle, and after him

godlike Leonteus of strong heart, and Aias son of Telamon, and divine Epeios. They stood in a row, and divine Epeios took the solos, whirled around, and threw it. And all the Achaians laughed at him.

Secondly Leonteus, born of the stock of Ares [=god of war], and third, great Aias the son of Telamon threw with his mighty arm, and he overthrew the markers of the others. But when Polypoites, steadfast in battle, took the *solos,* he threw as far beyond the crowd as a cattle herder throws his staff and it flies whirling through the grazing cattle. And they all shouted. And standing up the companions of mighty Polypoites carried the king's prize to the hollow ships. 841

The Archery (lines 850–883)

Then for the archers he set out a prize of dark iron, and laid down ten double-bladed axes and ten single-bladed axes and set up the mast from a ship with dark bow far off in the sands and tied to it with a slender cord a trembling dove by the foot, which he ordered them to shoot at. "Whoever hits this trembling dove, let him take and carry away home all the double axes. And whoever shall hit the cord but miss the bird—since he is less skillful—let him take the single axes." 850

So he spoke, and then up rose mighty Teukros, a chief, and then Meriones, stood up, the brave companion in arms of Idomeneus. And taking their lots they shook them in a bronze helmet, and Teukros was chosen by lot to go first. Straightway he shot an arrow with great force but he did not vow to Apollo, the lord of archery, a glorious sacrifice of firstborn lambs. And he missed the bird, for Apollo begrudged this to him. But he hit the cord beside the foot, with which the bird was tied, and the sharp arrow completely severed the cord. And the bird then flew up to heaven, but the cord dangled toward the ground. And the Achaians roared aloud. Then Meriones in haste seized the bow from the hand of Teukros. But he had made his own arrow ready while Teukros was aiming. And straightway he vowed to Apollo the far-darter a glorious sacrifice of firstborn lambs. He saw the trembling dove high under the clouds. And he struck her in the middle, as she circled around, under the wing, and the shaft went straight through her and falling to earth it stuck in the ground near the foot of Meriones. But the bird sitting on the mast from the ship with dark bow hung down her head, and her wings thick with feathers drooped. And her spirit quickly fled from her body, and down from the mast she fell. And the people again watched and were amazed. And Meriones took all ten of the double axes, and Teukros carried the single axes to the hollow ships. 859

The Javelin (lines 884–895)

Then the son of Peleus [=Achilleus] set out a spear that cast a long shadow and a cauldron that had not been used over fire, with a design of flowers, the value of an ox. And then the javelin throwers arose. Up stood broad and mighty Agamemnon son of Atreus, and up stood Meriones, the brave companion in arms of Idomeneus. And to them swift-footed divine 884

Achilleus said, "Son of Atreus [= Agamemnon], since we know how much you excel us all and how superior you are in strength and in throwing, take this prize to the hollow ships, and to the hero Meriones let us give this spear, if you are willing in your heart. For I do urge it."

895   So he spoke, and Agamemnon, lord of men, did not refuse, but gave the fair prize to the herald Talthybios.

(a) In lines 690–695, what seems to have constituted victory in the boxing match? How open was the competition?
(b) In line 703, one gets the woman, the other gets a tripod, an equal prize. Comment.
(c) Compare the apparent value of the prizes in the foot race.
(d) Three events (fighting in armor, throwing the solos, and the archery) in lines 798–883 are considered by many scholars to be late (but ancient) additions to the poem. One argument is that the events are confused and improbable. Comment.
(e) Why in line 840 did the Achaians laugh at Epeios?
(f) How far did the solos seem to be thrown? What was its apparent weight?
(g) How far does luck play a part in these contests?
(h) In some ways these games are like our modern sports but with modern differences. In other ways, they are entirely different. One major goal of this course is to teach the reader how to compare the resemblances and differences in these and other sports and recreational activities. List some of the resemblances and some of the differences.

Further Readings

Athletics in Homer
Gardiner AAW, pp 18–27.
————GASF, pp 8–26.
Willcock, M.M., "The Funeral Games of Patroclus," *Bulletin of the Institute of Classical Studies* 20 (1973), pp 1–11.
Yalouris, pp 24–35.

The Homeric Question
Lesky, A. *A History of Greek Literature* (New York 1966), pp 32–40.

3

Running Events

There are five chief differences between ancient and modern events:

1. starting gate [*husplex*]
2. turning post [*kampter*]
3. race in armor
4. limited number of distances
5. lack of hurdle events

There is considerable controversy over how the kampter and the husplex were used.

The *dromos* (= running track) on which the Greek footraces were held was a *stade* long. A stade was 6 *plethra*. A plethron was 100 feet; thus a stade was 600 feet. However, because the Greek foot varied from one locality to another, the stade at Olympia was 192.27 meters long, at Epidauros it was 181.3, at Delphi 177.5, and at Pergamon 210. The word "stadium" comes from the Greek word "stade." The stade race was a straightaway dash, whereas the other races were all multiples of the stade.

1
Best in the stade was Oionos son of Likymnios, running a straight course.

Pindar, *Olympian Odes* 10.64–66

[The *scholiast* (= ancient editor) on this passage says " 'Straight,' meaning not having a kampter like the *diaulos.*"]

In the longer races there were turning posts called *kampteres* to assist the runners in making their turns (Pl 4). The starting line, called the *balbis* (Pl 5), was a stone slab with two grooves:

2
Just as with runners, so in the orchestra there are lines marked out so that the chorus will stand in a straight line.

Eustathius 772.9

[The "orchestra" was the round section of a Greek theater in front of the stage.]

27

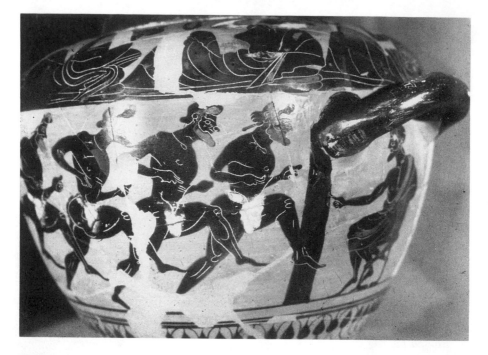

Plate 4 Athletes about to turn around kampter (= turning post). Official watches for foul. Black figure amphora.

3

The balbides [plural of balbis] are grooves at the starting line where the runners stand so that they may all be in a straight line. For this reason the heralds still say to the runners, "Put your feet side by side at the balbis."

Moeris 193.4

[Sometime in V BC the balbis was replaced by a starting gate called a *husplex:* each runner was restrained at the starting point by a horizontal bar, held up by a cord whose tail end was held by the starter. When the starter released the cords, all the bars dropped simultaneously (Pl 6).]

4

The man who is slandered is usually one who has been particularly honored and is therefore an object of envy to his inferiors . . . Much the same kind of thing happens in athletic contests in the races. For there, once the husplex goes down, the good runner puts his mind only on going forward, and concentrating on the finish, puts his hope of victory in his legs. He does not foul the man next to him nor does he waste time thinking up tricks against his opponents. The immoral, unskilled athlete, however, turns his hope of success from speed to unsportsmanlike conduct, and the only thing in the world he thinks of is how to hold his opponent or check him by tripping, feeling that if he should fail to do this, he could never win.

Lucian, *On Slander* 12

Plate 5 Balbis (= starting line) at Olympia. Note hole for turning post.

Plate 6 Custodian at excavation in Isthmia has just released cord, and husplex (= starting gate) has begun to drop.

(a) In modern horse racing, the restraining bar goes *up*. What does this testimonium tell us?

The start seems to have been a standing one, although there is some evidence for a crouching start. A puzzling passage in Herodotus indicates that athletes who start too soon are whipped:

5

The Corinthian general Adeimantes son of Okytos said, "O Themistokles, in the games those who start too early [=jump the gun] are whipped." And Themistokles said in answer, "Yes, and those who are left standing win no crowns."

Herodotus 8.59

Lanes were marked out in some way; at Olympia and Delphi there were twenty lanes, and at Epidauros, eleven.

There were four types of running events in the ancient Olympic Games: *stade, diaulos, dolichos,* and *hoplitodromos.* At first the only footrace was the stade, and some authorities believed that later games began with this event.

6

The herald in the Olympic Games, as you know, first announced the stade, just as he does now to us [in the Panathenaic Games].

Plato, *Laws* 8.33a

The stade remained the only event until the fourteenth Olympic Games (724 BC), when the diaulos (=two-lap race) was added. Diaulos also means "double flute," referring to the two legs of the race, for this race was 2 stades, down and back again. There were no gradual curves as in our modern track; to assist the sprinters in making the hairpin turn, there was a turning post called a kampter. There is a difference of opinion as to whether there was a single post around which all runners ran, or whether each runner turned around his own post. It would appear, however, that there must have been a separate post for each runner. Although Plate 4 shows only one turning post, this was an artistic convention; it would have been virtually impossible to show all the kampteres at once. Experiments done at The University of Michigan have shown what common sense suggests: if even a few runners try to turn around a single post, almost invariably one or more of the runners will be knocked down. An inscription[1] listing the cost of repairs on the stadium at Delphi includes 36 kampteres, which suggests multiple posts. The archeological evidence at Nemea shows that there were individual turning posts.[2] There is no evidence to show whether the turns were clockwise or counterclockwise. However, because the athlete in a race in armor had to carry his shield in his left hand, he would have to make the turn grasping the post with his right hand, and go around the post clockwise. We may assume that the other runners made their turns in the same direction.

The *dolichos* (=long-distance race) was added in the fifteenth Olympic Games (720 BC). This varied in length at different sites; we hear of races of 7, 12, 20,

Plate 7 Hoplitodromos (= race in armor). Red figure kylix (= drinking cup). Red figure vases
have red figures on a black background.

and 24 stades; that is, the shortest race was under 1 mile, the longest about 3
miles. The distance of this race in the Olympic Games is not definitely known;
some scholars think it was 24 stades.

The *hoplitodromos* (= race in armor) was added to the Olympic program in the
sixty-fifth Olympic Games (520 BC) (Pl 7). The race was not in full armor; the
competitors wore a helmet and greaves (= shinguards) and carried a shield:

7
Those running the double-stade race in armor have a crest ⟨of a helmet⟩ on
their heads.

Scholiast on Aristophanes, Birds 292

8
There [in the temple at Olympia] are kept the 25 bronze shields, which are
carried by the competitors in the hoplite race.

Pausanias 5.12.8

Eventually, helmets and greaves stopped being worn. The distance of this race
varied from place to place. At Olympia and Athens the distance was 2 stades, at
Nemea 4 stades, but at Plataia it was 15 stades.

9
The hoplite race at Plataia in Boiotia is considered to have the most prestige because of the length of the race and because the equipment [the

shield?] reached to the ground and protected the competitor as if he were actually fighting.

Philostratos, *On Athletics* 8

Heats were run in the stade. To advance to the final, it was necessary to win a trial heat.

10

Each of the runners is put ⟨into a heat⟩ by lot, and they do not compete in the stade at the same time. They compete in separate heats and then run again ⟨in the final⟩ for first place. And so the man who wins the stade wins two races.

Pausanias 6.13.4

[We are told that seven athletes from the city of Kroton qualified for the finals in the stade (Strabo 6.12), and that in the games the Ten Thousand held at Trapezos more than sixty Cretans competed in the dolichos (Xenophon, *Anabasis* 4.8.27).]

In the case of a tie the prize was presented to the god:

11

We ended in a tie, something which rarely happens with runners.

Seneca, *Moral Epistles* 83.5

[In this excerpt the Latin author was talking about his workout with a young slave. The word we translated as "tie" means "sacred."]

At Isthmia, Nemea, Athens, Epidauros, Argos, Plataia, and other sites there was also a 4-stade race; it was called the *hippios* (= horse race), perhaps because the length of the racetrack for horses was twice as long as the stadium.

　　Relay races were common in local festivals but were not part of the Crown Games; there were often eight to ten runners on a team. Instead of a baton, the runner passed a torch [Pl 8]. The winner's torch lit the sacrifices. For this reason, a team was disqualified if its torch went out.

12

Torches and torch carriers: the Athenians hold torch races on the feasts of the Panathenea, Hephaistos, and Prometheus.

Anecdota Graeca 1.277.22

13

There he [= Alexander the Great] made sacrifices in the traditional manner and held torch races and athletic contests.

Arrian, *Anabasis* 3.16.9

14

In the Academy is an altar to Prometheus, and they run from it to the city with lighted torches. The contest consists both in running and in keeping the torch lit. The runner who finishes first does not get the prize if his flame has gone out, but it goes to the second runner instead. And if *his* torch is

Plate 8 Passing the torch in a relay race. Red figure oino-choe (= wine pitcher).

not still burning, the winner is number three. And if everyone's torch is blown out, then no one wins.

Pausanias 1.30.2

[The Academy was an area outside the ancient city walls of Athens. The racing with torches commemorated the gift of fire to man by Prometheus.]

(a) What were five chief differences between ancient and modern running?
(b) How long was a plethron?
(c) Describe the kampteres.
(d) Describe the balbis.
(e) Which event in the Olympic Games came first?
(f) What is the controversy about the kampter? What is the evidence?

(g) What event had qualifying heats?
(h) What would cause disqualification in a relay race? Why did this seem reasonable to the Greeks?

It may come as a surprise to learn that the marathon was not an event in the ancient Greek games. This long-distance race of 26 miles and 385 yards was created in modern times for the 1896 Olympics in Athens to commemorate the legendary feat of an Athenian runner named Phidippides, who supposedly ran from Marathon to Athens to announce that the great Persian army had been defeated. According to legend, he uttered the immortal words, "Rejoice; we have won," and then dropped dead. This is a dramatic and inspiring story, but ancient evidence does not support it. The following accounts by five ancient authors make this clear.

The first of these authorities is the historian Herodotus, born about 484 BC, who covered in great detail and accuracy the period of the V BC wars between Greeks and Persians. Here is his version of the Phidippides story. When the Athenian generals realized that a battle was imminent, they sent a professional long-distance runner named Phidippides to Sparta for help. He arrived in Sparta, a distance of 145 miles, on the second day. The Spartans voted to send aid, but because their religion forbade them to leave until the full moon, they missed the battle of Marathon. On his return, Phidippides reported that on his way to Sparta he had met the god Pan, who addressed him by name and complained that the Athenians had neglected to worship him. The Athenians obeyed his command: after the war they built him a temple at the foot of the Acropolis. This is all Herodotus has to say about Phidippides; there is nothing about a run from Marathon to Athens and no dying words about the victory.

If Phidippides did not bring the great news, who did? Here is what Plutarch has to say 600 years after the battle:

15

According to Herakleides Ponticus, Thersippus of Eroeadai brought the news about Marathon, but most authorities say it was Eukles, who ran in full armor still heated from battle, into the homes of one of the city's leaders, and said only, "Rejoice; we have won" and died on the spot.

Plutarch, "Fame of the Athenians" (*Moralia* 347C)

(a) Who are the two runners credited with the run?
(b) What did Thersippus probably do with his armor?

Lucian, who lived about the same time as Plutarch, has this to say:

16

The long-distance messenger Philippides [sic] is said to have been the first who used this word [=rejoice] when he announced the victory to the officials who were sitting in session and were concerned about the outcome of the battle; and with the words "Rejoice; we have won," he expired with this dying word "Rejoice."

Lucian, *A Slip of the Tongue* 3

Here is Pliny the Elder, who died in 79 AD:

17
The feat of Philippides [sic] in running 1160 stades [= 145 miles] from Athens to Sparta in two days was a great accomplishment.

Pliny, Natural History 7.84

(a) What does Pliny say about carrying the news of the victory?

Cornelius Nepos, a Latin writer of I BC, has this variation:

18
Although the Athenians were disturbed by the invasion, they sought help from no one except the Spartans and sent Phidippus [sic], a runner of the type called "all-day runners," to say they needed help as soon as possible.

Cornelius Nepos, Lives 1.4

(a) Is there any mention in these authors of a run from Marathon?

Here is a story in Plutarch, which parallels the legend of Phidippides, describing how in 479 BC Euchidas ran from Delphi to Plataia:

19
Then he took the sacred fire from the altar and ran back to Plataia. He finished before sunset, doing 1000 stades [= 125 miles] in 1 day. He greeted his fellow citizens, handed over the sacred torch, and with that fell down and shortly expired.

Plutarch, Life of Aristides 20.5

(a) In what way does this exploit imitate the Marathon story?
(b) What evidence is there for the run from Marathon?
(c) List the names given to the runner in these accounts.

Further Readings

Running
Bronner, O., "Balbis, Husplex, Kampter," *Isthmia* II (1973), pp 137–142.
——— "Starting Devices in Greek Stadia," *American Journal of Archaeology* 76 (1972), pp 205–206.
Drees, pp 78–80.
Gardiner AAW, pp 128–143.
——— GASF, pp 251–294.
Harris GAA, pp 64–77.
——— SpGR, pp 27–33.
Matthews, V.J., "The Hemerodromoi," *Classical World* 68 (1974), pp 161–167.
Miller, S.G., "Turns and Lanes in the Ancient Stadium," *American Journal of Archaeology* 84 (1980), pp 159–166.
Yalouris, pp 128–133; 155–175.

Relay Races
Yalouris, pp 248–251.

Sequence of Events
Drees, pp 66–69.

Marathon
Lee, H.M., "Modern Ultra-long Distance Running and Philippides' Run from Athens to Sparta," *Ancient World* 9 (1984), pp 107–113.

4

Pentathlon

The ancient Greek pentathlon consisted of five events: a run of unknown distance (generally assumed, although without evidence, to be the stade), diskos, long jump, javelin, and wrestling. The diskos, long jump, and javelin were not (usually) held as separate events but rather as part of the pentathlon:

1

Diophon, son of Philo, won at Olympia and Delphi in the jump, the sprint, the diskos, the javelin, and the wrestling.

Semonides, fragment 151D

2

"Pentathlete" is a word for "competing in five events," namely, wrestling, running, javelin, diskos, and pankration.

Scholiast on Aristeides 3.339

3

The pentathlon has in one competition these five events: boxing, wrestling, jumping, diskos, and running.

Scholiast on Pindar, *Olympian Odes* 13.39

4

No one was thrown quicker than I in the wrestling, nor ran any slower in the stade. In the diskos, I never got close at all, and as for those feet of mine, I couldn't lift them ⟨off the ground⟩ at all. Cripples used to beat me in the javelin. Out of the five events of the pentathlon I was the first who was proclaimed by the heralds as "Beaten in all five."

Lucillius, *Greek Anthology* 11.84

(a) Which two of these authors have the events wrong?

The events of the pentathlon that the great Jim Thorpe won in 1912 were the long jump, javelin, 200-meter dash, discus, and 1500-meter run; however, this pentathlon is no longer an Olympic event. The "modern pentathlon" in the Olympics is a test of qualities presumably needed by a courier carrying a dispatch: horse riding (800 meters), fencing (épée), shooting with pistol (25 meters), swimming (300 meters), and cross-country running (4000 meters). The performance of each competitor is graded according to a scoring table introduced in 1956. Formerly places were counted (ie, one point for a first place, ten for tenth place, etc.). The pentathlon is no longer an Olympic event for women, but has been superseded by the heptathlon. The events are the 100-meter hurdles, shot put, high jump, long jump, javelin, 200-meter run, and 800-meter run. Points are awarded according to a scoring table.

The modern decathlon has the following events: 100-meter dash, long jump, shot put, high jump, 400-meter dash, 110-meter hurdles, discus, pole vault, javelin, and 1500-meter run. As in the pentathlon, performance is measured by a scoring table.

(a) Which events in the modern decathlon were in the ancient pentathlon?

There is no conclusive evidence about the order of events in the ancient pentathlon, although it is clear that wrestling came last:

5
They had already finished the horse races and the run in the pentathlon. The competitors who had advanced to the wrestling were no longer in the stadium but were wrestling between the stadium and the altar.

Xenophon, History of Greece 7.4.29

[Xenophon was describing the situation that existed in the Olympics of 364 BC when the Eleans tried by force of arms to recover control of the games, which had been seized by the Arkadians.]

Pindar says that victory in the javelin could mean that the athlete need not compete in the wrestling:

6
O Sogenes of the Eunexid family, I swear that when I shot forth my fast tongue I did not step over the line like the ⟨thrower of the⟩ javelin with point of bronze, ⟨the victory in the javelin⟩, which removes ⟨the threat to⟩ the neck and muscles from the sweat of wrestling before one's limbs enter the bright sunshine.

Pindar, Nemean Odes 7.70–73

[This seems to mean that the javelin came fourth. But even if we agree that the javelin was fourth and the wrestling fifth, there is no evidence about the order of the first three events. However, the meaning of this passage is disputed by scholars.]

The all-around athlete was considered by many to be superior to the specialist:

7
The pentathletes have the most beautiful bodies, because they are constructed for strength and speed together.

Aristotle, Rhetoric 1.5, 1361b

Others preferred athletes who excelled in some one event:

8

You seem to me to be explaining the relative merit of the pentathletes and the runners or wrestlers. For the first group [the pentathletes] are left behind by the others in their specialties and are second-raters, while the second group are first among all the athletes and beat them.

Pseudo-Plato, *The Lovers* 135e; not written by Plato, but perhaps by a pupil

[That is, the performance of a runner or wrestler in the pentathlon was not the equal of the specialist in these events.]

(a) List the five events of the ancient Greek pentathlon.
(b) List the five events of the modern Olympic pentathlon, which is sometimes called the military pentathlon.
(c) What was the basis of the belief that pentathletes had the most beautiful bodies? What was the argument that pentathletes were inferior to contestants in other sports?

Further Readings

Drees, pp 72–77.
Harris GAA, pp 77–80.
———— SpGR, pp 33–35.
Yalouris, pp 214–215.

5

Diskos

The modern discus weighs 2 kilograms (4 pounds, 6.4 ounces), is 8⅝ inches in diameter, and is made of either metal or wood and metal. The modern discus thrower must stay within an 8-foot circle, and the discus must land in a fair area within a sector of 40 degrees. The present world's record is over 230 feet.

The ancient *diskos* was made of stone in early times, but seems later to have been changed to bronze.

1

And Nikeus, whirling around, threw the stone with his arm farther than all the others.

Pindar, *Olympian Odes* 10.72

2

Whenever they throw the stone diskos.

Pindar, *Isthmian Odes* 1.25

3

In the gymnasium you also saw another athletic implement, bronze, circular, like a tiny shield.

Lucian, *Anacharsis* 27

The ancient diskoi that have been discovered (eight diskoi at Olympia) vary widely in size and weight, and are made of either stone or bronze. It has been suggested that some of the bronze diskoi, which seem to have edges too sharp to be throwing implements, were actually votive objects celebrating a victory, whereas the small diskoi may have been used by boys. A diskos in the Museum of Fine Arts in Boston weighs 14 pounds, 10 ounces, and is inscribed "From the games." A diskos weighing almost 19 pounds has recently been discovered at Nemea. The diameter of the diskoi that are represented on Athenian red-figured vases seems to

Plate 9   Diskos thrower and javelin thrower. Pickaxe and pair of weights are symbols of pentathlon. Interior of red figure kylix.

be about 12 inches, coming up to the elbow when grasped (Pl 9). Gardiner (AAW, p 156) gives the dimensions of eleven diskoi.

The diskos was thrown from an area of unknown size, called the *balbis*.

4

The balbis is small, large enough for one man standing erect, and marked off ⟨in all directions⟩ except at the rear. The right leg supports the front upper part of the body leaning forward and takes the weight off the other leg, which moves at the same time as the right arm and follows through with it. The form of the thrower of the diskos is as follows. He must turn his head to the right far enough so it is possible to see the ⟨right-hand⟩ side of his chest, pulling ⟨against the diskos⟩, and throw the diskos employing all the right-hand parts of his body. Apollo threw the diskos like this, for he could have done it in no other way.

Philostratos, *On Statues* 1.24 (not the author of *On Athletics*)

(a) What two meanings does balbis have?

It is assumed that the diskos had to land in a fair area, and we know that the spot where it landed was marked by a peg.

5

He means the mark where the diskos first landed.

Eustathius

[Eustathius is commenting on Homer's expression, "He surpasses the marks of all," in *Odyssey* 8.192.]

It sometimes happens that the ancient scholars made serious errors. Here is an example:

6

The diskos was made of stone. Eratosthenes in his list of Olympic victors mentions the *solos,* saying that it was made of iron or wood or bronze, with a hole in the center and a cord running through it, which the contestants held on to when they threw it.

Scholiast on Odyssey 8.190

7

The diskos is different from the solos. For the diskos is a stone with a hole bored through it, as Tryphon (I AD) says in the fifth book of his *Correct Greek,* but the solos was beaten out of bronze.

Ammonius

8

The diskos was made of stone and circular, with a hole in the middle, through which a cord was passed for throwing it up in the air. And in the *Odyssey* Homer says, "The stone (that is, the diskos) hummed."

Scholiast on Iliad 23.826

Reliance on Testimonia 6, 7, and 8 led to the following erroneous entry in Liddell and Scott's *Greek-English Lexicon* (8th edition, 1882) under *diskos:* "a sort of quoit. . . . It had a hole in the middle for a wooden helve, or leathern strap, to swing it by, whereas the *solos* was a solid piece of metal. . . . Pitching the diskos was a very ancient Grecian game, esp. at Sparta. In Hom. there is no mark to aim at: the trial being simply who can pitch furthest, as in the North-country game of *puttin' at the stane.*"

The noise made by the diskos mentioned in Homer (Testimonium 8) was formerly identified with the noise of which Cicero spoke:

9

The students of teachers in the Greek gymnasia prefer to hear the diskos than to hear the professor.

Cicero, On the Orator 2.5.21

But the noise of the diskos is explained by these testimonia (Pl 10):

10

The diskos sounded, and this was the signal that my father had already entered the baths.

Letters of Fronto to Marcus Aurelius (II AD), 4.6

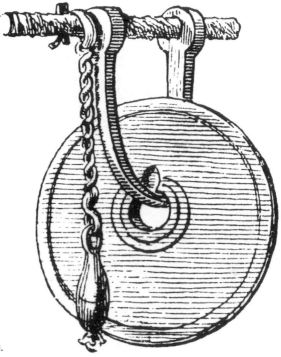

Plate 10 Diskos-shaped gong.

Sextus Empiricus, *Against the Mathematicians* 5.28, says that to obtain an accurate horoscope the Chaldean astrologers would sit on a mountainside with a woman in labor, and when she gave birth,

11
[They] immediately signaled with a diskos to a person on the peak of the mountain,

who noted the rising constellations for the horoscope. It is now clear that the word "diskos" meant not only the athletic implement but also a gong. The entry of "diskos" in the current (ninth) edition of Liddell and Scott's *Lexicon* (published in 1940) has added this meaning and has also kept the misleading translation of "quoit," which is a ring of metal or rope used in a game like horseshoes.

The statue by Myron (Pl 11) is typical of ancient representations, whether statues, coins, or vases, in showing the warm-up swing before the diskos is thrown.

In Appendix 297 of the *Greek Anthology* there is evidence for the distance of a diskos throw.

Plate 11 Bronze statue of diskos thrower.

12

Phaÿllos jumped five feet more than fifty and threw the diskos five feet less than a hundred.

Three factors are essential in trying to find out if 95 feet was a reasonable distance:

1. How heavy was the diskos?
2. How much room was given the thrower in the balbis?
3. How many turns, if any, did the thrower use?

Ninety-five feet is a reasonable distance if we assume a 15-pound diskos, because the modern 16-pound shot put record is over 70 feet. At Olympia, in order to ensure that the diskoi were equal, three diskoi were stored in a temple for use in the games.

13

In this treasury of the Sicyonians at Olympia there are stored three diskoi which they use in the pentathlon competition.

Pausanias 6.19.4

The following aspects of the diskos event are unknown: the origin of the event (stone used as weapon?), the order in the pentathlon, and the number of throws.

(a) Which of the preceding testimonia clearly contain errors?
(b) Could a competitor use his own diskos?
(c) Explain the belief that a diskos was thrown by a strap.
(d) What important features about throwing the diskos are unclear?
(e) What is the evidence for multiple turns in the diskos?
(f) How large was the balbis?
(g) What features of the ancient and modern diskos are alike? Which are different? What difference in spelling appears for the ancient and the modern event?
(h) How reliable a source is Lucian? When did he live?

Further Readings

Drees, pp 72–74.
Gardiner AAW, pp 154–168.
———— GASF, pp 313–337.
Harris, H.A., "An Olympic Epigram," *Greece and Rome* 7 (1960), pp 7–8.
———— GAA, pp 85–92.
———— SpGR, pp 38–39.

6

Jump

The essential equipment in both the ancient and the modern long jump consists of runway, takeoff board, and landing pit. The dimensions and composition of the ancient takeoff board (*bater,* in Greek) are unknown (Pl 12).

1

The bater is the beginning of the *skamma* [= landing pit] of the pentathletes, from which they first jump, as Seleukos says. Symmachos says that the bater is the middle from which those jumping make a second jump. The explanation of Seleukos is better.

Anecdota Graeca, entry for "bater"

[Seleukos lived in I AD, and Symmachos lived a century or two later.]

The athletes were expected to prepare pits for the long jump and for wrestling, and vase paintings often showed them using a pickaxe. Jumps were measured by a rod.

2

The instrument used to measure the jump is called a *kanon* [= rod].

Pollux, *Dictionary of Names* 3.151

The greatest difference between the ancient and the modern event is that ancient jumpers used *halteres* (Pl 13), which were weights of stone or metal, shaped much like a modern telephone or in some cases like a dumbbell or a clothes iron.

3

The *halteres* are an invention of the pentathletes and were invented for jumping (*halma,* in Greek), from which they take their name. Considering the jump to be one of the most difficult events in competition, the rules permit encouragement of the jumper by means of a flute and also assist him even more with the halteres. For then guidance of the hands is unfailing and brings the feet to the ground without wavering and in good form. The

Plate 12   Athlete jumping from bater (=takeoff board). Red figure kylix.

rules show how important this is, for they refuse to have the jump measured if the mark is not correct.

Philostratos, *On Athletics* 55

4

Epainetos won the jump and therefore ⟨dedicated⟩ these halteres.

IAG 1

[This inscription is on a halter made of lead, weighing 2.199 kilograms, dated by Moretti as 580–570 BC.]

Some of the information in this book comes from inscriptions, which are written on durable material such as stone or metal. Because of the expense of the material and the difficulty of carving the letters, inscriptions were used for matters considered important, such as dedications or laws. The study of inscriptions is called epigraphy. Because inscriptions are often found in a fragmentary state, an epigraphist must often restore missing sections. The greatest collection of Greek inscriptions is the *Inscriptiones Graecae* (abbreviated as IG), whereas *Sylloge Inscriptionum Graecarum* (abbreviated as Syll[3]), is a much smaller selection. Ninety inscriptions concerning Greek athletics are collected in Luigi Moretti's *Iscrizioni Agonistiche Greche* (abbreviated IAG). Another collection is the *Corpus Inscriptionum Graecarum* (abbreviated CIG). The location of the inscriptions is given for the benefit of teachers who want to consult the Greek.

Plate 13   Athlete in middle of "float," using halteres (= jumping weights), has just cleared rod held by coach to help in gaining height. Athlete on left is exercising with halteres. Red figure kylix.

5
A pentathlete using halteres jumps farther than one without them.

Aristotle, *On the Movement of Animals* 3.705a; repeated in almost the same words
in *Problems* 5.8.8816

A German scholar, Joachim Ebert, conducted an experiment with athletes using weights weighing 2.5 kilograms each. His results, as reported by Drees (p 75), are surprising: "In the running jump the weights proved a hindrance, reducing normal performance more than a meter. In the standing jump, however, performances were improved by fifteen to twenty centimetres." Considering Testimonium 5 by Aristotle, we can draw only one conclusion: Ebert's athletes did not use the same techniques as the Greeks.

The halteres were often used as training devices. Indeed, a Dr. Leonard Schwartz has written a book entitled *Heavyhands* (Boston, Little, Brown, 1983) featuring exercises using implements like the Greek halteres.

Even if we grant that the use of weights in some way added enormously to a jump (let us say 10 feet), we still cannot explain the reported jumps, one of 52 feet, one of 55 feet, and one of more than 50 feet (Testimonia 6, 7, and 8, respectively).

6
In the 29th Olympics (664 BC) Chionis of Sparta won the stade; in the jump he did 52 feet.

Sextus Julius Africanus

7

Phaÿllos jumped five feet more than 50 feet and threw the diskos five feet less than 100 feet.

Greek Anthology, Appendix 297

[This short poem was preserved in a collection of poems and is found in the notes of six different editors. All these sources, however, were written centuries after the alleged event. There are so many references to Phaÿllos that some scholars think there must have been two people with the same name. One Phaÿllos is known to have been an athlete and to have fought in the Persian Wars.]

8

"To jump over the *skamma"*: 50 feet was the length of the skamma (jump-ing pit) in ancient times . . . Phaÿllos in jumping over the skamma, jumped more than 50 feet.

The *Suda,* entry for "skamma"

Here are some of the theories that have attempted to explain the reported length of some ancient jumps.

1. The Phaÿllos poem, the *Victor List,* and the *Suda* are all errors.
2. The Greeks were physically superior to modern athletes.
3. The bater was a type of trampoline.
4. The skamma was lower than the bater.
5. The halteres were much more efficient than modern experiments have shown.
6. The jump was a double or triple (hop, skip, and jump).
7. The record jumps were a deliberate fabrication.
8. The Phaÿllos jump was a joke whose point eludes us.
9. The "feet" used in measuring were much shorter than our modern foot.

Here follows a brief critique of some of these suggestions.

1. In evaluating historical evidence, one should not dismiss it as false until all other explanations have been examined. The question of the accuracy of these records is complicated. In the *Victor List,* for example, an Armenian transla-tion gives the distance of a jump as 22 feet. It should be noted that in Greek the numerals for 22 and 52 can be easily confused ($22 = \kappa\beta$; $52 = \nu\beta$). How-ever, it should also be noted that the evidence about Phaÿllos occurs in a poem with a fixed metrical form, which makes any accidental substitution most un-likely.
2. There is no evidence to support the assumption of physical superiority of the Greeks.
3. There is no evidence supporting use of a trampoline.
4. Unless the jump was made on a steep slope, the effect of a lower landing place would be small.
5. Even if we assume a much more effective use of halteres, such assistance could not account for a 52- or 55-foot jump.

Plate 14 Jumper still holds halteres when landing. Black figure lekythos.

6. The multiple jump is the favored solution of the majority of scholars, because the modern triple jump (also called the hop, step, and jump) is over 58 feet. However there is no solid ancient evidence, either literary or pictorial, to support this theory of multiple jump; the following testimonium is hard to understand.

9

For those jumping in the pentathlon do not make a continuous movement, because they interrupt part of the interval in which they are moving.

Themistius, *Notes on Aristotle's Physics* 5.3

The weight of modern scholarship favors some kind of multiple jump, perhaps taking the distance of two separate jumps added together. Or perhaps it was like our hop, step, and jump. One of the strangest things about the ancient jump is that flutists were often brought in to play for the jumpers (Pl 14). How this instrument could have been any help to jumpers is impossible to guess.

The number of trial jumps is not known. There are pictures of standing jumps and vaulting onto horses, and references to running high jumps as training exercises:

10
Useful exercises are jumping, either for height or distance.

Seneca, *Moral Letters* 15.4

There are scattered references to vaulting with a spear to escape an animal, but no record of vaulting in competition.

11
Perhaps Nestor would have died before the Trojan War, but he planted his spear and with a mighty effort leaped into the branches of a nearby tree and in safety looked down from his position on the enemy [=boar] which he had escaped.

Ovid, *Metamorphoses* 8.365–368

(a) What were the differences between the ancient Greek long jump and the modern jumps?
(b) What was the longest jump in ancient Greece?
(c) What implement was commonly shown in vase paintings?
(d) Give several explanations of the Phaÿllos jump, and give reasons for either accepting or rejecting them.

Further Readings

Drees, pp 74–75.
Ebert, J. "Zum Pentathlon der Antike," *Saxon Academy* 56.1 (1963), pp 2–34. (In German)
Gardiner, E.N., ""'Phaÿllos and his Record Jump," *Journal of Hellenic Studies* 24 (1904), pp 70–80.
———— AAW, pp 144–153.
———— GASF, pp 295–312.
Harris GAA, pp 80–85.
————SpGR, pp 35–36.
Yalouris, pp 176–187.

7

Javelin

The modern javelin is made of metal and must not be less than 8½ feet long or weigh less than 1.765 pounds. It has a whipcord binding at the point of balance and a metal tip. No throwing aids are permitted. There is a balkline over which the thrower must not step. The javelin must land in a fair area, a sector of 30 degrees, and must land tip first. The world record is over 340 feet.

The ancient Greek javelin was made of wood, with a metal ferrule or point to permit the weapon to stick in the ground and protect the shaft.

1
Now the god gave victory to Automedon. For he surpassed the other competitors in the pentathlon as the bright moon on the night when it is full surpasses the stars in its light. So in the countless number of the Hellenes did he appear as a wondrous figure. He aroused the shouts of the people when he threw the circular diskos, or when he cast high into the air a shaft made from dark-leafed elder tree, or when he finished the flashing wrestling.

Bacchylides, *Odes* 8.25–36

2
O Sogenes of the Euxenid family, I swear when I shot forth my fast tongue I did not step over the line like the ⟨thrower of the⟩ javelin with point of bronze, ⟨the victory in the javelin⟩ which removes ⟨the threat to⟩ the neck and muscles from the sweat of wrestling before one's limbs enter the bright sunshine.

Pindar, *Nemean Odes* 7.70–73

The athlete in the image stepped over the balkline and therefore was disqualified from further participation in the pentathlon. It is not clear whether the athlete had only one throw, nor does it say that the javelin came just before the wrestling, although it does suggest this. From vase paintings, the shaft appears to have been

Plate 15 Two athletes brandishing javelins with mesagkylon (= throwing strap). Amphora.

about 6 feet long and as thick as a finger. The javelins used in athletic events may have been lighter than those used in war and lighter than the modern javelin. The greatest difference between the ancient and modern event is that the Greeks used a throwing strap (Pl 15) about a foot or foot and a half long, wrapped around the shaft at the point of balance.

3

A *mesagkylon* is a kind of javelin with a cord wrapped around the middle, which the athletes hold on to as they throw.

Scholiast on Euripides, *Andromache* 1133

[According to Gardiner AAW, p 174, the Emperor Napoleon III, a student of ancient history, reported that untrained men, who could throw the javelin only 25 meters, increased their performance to 65 meters when using this strap.]

We have some indirect evidence about the distance an athlete could throw, and it appears that the Greeks could throw over 300 feet. There was a balkline (see Testimonium 2) and a fair area in which the javelin must fall.

4

The track ⟨for horses⟩ has a distance from one end to the other of four throws of the javelin or three bow shots.

Statius, *Thebaid* 6.353–354

[The race course varied in distance from 200 to 600 yards. Records of arrow flights vary from 200 to 500 yards. See Harris (SpGR, pp 96–99).]

The javelin had to fall in a fair area:

5

As for this bronze-pointed javelin which I am shaking in my hand, I hope I will not, as the expression goes, throw it out of bounds but rather hurl it a long distance, so as to surpass my competitors.

Pindar, *Pythian Odes* 1.44–45

It appears from vase paintings that in the Panathenaic Games there was a contest in throwing the javelin at a target, but there is no evidence that this event was used in the Crown Games:

6

Phrastor struck the mark with his javelin.

Pindar, *Olympian Odes* 10.85

[Pindar is describing the winners in the legendary first Olympic Games founded by Herakles in the Heroic Age, before the Trojan War and before the reorganization of the games at Olympia in 776 BC. Furthermore, according to Liddell and Scott, the standard Greek–English dictionary, the verb that we translate as "strike" means to strike with a weapon (like a sword) but never with a missile like a javelin. The word "mark," as used here then, is probably a metaphor meaning "throw to the spot he needed to reach for victory."]

Plate 16 Athlete completing approach run uses rear cross step to initiate javelin throw. Red figure amphora.

The Greeks used measuring rods for performance in diskos, jump, and javelin. It is sometimes difficult to tell whether the athletes are holding javelins or measuring rods, but if the implement has a metal tip it is a javelin.

Vase paintings do not tell us much about the technique of throwing. The vase painters generally chose to show the thrower in a position of rest, perhaps cleaning the point. However, it appears that except for the use of the throwing strap, ancient and modern techniques were similar (Pl 16). The number of trial throws is not known. The javelin may have been the fourth event, just before wrestling, in the pentathlon.

(a) Compare the ancient Greek javelin with the modern javelin. What is the greatest difference between the two?
(b) How far could the ancient javelin be thrown? How good is the evidence?

Further Readings

Drees, pp 75–76.
Gardiner AAW, pp 169–176.
——— GASF, pp 338–358.
Harris GAA, pp 92–97.
——— SpGR, pp 36–38.
Lee, H.M., "The *TEPMA* and the Javelin in Pindar," *Journal of Hellenic Studies* 96 (1976), pp 70–79.
Yalouris, pp 196–201.

8

Scoring the Pentathlon

How the pentathlon was scored has been perhaps the most puzzling problem in all Greek athletics. As E. Norman Gardiner wrote in 1903, "The difficulty of this question is due to the scanty and unsatisfactory character of the literary evidence." Almost all we know from ancient evidence is that there were five events (diskos, jump, javelin, run, and wrestling), that three victories were required to win, and that wrestling was the last event.

1

Pentathlete is used instead of "those competing in the five events" or "those winning in the five events," because not all the pentathletes win all five events. For three of the five events are sufficient for them to win.

Scholiast on Aristeides 3.339

2

Akmatides the Spartan dedicated this after winning the five events *akoniti.*[1]

IAG 8 (inscription on *halter* found at Olympia, dated about 500 BC)

3

Competing in the pentathlon he [= Tisamenos] was within one wrestling match of winning the Olympic crown against Hieronymos of Andros.

Herodotus 9.33

4

Tisamenos received a prophecy that he was going to gain the five most glorious crowns. Therefore he trained for the Olympic pentathlon but was defeated, although he did win two events. For he defeated Hieronymos of Andros in running and in jumping. But he was defeated by Hieronymos in wrestling and, in failing to gain the victory, he understood the prophecy—when he consulted the oracle the god had promised him that he would win five *military* victories.

Pausanias 3.11.6

5

Before the time of Iason and Peleus, jumping was a separate event, the diskos was a separate event, and winning the javelin throw was enough for a victory at the time of the voyage of the Argo. Telamon was the best at the diskos, Lynkeus best at throwing the javelin, and the sons of the North Wind excelled at running and jumping. Peleus was second in these events but was superior to all in wrestling. Therefore, when they held games in Lemnos they say that in order to please Peleus, Iason combined the five events and that Peleus won the victory.

Philostratos, *On Athletics* 3

Gardiner published a comprehensive article, "The Method of Deciding the Pentathlon," refuting all previous theories up to that time. George E. Bean discussed subsequent theories advanced since Gardiner in his article, "Victory in the Pentathlon." Joachim Ebert proposed in "Zum Pentathlon der Antike" a solution that counted second places. This theory was discussed by R. Merkelbach in "Der Sieg im Pentathlon." Gardiner and Lauri Pihkala put forth their own theory, "The System of the Pentathlon," a journal article that was summarized in Gardiner's AAW (pp 178–180). All these scholars bring conclusive proof that their predecessors' solutions will not work. Since Gardiner's theory is best known, we will examine it briefly. Here is his explanation, given on page 180 of AAW:

Any competitor who is defeated by any other in three events is cut out. If one competitor is actually first in three of the four events, he alone is left in and must be the winner. Similarly, any competitor who is actually first in two events must be left in. It will generally happen that the events are divided between three or four competitors. The usual result is that from two to four competitors are left in, each of them having defeated each of the others in two, not necessarily the same, events; a larger number is possible but very improbable. These then compete in wrestling, and the winner in the wrestling is the winner of the pentathlon; he is indeed a triple victor, for he has defeated each of his rivals in three events. The working of this scheme is clear from the following table, giving the imaginary performances of 6 competitors A B C D E F placed in order of merit in the four events I II III IV:

	I	*II*	*III*	*IV*
1	A	B	C	D
2	E	A	B	F
3	B	D	E	C
4	C	E	A	A
5	F	C	D	B
6	D	F	F	E

Comparing A with each of the other five, his score is A 2, B 2——A 2, C 2——A 3, D 1——A 3, E 1——A 3, F 1. D E F therefore drop out. Similarly B has defeated C in two events, lost in two events. No one has defeated A B C in more than two events. These three all tie and qualify for the wrestling match.

That this was the actual method of deciding the pentathlon cannot be proved, but it so completely satisfies all the conditions imposed by such evidence as we possess that we may safely accept it as approximately correct.

Gardiner's system is complicated, as anyone will agree who has tried to apply it. Worse than this is the fact that there are combinations where there will be *no* winner. If, for example, at the end of the first four events, the standings were as follows,

Jump	Diskos	Javelin	Run
A	B	C	D
B	C	D	A
C	D	A	B
D	A	B	C

then there would be no one qualified for the wrestling, since each pentathlete would have been beaten by three competitors in an event, which, according to Gardiner's theory, eliminates them.

Other systems that have been proposed include the following:

1. Five (or three) outright victories.
2. Tournaments in which pairs compete in all five events and winners advance as in a modern tennis tournament.
3. Points, as one for first place, ten for tenth place; lowest score wins.
4. Weighting some event, such as having some athletes compete in two wrestling matches.
5. Progressive elimination, such as eliminating in the first event all competitors who fail to meet a certain criterion.
6. Counting second place.
7. *Repechage*, that is, matching athletes who are tied to eliminate one of them.

Some systems use more than one method.

The refutation of Ebert's theory lies first in the fact that the Philostratos citation (Testimonium 5) should be accepted with great caution. Philostratos is a notoriously inaccurate authority. Second, the event he describes occurred in mythological times, a generation before the Trojan War. There is no suggestion of any pentathlon in Homer. Finally, Merkelbach shows that grotesque results can occur when using Ebert's system. Consider, for example, these results:

Jump	Diskos	Javelin	Run	Wrestling
A	A	B	B	C
C	C	C	C	A
B	B	A	A	B

A with victories in two events and B with two are beaten in Ebert's system by C, with only one victory.

We propose the following solution. All competitors competed in the first three events. If the same athlete won all three events, he was the outright winner, and events four and five were cancelled. If there was no winner at the end of event number three, all contestants competed in event number four, at the end of which there could have been only four combinations:

1. One athlete had won three of the four events; he was the winner, and the fifth event (wrestling) was cancelled.
2. Two athletes had each won two victories; they proceeded to the wrestling, where one of the two would win his third victory.
3. One athlete had scored two victories, and two other athletes had scored one apiece.
4. There had been a different victor in each of the four events.

When there had been a different winner in each event, as in item 4 in the list, the four athletes, whom we designate as A, B, C, and D, were matched by lot. Each pair then competed in an event selected by lot from an event *that neither athlete had won* in this competition. For example, let us assume that A had won the diskos and his opponent B had won the running. They would compete against each other in *either* the javelin *or* the jump, as the lot decided. Athletes C and D then competed in an event chosen by lot in which neither had been victorious, that is, in either the javelin or the jump. The victors in these pairs would then have two victories each, and they would proceed to the wrestling, which would decide the winner.

If there was one athlete with two victories and two with one win, as in item 3 in the list, the two with one victory would compete against each other in an event that neither had won; the winner of this match, who now had two victories, met in the wrestling with the other athlete with two victories, to determine the victor.

Such use of lots was common in Greece. An opportunity to compete a second time is used in some modern sports, as in crew; it is known as *repechage*.

(a) Explain the system of scoring the pentathlon that has just been described. Was there any way in which there could have been no victor?

Further Readings

Bean, G.E., ''Victory in the Pentathlon,'' *American Journal of Philology* 60 (1956), pp 361–368.

Drees, pp 76–77.

Ebert, J., ''Zum Pentathlon der Antike,'' *Saxon Academy* 56.1 (1963), pp 2–34.

Gardiner, E.N., ''The Method of Deciding the Pentathlon,'' *Journal of Hellenic Studies* 23 (1903), pp 54–70. Of great interest; contains a survey of previous scholarship.

——— AAW, pp 177–180.

——— GASF, pp 359–371.

Gardiner, E.N., and Pihkala, L., ''The System of the Pentathlon,'' *Journal of Hellenic Studies* 45 (1925), pp 132–134.

Sweet, W. E., ''A New Proposal for Scoring the Greek Pentathlon,'' *Zeitschrift für Papyrologie und Epigraphik* 50 (1983), pp 287–290.

9

Combat Sports

The Greeks had three types of contests that simulated hand-to-hand fighting. One was wrestling, in which the opponents grappled with and tried to force each other to the ground, but without striking. A second type of combat competition was boxing, in which striking was permitted, but not grappling or tripping. The third type was the *pankration,* whose name suggests its nature (*pan* = all, *kratos* = strength): the participants could both grapple and strike. There is visual evidence for these sports, particularly paintings on ancient vases. We cannot always tell whether what is shown in the painting is a legal move, a foul, or a practice maneuver. Usually it is possible to tell wrestling from boxing, but both may be easily confused with the pankration.

None of the three events had weight classes as we have today. Consequently big men had an advantage in combat sports, which were termed "heavy" events, as opposed to "light" events like running and jumping. There were however divisions according to age, that is, men and boys competed separately in all events at the Olympic Games (except for the boys' pentathlon, which was held once and then abandoned). For other games there were three age classes: boys, youths, and men. Contestants in a combat event drew lots to determine their opponents in the first round. The victors in this round then drew lots to determine the pairing in the second round, and so on. Here is an explanation of the method:

1

Lykinos: You know, don't you, how they choose by lot one's opponent in wrestling or pankration?

Hermotimos: I do.

Lykinos: Since you have seen it firsthand, you can describe it better than I can.

Hermotimos: On the one hand, in the old days when Herakles was the chief official, they took laurel leaves . . .

Lykinos: Skip the old days, dear Hermotimos, and tell us what you know firsthand.

Hermotimos: A silver vase sacred to the god is put out in front. Into it are thrown small lots, as large as a bean with letters on them. There are two marked with an alpha on each, two with a beta, and so with the others, two gammas, and so on in order; if there are more competitors, two lots are always marked with the same letter. Then each of the athletes comes up and with a prayer to Zeus puts his hand in the vase and pulls out one of the lots. After him, another does the same thing. Standing by each athlete is an official with a whip who holds his hand and keeps him from reading the letter which he has drawn. Then the *alutarches* [= head of the police], I think, or one of the Hellanodikai (for I don't remember this) goes around the athletes, who are standing in a circle, and looks at their lots and in this way he matches in wrestling or pankration the man holding an alpha with the person holding the other alpha. Then in the same way he matches beta with beta and the others holding the same letter in this manner. He does it this way, if the competitors are even in number, like eight, four, or twelve, but if they are odd, say five, seven, or nine, he mixes in with the other matched lots an odd lot with a letter on it which does not match any other. Whoever draws this lot waits as an *ephedros* [= athlete waiting to fight winner of bout in progress] while the other pairs fight. And this is a considerable advantage to an athlete, to be able to compete fresh against competitors who are fatigued.

Lucian, Hermotimos 39–40

What seems like a curious feature is that lots were drawn by *all* contestants at *each* level. A person who achieved a bye in the first round also drew for the next round and sometimes progressed to the finals without ever competing in a single round:

2

He gained the victory at Olympia in a boys' pankration without the benefit of drawing a bye, engaging in three bouts with his competitors. . . . He did not win the crown by luck of the draw but he won without getting a bye.

IAG 64

We learn from Pindar that in one wrestling contest the winner defeated four opponents:

3

And from above, you fell with cruel purpose at the Pythian Games on the bodies of four opponents, for whom no happy homecoming was decreed as there was for you, and as they returned to their mothers, no sweet laughter brought pleasure, but they crept through the back streets, avoiding their enemies, crushed by their misfortune.

Pindar, Pythian Odes 8.115–122

[In the contest referred to above, there would have been sixteen competitors in the first round. If a victor won all matches with no falls against him, he would have won twelve falls in 1 day.]

There are inscriptions that record ties in wrestling:

4

⟨This inscription honors⟩ Aurelius Lucillius and Aurelius Dionysius, son of Zosimos, who fought with distinction and were awarded first place together in the men's wrestling at the Augustan Games.

Inscription (from Olbasa in Asia Minor, a town founded by the Emperor Augustus),
published by *Wiener Studien* (1902), 24

[We do not know what circumstances produced a tie. Perhaps the two who qualified for the final were injured and were unable to compete. The Greek word for "tie" was *hiera*, which also means "sacred"; in case of a tie, the prize was dedicated to the god in whose honor the games were held; hence it was called sacred. In the funeral games for Patroklos (see Chapter 2), Odysseus and Aias tie in wrestling.]

In all three combat sports an athlete could win *akoniti* [without dust]:

5

A man named Dromeus from Mantineia was said to have been the first we know of to have won the pankration by default [= akoniti].

Pausanias 6.11.4

An athlete could win akoniti by luck of the draw or by withdrawal of an opponent because of injury or some other reason. Pausanias considered this type of victory worthless:

6

I shall not even describe all the statues which have been set up since. I know which ones got the wild olive not by strength but by the luck of the draw.

Pausanias 6.1.1

[An athlete could also win akoniti if his opponents recognized his superior ability and withdrew to avoid injury. This kind of victory was considered laudable and is mentioned prominently in inscriptions, as in Testimonium 6 in Chapter 21.]

The word akoniti also had a metaphorical meaning, as this quote shows:

7

Akoniti means "without contest or battle," that is, "easily," taken from the language of athletes who win so easily that they do not get dusty.

The *Suda*, entry for "akoniti"

(a) What were the three combat sports in ancient Greece?
(b) At the Olympic Games the athletes were divided into two classes. What were they?
(c) Which events were called "heavy"?
(d) Describe the drawing of lots.
(e) What was unfair about the drawing of lots, as the Greeks did it?
(f) What three meanings did akoniti have?

Further Readings

Poliakoff, M., *Studies in the Terminology of the Greek Combat Sports* (Königstein 1982).

10

Wrestling

There are three kinds of amateur wrestling in the United States: catch-as-catch-can, free style, and Greco-Roman. We will ignore the "professional wrestling" shown on television. The type of wrestling done in high schools and colleges in the United States is mainly "catch-as-catch-can." In this type of wrestling, the competitors spend about half their time in an upright position and about half the time on the mat. The victor is determined by a complicated system of points.

One type of wrestling in the modern Olympics is free style. It is similar to catch-as-catch-can, but wrestlers tend to remain on their feet more of the time. Victory in Olympic free style is also decided by points. Greco-Roman wrestling, also used in the modern Olympics, is all upper-body wrestling. Use of the legs is prohibited. Victory is determined by points. Uncommon in the United States, it derives its name from the fact that the rules were drawn up in the mistaken belief that this kind of wrestling was that of the ancient world.

Plates 17–19 illustrate several features of ancient Greek wrestling. The victor was the one who threw his opponent in three out of five bouts.

1

Milo ⟨of Kroton⟩ was once the only wrestler to show up at the sacred games. The official in charge at once called him forward to receive the crown. As he approached he slipped and fell on his hip. The spectators shouted that he should not be crowned since he fell when he was all alone. Standing up in the middle, Milo shouted in reply, "That is not three falls. I fell only once; let someone give me the other two falls."

Anonymous author, *Greek Anthology* 11.316

What constituted a fall is the most debated point in ancient wrestling. There is evidence that a wrestler was thrown if his back or one hip or both shoulders touched the ground:

Plate 17 Athletes starting bout. Black figure Panathenaic amphora.

Plate 18 Wrestler applying side body lock. Bronze statuette.

Plate 19 Wrestler using flying mare to throw opponent, a move forbidden in modern wrestling. Red figure kylix.

2

If you ever heard of Damostratos of Dinope, who six times carried off the pine crown at the Isthmian Games, you are looking upon him now. In the twisting sport of wrestling he was never thrown nor did his back ever leave its mark in the sand.

Philippos, Greek Anthology 16.25

The main controversy about the fall, however, concerns the knee. A poem by Semonides suggests that it was a fall if *both* knees touched:

3

This is the glorious statue of glorious Milo, who in fighting seven times at Olympia never fell to his knees.

Semonides, fragment 153D

[Note that Semonides says "knees" in the plural. Some authorities believe it was a fall if only one knee touched.]

Closely connected with this question is whether wrestling continued when the opponents were on the ground:

Plate 20   Wrestler putting dust on opponent. Red figure kylix.

4

But if one of them fell on his back, he pulled his opponent with him and thrust him up and behind him, just as happens in wrestling.

Dio Cassius, 71.7

[It should be noted that this excerpt describes the fighting of *Roman* soldiers, not Greek athletes. The question is further confused by the fact that some of the activities may have been practice exercises.]

Athletes wrestled in a pit that, like the pit for the long jump, was called the *skamma* and was dug by the athletes themselves. For practice the pit was often flooded with water, but in competition the pit was sandy soil. The wrestlers rubbed themselves with olive oil and then, just before their match, covered each other with dust to furnish a good grip (Pl 20).

(a) What are the three most common types of wrestling today?
(b) How many falls decided the victor in Greek wrestling?
(c) What were some possible ways to win a fall?
(d) What is the controversy about falling to the knees?

Further Readings

Drees, pp 80–81.
Gardiner AAW, pp 181–196.
———— GASF, pp 372–401.
Harris GAA, pp 102–105.
———— SpGR, pp 21–23.
Yalouris, pp 202–213.

11

Boxing

Modern boxing resembles the Greek combat sport of boxing only in some ways. Modern scholars frequently say that Greek boxers did not have a ring. It is true that there were no taut ropes for the athletes to bounce against, but there must have been some way of holding back the spectators, and the surrounding crowd would necessarily limit the territory within which the boxers fought. Moreover, a vase in Taranto seems to show officials marking off the boxing area with measuring rods (Pl 21).

There were no rounds, so fighters could not rest except by mutual consent. There are references to different types of equipment used in training, such as punching bag, ear guards, and padded gloves:

1

In order to imitate as nearly as possible the fighting in the ring, instead if *himantes* we would put on *sphairai* so that we could practice striking and the avoidance of blows as much as possible.

Plato, Laws 8.830B

2

For in the palestra they put *episphaira* on the hands of the competitors, so that the bout may not have any serious consequences, since the blows are soft and painless.

Plutarch, "Precepts of Statecraft" 32 (Moralia 825e)

The meaning of the word *sphairomachia* in the next testimonium, written by a Roman, is unclear, because *machia* means "fighting" and *sphaira* means either "round padded glove" or "a ball:"

3

Today I am at leisure due not only to my own efforts but to the show, which has called all the dull people to see the *sphairomachia*.

Seneca, Moral Letters 80.1

Plate 21 Officials marking ring. Black figure Panathenaic amphora.

4

For this reason (so that children will not hear what is improper) Xenokrates recommended that we put *amphotides* [= ear guards] on the children rather than the athletes, because the athletes have only their ears disfigured by the blows they receive, while the children have their characters deformed by what they hear.

Plutarch, "On Listening to Lectures" 2 (Moralia 38B)

5

Boxers' himantes of leather were wrapped around their hands to make them better for striking and to hold the fingers together, binding them stiffly into a round shape, like some sort of club.

Eustathius, 1324.18

The greatest difference between ancient and modern boxing is the gloves. In amateur boxing today, gloves usually weigh 10 or 12 ounces. Professional fighters wear 8-ounce gloves, except during championship bouts, when they use gloves that weigh only 6 ounces. The heavier gloves are used to give more protection, both for the person striking the blow, who needs to protect his hands, and for the recipient of the blows. Until around the end of V BC, fighters' only protection was straps of leather, which appear in vase paintings to be 10 to 12 feet long (Pl 22). Called himantes, they offered little protection for the hands. They were replaced by "sharp gloves" (Pl 23), which offered more protection for the hands but must

Plate 22 Boxer preparing to wrap leather thongs around fists for himantes (= gloves); pentathlete digging skamma (= pit). Red figure kylix.

Plate 23 Detail of bronze boxer statue, showing "sharp gloves."

have increased the damage of the blows. As may be imagined, injuries were frequent and severe:

6

O Augustus, this man Olympikos, as he now appears, used to have nose, chin, forehead, ears, and eyelids. But then he enrolled in the guild of boxers, with the result that he did not receive his share of his inheritance in a will. For in the lawsuit about the will his brother shows the judge a portrait of Olympikos, who was judged to be an imposter, bearing no resemblance to his own picture.

Lucillius, *Greek Anthology* 11.75

7

And I know a similar story about what the judges of Argos did in the case of Kreugas from Epidamnos in boxing. For the Argos judges gave the prize of Nemea to Kreugas although he was dead, because his opponent, a Syracusan named Damoxenos, broke the special rules which the two athletes had agreed upon. For darkness was about to occur as they were fighting, and they agreed in the presence of the judges that each would submit to one blow from the other. The fighters in those days did not have the "sharp gloves," extending up the wrists on both hands but they were fighting with the "soft gloves" with slim strips of rawhide from an ox, and they were crisscross around the hands in the old-fashioned manner. Well then, Kreugas struck his opponent on the face; Damoxenos then told Kreugas to raise his arm to protect his head, and when Kreugas did this, Damoxenos struck him under the ribcage with fingers stiff. Because of the pointed fingers and the force of the blow he drove his arm into the abdominal cavity of his opponent, seized the entrails, and tore them out. Kreugas expired on the spot, and the Argive judges disqualified Damoxenos because he had not followed the agreement, since instead of one blow he had used several against his opponent. They gave the victory to the deceased Kreugas and set up a statue in Argos, which in my day was located in the sanctuary of Lycian Apollo.

Pausanias, 8.40.3–5

[This unlikely story is not found elsewhere. The meaning of the epithet "Lycian" applied to Apollo is not agreed upon.]

8

Kleoxenos of Alexandria won the boxing in all the Crown Games and finished *atraumatistos* [= without being injured].

Sextus Julius Africanus, *Victor List,* under the year 240 BC

We learn that the rules for boxing were drawn up in 688 BC. We are told that holding was a foul, as were scratching and biting:

9

Boxing was added and Onomastos of Smyrna won; he also wrote the rules for boxing.

Sextus Julius Africanus, *Victor List,* under the year 688 BC

10

The referees do not permit boxers to seize one another even though they may wish to do so.

Plutarch, "Table-talk" 2.4 (*Moralia* 638E)

11

In a bout our opponent may have scratched us with his nails or butted us hard.

Marcus Aurelius, *Meditations* 6.20

A good defense was praiseworthy:

12

Hippomachos of Elis won the boys' boxing . . . . They say he fought three bouts and won without being hit once and without having a mark on his body.

Pausanias 6.12.6

Victory was awarded to the athlete whose competitor was unable or unwilling to continue. The signal for surrender was an upraised hand (Pl 24). Presumably the judge could stop the fight to avoid unnecessary injury.

Vase paintings often show boxers in abnormal postures (Pl 25), but we should not think that the Greeks fought in such an unnatural way. We have here an artistic convention. Although the Greeks knew about perspective and foreshorten-

Plate 24 The signal for surrender in both boxing and pankration was an upraised hand. Because contestants here are not wearing gloves, this is probably the pankration. Black figure Panathenaic amphora.

Plate 25 Boxer at left binding thongs around fists. Judge, identified by clothing and rod, signals start of fight. Boxers are shown holding their arms at an impossible angle, according to artistic convention. Athlete on right exercises with halteres. Red figure kylix.

ing, they generally ignored it in their art. On vases the painter usually shows the torso from a front view, and the head, shoulders, arms, and legs in profile; the face is in profile, whereas the eyes are shown from the front. Showing the boxers with their arms held in front in a normal manner would have covered the chest to the detriment of the painting, so the artist rotated the arms 90 degrees. In a marble relief (Pl 26), if the artist had put the arms in their natural position, they would have protruded from the rest of the carving.

(a) What were the different types of boxing gloves?
(b) Did they offer more or less protection than modern gloves?
(c) What constituted a foul?
(d) What was the normal sparring position?
(e) In Testimonium 8, what was unusual about the career of Kleoxenos?
(f) How dangerous was ancient boxing?

Dio Chrysostomos (= Dio with the golden voice) lived in I and II AD. It has been suggested that his description of the boxer Melankomas, given as Testimonium 13, was actually delivered as a funeral oration. It has also been thought that the games described in this discourse were the Ludi Augustales given in honor of Augustus in Naples in the year 74 AD. Titus, who was to become emperor in 79 AD, was an official in these games. On the other hand, some believe that the

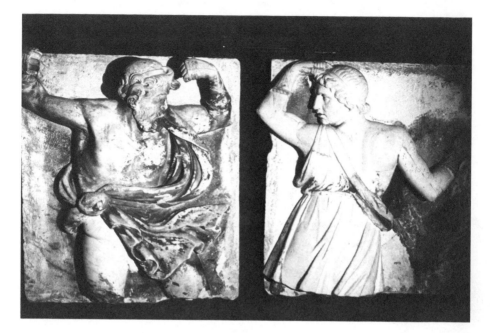

Plate 26   Boxers with arms in abnormal pose. Marble relief.

whole discourse describes an imaginary person. Whatever the truth of the matter, the selection is of considerable importance in trying to understand ancient boxing.

13

After we had come up from the harbor, we at once walked over to see the athletes, as eagerly as if this inspection was the whole reason for our trip. When we got to the gymnasium we saw some of the athletes running outside on the track, as the spectators cheered them on, while other athletes were practicing other events. There seemed to be little point in watching these, and we went wherever we saw the biggest crowds.

Consequently, we observed a large number of people standing near the *exedra* [=portico with curved benches] of Herakles. Others were continually joining the throng, while still others were leaving when they found that they could not see what was going on. At first we tried to see by craning our necks, and with some difficulty we were able to get a glimpse of the head of an athlete exercising, with his hands held out in front of him. After a bit we worked our way in closer. We found him to be a young man of great height and beauty, and of course his body seemed larger and more beautiful because of the exercise he was doing. He was putting on a splendid performance, with such enthusiasm that he seemed more as if he were really fighting an opponent.

When he ended his exercise and the crowd began to disperse, we observed him carefully. He looked like a skillfully carved statue, and his skin was the color of bronze.

When he was gone we asked an old man who had been one of the audience who he was. He gave a sad look and answered, "If you must know, that is Iatrokles, rival of Melankomas. He was the only opponent of Melankomas who would not yield to him—at least not until he was unable to continue. But he never beat Melankomas, for he always lost, although sometimes they used to fight all day. But Iatrokles had finally given up trying; consequently at the last contest held in Naples, Melankomas defeated him quicker than he did anyone else. But now you see how high his morale is and what a crowd comes to watch him. I know that my own feeling is that he is glad about what happened to Melankomas. That's natural, for he knows that not only will he win the crown in these games but also in all the other games."

"What's that?" I cried, "Melankomas dead?" You see, we knew him by reputation, though we had never seen him.

"Yes," he replied. "He died a little while ago, and his funeral was the day before yesterday."

"In what way," I asked, "was he superior to Iatrokles and all the others? Was it in size or in courage?"

"My friend," he said, "he was more courageous and larger than any of his opponents, than any man alive, and was the most beautiful as well. If he had stayed out of athletics and never accomplished anything noteworthy, he would still have been famous for his looks alone. As it was, he attracted the eyes of everyone, no matter where he went, including those who did not know who he was.

"However, he did not dress in fine clothes nor try any other way to attract attention but he tried rather to escape notice. But when he had stripped, no one looked at anyone else although there were many other competitors, both boys and men. Although beauty usually leads to lack of vigor, even in those who are only moderately handsome, Melankomas, beautiful as he was, kept his sense of values. And although he held his beauty in low esteem, he nevertheless kept it undamaged in spite of the rough activity he had taken up.

"Although he competed in boxing, he was as unmarked as any runner. And he had trained so hard and had gone so far beyond his competitors in enduring fatigue that he could stand for two whole days with his arms extended, and no one could see him lowering them or taking a break, as other boxers do. He used to compel his opponents to surrender before they landed a single blow. More surprising than that, they surrendered before he had ever struck them. For he did not think it showed courage to strike them or receive a painful blow, but thought that such tactics were used by boxers who had no tolerance for fatigue and wished to get the fight over with.

"But to hold out as long as required, not to be worn down by the weight of the arms, not to become short of breath, not to be exhausted by the heat—this he thought required the greatest skill."

"And he was right," I cried, interrupting. "For in battle, it is the poor soldiers who throw away their armor, although they know well that without protection they are more liable to be wounded. It is clear that they are more exhausted by their fatigue than by their wounds."

"And that's the reason," the old man answered, "why Melankomas was the first man we know of to stay unbeaten since he first competed in the Pythian Games, acquiring many crowns in important games,[1] meeting many famous opponents. His father, a most distinguished man from Karia, also named Melankomas, was winner in the Olympic Games and in other games, but the son surpassed his father before he reached maturity, for the father was not undefeated.

"With all these wonderful qualities he came to an unhappy end, having endured the agony of athletics without experiencing the pleasures of life. And he was so eager to win that when he was dying he asked his friend Athenodoros, the pankratiast, a childhood friend, how many days of competition were left." And as he said this, the old man began to cry.

"No one blames you for crying so hard," I said, "since he was obviously so closely connected to you."

"By the gods," said he, "we had no connection. He was neither a relative nor a pupil of mine; I happen to coach one of the boys in the pankration. But he was such a person that all who knew him grieved when he died."

"In that case," said I, "you should not say he came to an unhappy end. Quite the opposite: he was happy and blessed beyond all others if he was what you say he was. He happened to come from a distinguished family, was beautiful and, more than that, was strong and courageous, with a good sense of values, and these qualities are the greatest gifts we can have. The most amazing thing about the man was that he was not only superior to his opponents but also overcame fatigue and blazing heat and the urging of his stomach and his sexual drives. For the man who intends not to yield to an opponent must first not yield to these.

"You spoke about the pleasures he has missed. Whoever enjoyed more pleasure than an athlete eager to win who was always victorious and who knew that he was an object of admiration? In my opinion, the gods loved him very much, and they especially honored him by this death, so that he might experience none of the sorrows of life. For it is certain that if he had continued to live he would have become uglier rather than more beautiful, weaker instead of stronger, and in the same way might sometime have suffered defeat. But any man who dies in the midst of the greatest honors after he has done mighty deeds has died the happiest of deaths. One can find in past generations people beloved by the gods who died young."

"To whom do you refer?" he asked.

"Achilleus, for one," I said, "and Patroklos and Hektor and Memnon and Sarpedon,"[2] and I was about to mention still others when he said, "What you have said is a comfort for those who mourn, and I would like to hear more of what you have to say, but it is now time for me to train my young athlete, so I must leave."

Dio Chrysostomos, *Discourse* 28

(a) What seems to have been the standing of Greek athletes in Naples at this time?
(b) Was Naples a typical Roman city?
(c) From the description of Melankomas' style, we can draw some inferences about footwork. To fight in this way, would he stand still or would he dance in and out of reach of his opponent?
(d) How long did some of the boxing matches last?
(e) Why was Melankomas not marked?
(f) How long could Melankomas keep his guard up? Does this sound realistic?
(g) What does Dio think of the importance of defense in boxing?
(h) What is the attitude of this author about athletics?

The following excerpt from Theokritos is probably the best description of Greek boxing that we have. As appears from his poems, Theokritos lived in Sicily in the city of Syracuse in III BC. His poems are called "idylls"; the people in them are usually supposed to be simple herdsmen, but their language is highly educated. This type of literature, called pastoral poetry, artificial as it is, has been much imitated down through the years, particularly by the Roman poet Vergil. The Dioskoroi are the twins Kastor and Polydeukes, brothers of Helen of Troy. In this poem they are on the ship Argo along with other famous heroes of the generation before the Trojan War, searching for the famous Golden Fleece. We have omitted the first twenty-six lines, which are an introduction.

14

The Argo with its burden of the beloved children of the gods had escaped the Clashing Rocks and come to the fearful mouth of the snowy Pontos [= Black Sea] and the country of the Bebrykians. Then the men went down the ladders in crowds on either side of Iason's ship. When they had landed on the deep sand of that protected shore, they spread their beds and kindled a fire with rubbing sticks. Then Kastor, master of swift horses, and Polydeukes, whose skin was as dark as wine, separated themselves from the others and wandered alone, exploring the wild forest of the mountains, full of trees of all kinds. And under a rocky cliff they found a never-failing spring flowing with pure water. The stones at the bottom shone from the depths like crystal and silver. Beside it grew tall poplars and other trees, pines and cypresses with pointed tips, and plants with sweet-smelling blossoms, which furnish happy employment for the shaggy bees, the kind of flowers that bloom in the meadows at the beginning of summer.

And in this spot sitting out in the sun was a man of tremendous size, horrible to look at, with ears beaten into shapelessness by blows from fists as hard as rock. His great chest and broad back were ridged with flesh seemingly made of iron, like a giant statue fashioned by a hammer, and the muscles of his mighty arms swelled up to his shoulders like rounded rocks which a wild winter flood has polished in great whirlpools. More than this, over his shoulders and back hung a lion skin, suspended by its claws.

Polydeukes, winner of contests, was the first to speak and addressed him thus: Good day, sir, whoever you are. Tell me, who are the people who live here?

Amykos: How can it be a good day when I see men I have never seen before?

Polydeukes: Be of good cheer. Believe me when I say that we are law-abiding and so were our forefathers.[3]

Amykos: I am cheerful enough, but it does not appear that you have made me so.

Polydeukes: Are you a rustic boor, haughty and spiteful toward all?

Amykos: I am just what I appear to be, and I am not standing on *your* property.

Polydeukes: Step on mine then, and you will leave with suitable presents of friendship.

Amykos: Keep your friendship presents; I have none ready for you.

Polydeukes: My friend, won't you at least let me drink this water?

Amykos: You will find out when thirst parches your blistered lips.

Polydeukes: Do you want silver or something else of value? Tell me, what will persuade you?

Amykos: Stand there and raise your hands to me, man to man.

Polydeukes: Boxing, you mean? Or do you wish to fight also with feet and legs? I warn you, my eyesight is good.

Amykos: Put up your fists and use all of your skill.

Polydeukes: But who are you, against whom I will wrap my hands with thongs?

Amykos: You see him before you. Your opponent is no effeminate man, and is called The Boxer.

Polydeukes: And is there a prize ready for us to compete for?

Amykos: If I defeat you, you will be my property, and I will be yours if you win.

Polydeukes: These are the rules of fights between red-crested roosters.

Amykos: Whether we fight like roosters or lions, we will fight for no other prize.

So spoke Amykos, and he took his hollow seashell and blew a blast. Quickly the Bebrykians, who always wear their hair long, obeyed the call of the shell and gathered in numbers under the shady plane trees. In similar fashion, Kastor, great in battle, went and summoned all of the heroes of the ship from Magnesia. And after the two contestants had protected their hands with strips of leather and wrapped the long thongs around their forearms, they came together in the center, breathing destruction against each other.

At this point each tried hard to maneuver so as to have the sun at his back. But through your skill, O Polydeukes, you got around this huge man, and Amykos had the rays of sun full in his face. Then he rushed forward, full of anger, and aimed blows at Polydeukes. The son of Tyndaris[4] struck him on the tip of the chin as he advanced. At that Amykos was more aroused than before, and he began to swing wildly and, being so tall, leaned on the shorter Polydeukes. The Bebrykians broke into shouts, and the heroes for their part encouraged their mighty Polydeukes, for they were afraid that possibly this man so like Tityos[5] might defeat him by using his weight in this narrow place.

But then the son of Zeus, shifting now this way and now that, cut him, first with one hand, then with the other, and this slowed down the attack of the son of Poseidon, formidable as he was. These blows made him drunk and he spat out crimson blood. All the glorious heroes of the Argo shouted in unison, when they saw the damage Amykos had suffered around his mouth and jaw. As his face swelled, his eyes started to close. Then Polydeukes, commander of men, confused his opponent by feinting from all directions. And when he saw that Amykos was confused, he smashed his fist into his opponent's brow, right over the nose, and opened up his forehead to the bone. And Amykos lay stretched out on his back among the flowering petals.

When he regained his feet, the battle became fierce. The blows they aimed at one another with the hard gloves were meant to kill. The lord of the Bebrykians aimed his blows at the body, all below the neck. But Polydeukes the unbeaten pounded his opponent's whole face into a shapeless mass with disfiguring blows, and as Amykos sweated, his flesh seemed to shrink, and soon the man who had been so large became small, but the harder Polydeukes fought, the stronger his body seemed and the better the color of his skin.

O Muse, how did the son of Zeus destroy that greedy man? Tell me, for thou knowest the answer, and I who interpret these things to others will sing whatever and however thou wouldst.

And then Amykos, trying to win by some one great effort, seized the left hand of Polydeukes with his own left hand. Moving to the right as he lunged forward, he came in with his right, bringing his great fist up from his hip. Had the blow landed, he would have hurt the King of Amyklai [= Polydeukes]. But Polydeukes avoided the blow by ducking his head and simultaneously with his powerful right arm hit him under the left temple, a straight blow from the shoulder. And from the open wound made in the temple dark blood flowed freely. Then with his left he smashed him in the mouth, and the close-set teeth rattled. With an ever-increasing barrage of blows, he hammered his face until it was a shapeless bloody mass. On the ground lay Amykos, all of him, with his wits wandering, and he held up both hands in surrender, for he was near death. But you, Polydeukes the boxer, although you won, you did nothing unseemly; you had him swear a powerful oath, calling on his father Poseidon in the sea, that he would never again knowingly be inhospitable to strangers.

Theokritos, "Hymn to the Dioskoroi," *Idyll* 22, lines 27–134

(a) Amykos and Polydeukes are contrasting types in several ways. Give illustrations of this.

(b) What serious sin, in the eyes of early Greeks, does Amykos commit?

(c) At what time of the day does the match occur?

(d) Comment on the style of the two contestants.

(e) Does the violence in this selection fit with other evidence about ancient boxing?

(f) How does Amykos foul his opponent?

(g) What type of gloves are used?

(h) Certain scholars (eg, K.T. Frost, 1906) have said that the Greek boxers had no knowledge of footwork but slugged it out toe to toe. Does this passage support or contradict this view?

Further Readings

Drees, pp 81–83.

Frost, K.T., "Greek Boxing," *Journal of Hellenic Studies* 26 (1906), pp 213–225. Use with caution.

Gardiner AAW, pp 197–211.

——GASF, pp 402–434.

Harris GAA, pp 97–101.

——SpGR, pp 22–25.

Papalas, A., "The Development of Greek Boxing," *Ancient World* 9 (1984), pp 67–76.

Yalouris, pp 216–225.

12

Pankration

The pankration was a combat sport that combined wrestling and boxing. It apparently resembled some of the oriental martial arts now becoming popular in America, particularly full-contact karate. The evidence for the pankration is not plentiful, and many scholars have not understood some of this evidence. Here is what we know. We are told that the contestants struck with hands and feet:

1
Athletes fighting with blows of the hands and feet.

> The *Suda*, entry for "pankratiasts"

As in boxing, an athlete won if his opponent could not, or would not, continue. The evidence is clear that the pankration was considered by the Greeks to be less dangerous than boxing:

2
The pankration has the same characteristics as boxing except it does not have the injuries.

> Artemidoros, *Book of Dreams* 1.62

Plate 27 seems to show that tripping was permitted, while Plates 28 and 29 shows obvious fouls. However there is some difference of opinion as to who is doing the fouling in Plate 29: is it the man on the right, who is biting, or the man on the left, who is about to deliver a deadly rabbit punch?

3
At the next Olympics (212 BC) Kleitomachos was a competitor in both the pankration and boxing. At the same games, Kapros of Elis wanted to enter the wrestling and pankration on the same day. After Kapros won the wrestling, Kleitomachos said to the Hellanodikai that it would be fair if the pankration were moved up ahead of the boxing before he got injured in the boxing. His suggestion was a reasonable one, so the pankration was moved

Plate 27 Pankratiast tripping opponent. His closed fists show that the contest is not wrestling. Black figure amphora.

Plate 28 Official on right signaling foul in pankration. Red figure kylix.

Plate 29 Here the official signals a foul with his rod. The question is, who is committing the foul? Black figure amphora.

up. He was defeated in the pankration by Kapros but fought with undiminished vigor and unimpaired body.

Pausanias 6.15.4–5

Biting was prohibited:

4

When he saw many of the athletes fighting unfairly and breaking the rules of the contest by biting instead of following the rules of the pankration, he said, "With good reason do the sport fans call these modern athletes 'lions'."

Lucian, *Demonax* 49

The next testimonium suggests that it was not clear whether bending the opponent's fingers was legal or not.

5

Next is a statue of a boxer from Ephesos, winner in the boys' class, named Athenaios, and beyond it is a statue of the adult pankratiast Sostratos of Sicyon, whose nickname was Fingertips, so called because he used to seize the end of the fingers of his opponent and bend them back, and he did not

stop until he saw that his rival had conceded. He won altogether 12 victories at Nemea and the Isthmus, two at Delphi, and three at Olympia. Next
to Sostratos is set up the statue of an adult wrestler named Leontiskos,
belonging to a Sicilian family from Messene on the Straits ⟨between Italy
and Sicily⟩. He was crowned once at Delphi and twice at Olympia, and they
say his style of wrestling was like the pankration form of Sostratos of Sicyon. They say he did not know how to throw the wrestlers but won by
bending the fingers.

Pausanias 6.4.1–3

[The base of the statue of Athenaios has been found.]

The most important evidence comes in a passage from Philostratos (probably not
the writer who wrote *On Athletics*). The speaker is guiding a group of young boys
through a picture gallery.

6

1   You have now come to the paintings of the Olympic Games and to the
most highly regarded event in them, the men's pankration. Arrichion is receiving the crown although dying at the moment of victory, and one of the
Hellanodikai is crowning him. Let's call this official Mr. Justice, for he is
concerned with the truth, and he is clothed like other judges. The terrain
provides a stadium in a natural hollow of the required length. The river
Alpheios flows lightly by—it is the only stream which flows on top of the
sea. On all sides grow beautiful wild olive trees, greyish green in color, with
leaves curved like parsley.

2   Later we will see the stadium and many other things, but let us now look
at Arrichion's performance before it is over. For he seems to have conquered not only his opponent but the Greek spectators as well. I mean they
are leaping up from their seats and shouting; some are waving their hands,
others parts of their clothing; they leap in the air or grab their neighbor and
hug him for joy. For the spectators cannot control themselves because of
the truly amazing thing they have seen. Is there anyone so without emotion
that he does not cheer for this athlete? For although he had already achieved
the remarkable record of two Olympic victories, what you see here is even
greater, winning this third victory at the cost of his life and going down to
the Land of the Blessed Dead still covered with the dust of the contest. Do
not imagine that this was accidental, for his strategy for victory was very
shrewd.

3   You say you want to know about the rules for this wrestling? The pankratiasts, my boy, engage in a dangerous kind of wrestling. For they have to
take blows in the face, which are considered too dangerous for a regular
wrestler, and they take holds where it is necessary to fall in order to win.
They also need to learn techniques of applying pressure to an opponent in
different ways at different times. A pankratiast may simultaneously grab his
opponent's ankle and wrench his arm in addition to hitting and jumping on
him. For these moves are permitted in the pankration, but not biting or pok-

ing. The Spartans, it is true, permit these last two; the reason is, I suppose, that they are training for war, but they are forbidden in the contests in Elis, although the use of pressure is permitted.

This is the reason why Arrichion's opponent had him seized around the waist and was intending to kill him, and already he had thrust his forearm under Arrichion's throat to strangle him, having previously wrapped his legs around the groin, winding the tips of his feet behind each of Arrichion's knees; and he forestalled his resistance by strangling him until drowsy death came over Arrichion's senses. But in letting up the pressure with his legs, he failed to defeat the plan of Arrichion. Arrichion kicked his foot free, and in doing so jeopardized his opponent's right side, since his knee hung without support; then he held him tightly to his groin—no longer an opponent—and bending to his left side, Arrichion locked the other [= left] leg of his opponent with his knee and forced the ball of the ankle free from its socket with this violent twist. Arrichion's body became weak as the soul left, but it still gave him strength to accomplish his purpose.

The man who was doing the strangling is painted to look like a dead man and was signalling his surrender with his hand, but Arrichion is painted to look like a victor, for his coloring is high, his body gleams with perspiration, and he is smiling just as living men do when they realize they have won.

Philostratos, *Pictures* 2.6

The description above by Philostratos is admittedly difficult to understand, but a person acquainted with modern wrestling will find the essential tactics familiar. Arrichion's opponent had at the outset a standing body scissors. Arrichion's only hope of breaking the hold was to put pressure on one of his opponent's leg joints (compare the collegiate tactic of locking the leg and sitting through on a figure four body scissors). Arrichion did this by first freeing his right leg, then hooking his opponent's left ankle in the bend of his right knee and, while drawing the ankle to the right side, falling with his body to the left.

In the third paragraph of this passage, Philostratos explains some of the ways in which the techniques of the pankration differed from those used in wrestling, in particular the moves that are permitted in the pankration but not in wrestling. After listing these, Philostratos adds that Olympic rules also forbade biting and poking, although these moves were permitted under Spartan rules. This passage, strange to say, has been held by some to mean that *everything* was permitted except biting and poking. There is no question that the pankration was a rough sport, though, as the Greeks specifically tell us, not as dangerous as boxing. The story about Arrichion, which also appears in Pausanias, is the only reported death in the pankration.

Triple victors (in wrestling, boxing, and pankration) were rare. This feat was accomplished first in 216 BC:

7

Just as you, stranger, see the courage in this bronze image of Kleitomachos, so Greece saw his might. For as soon as he had untied the bloody boxing thongs from his hands, he entered the fierce pankration. In the third event he did not soil his shoulders with dust but, wrestling without a fall, won three events in the Isthmian Games. He was the only Greek to gain this honor, and Thebes of the Seven Gates and his father Hermokrates also won crowns.

Alkaios, *Greek Anthology* 9.588

Both Lucian (*Anacharsis* 1–3) and Philostratos (*On Athletics* 50) mention "ground wrestling." This may mean that wrestlers and pankratiasts practiced ground wrestling as an exercise safer than upright wrestling.

The following is a modern description of the ancient pankration that is almost completely wrong, although the book from which it is taken won first place in a contest of "Epic Works" at the ninth Olympics in 1928. It is based on a misinterpretation of the story of Arrichion[1]:

> In the pankration the competitors fought with every part of their body, with their hands, feet, elbows, their knees, their necks, and their heads; in Sparta they even used their feet. The pankratiasts were allowed to gouge one another's eyes out . . . they were also allowed to trip their opponents, lay hold of their feet, nose, and ears, dislocate their fingers and arms and apply strangleholds. If one man succeeded in throwing the other, he was entitled to sit on him and beat him about the head, face, and ears; he could also kick him and trample on him. It goes without saying that the contestants in this brutal contest sometimes received the most fearful wounds, and not infrequently men were killed.

(We repeat, this account is *almost completely wrong.*)

The following description of a wrestling match (or is it the pankration?) comes from a novel called the *Aithiopika,* written perhaps in the middle of III AD by a writer named Heliodoros, about whose life we know little. Like Theokritos, Heliodoros describes a contest between the skill of the hero Theagenes and the brute force of a native.

8

10.30   An Ethiopian[2] was brought into the middle of the crowd. He looked about him in contemptuous and boastful fashion. He advanced slowly and then stopped, with his feet wide apart, and his swaying hands touched his elbows, first one and then the other.

10.31   When Hydaspes drew near the crowd, he looked at Theagenes and said in Greek, "Stranger, you must compete with this man, for the people have demanded it."

"Let the people's will be done," replied Theagenes. "But tell me, what kind of contest will it be?"

"You will wrestle[3]," said Hydaspes.

"Why can I not fight with sword and armor?" said the other. "Then, whether I won or lost I would impress my Charikleia, who has said nothing about me, or to speak plainly, seems to have forgotten all about me."

Hydaspes replied, "Why did you wish to bring up the name of Charikleia? But that aside, you must wrestle and not fight with a sword. For our religion forbids us to see blood spilled before the time of the sacrifice[4]."

At these words Theagenes realized that the king was afraid his victim might be killed before the sacrifice, and so he said, "You are quite right in saving me for the gods, for they will look after me."

Then he scooped up some dust and sprinkled it on his shoulders and arms, all wet with perspiration from his earlier contest with the bull. Shaking off the dust which did not stick, he extended both arms in front of him, set his feet firmly, and flexed his knees, curved his back and shoulders, bent his neck forward slightly, and tensed his whole body, trembling with excitement as he waited for the holds of "painful wrestling."

As the Ethiopian looked at Theagenes, he gave a mocking laugh, trying, it seemed, to intimidate him by his grimaces and leers. Suddenly he lurched forward, and slammed his forearm, stiff as a crowbar, into his neck. Hearing a murmur of approval for this blow, he started to strut and gave a slow smile.

Theagenes, being trained from his youth in athletics, used to olive oil[5], and a master of the art of Hermes [= patron deity of athletes], decided to give way at first and feel out the strength of his opponent, not choosing to close at this time with a monster so huge, so rugged, and so beastlike, but rather to use his experience to overcome this brute force.

Therefore, although a little shaken by the blow he had received, he acted as if he were more hurt than he was, and positioned himself so that his neck was vulnerable to a blow on the other side. When the Ethiopian struck again, Theagenes gave way a little under the blow and pretended he had almost fallen on his face.

When the giant saw this, he was much heartened and attacked for the third time, but carelessly. He struck with his arm again, and intended in this attack to throw his opponent. But Theagenes, who was crouching, suddenly ducked under the outthrust arm. With his right hand he seized the monster's left arm, pulled him toward him, and made him stagger. The Ethiopian had already lost his footing when his blow met with no resistance. Theagenes put his arms under the native's armpits and around his back.

10.32

Because of the giant's huge belly, Theagenes' arms could meet only with difficulty. Then he tried to upset the monster by striking vigorously behind his ankles with his heel, first one ankle and then the other. Forcing him to sink down on one knee, Theagenes held him in a scissors grip around his torso with his legs and thighs, grabbed by the wrists the Ethiopian's arms, which the giant was using to keep his body off the ground, and yanked them out from under him. Then wrapping his arms around his opponent's temples in a bear hug, he twisted the Ethiopian's back and shoulders, lifted him, and slammed him to the ground on his belly.

Heliodoros, *Aithiopika,* Chapter 10

[This concludes the fight, and the king of the Ethiopians grieves over the fact that their religion demands that this courageous youth be sacrificed.]

(a) Why is it appropriate that the hero's name is Theagenes? See Chapter 21.

(b) Identify Hydaspes and Charikleia.

(c) Why did Theagenes have to fight?

(d) Why was Theagenes not allowed to fence?

(e) Describe Theagenes' stance when he is ready to wrestle.

(f) Describe the various ways in which the Ethiopian tried to ''psych out'' Theagenes.

(g) What blows does the Ethiopian use?

(h) After the giant's initial attack, what tactics does Theagenes employ? How successful are they?

(i) Describe the fall. Is it one of the kinds of falls you met in your other readings about wrestling?

(j) How many falls constituted victory in this bout?

(k) Hydaspes says that Theagenes must ''wrestle'' the local champion. In what ways does the match differ from other accounts of wrestling?

(l) Either the local rules in Ethiopia differed from those in Greece, or Heliodoros has confused wrestling and the pankration. Which is more likely?

Further Readings

Brophy, R.H., ''Deaths in the Panhellenic Games, Arrichion and Creugas,'' *American Journal of Philology* 99 (1978), pp 363–390.

Drees, pp 83–84.

Forbes, C.A., ''Accidents and Fatalities in Greek Athletics,'' *Classical Studies in Honor of William Abbott Oldfather* (Urbana 1943), pp 50–59.

Gardiner AAW, pp 212–221.

———GASF, pp 434–450.

Harris GAA, pp 105–109.

———SpGR, pp 25–26.

Miller, *Arete* 59.

Yalouris, pp 226–231.

13

Horse Racing

Greek horse racing differed from other Greek sports in several ways. For one thing, participation was confined to those of great wealth. Some cities entered teams. Here is a selection from a speech written by Isokrates and delivered by Alkibiades, who discussed his father Alkibiades:

1
About this time (432 BC) my father saw that the Olympic Games were an object of love and admiration of the whole world, and that here the Greeks showed their wealth, their strength, and their training, and that not only were the athletes envied but also the victors brought glory to their cities; he believed moreover that, while the projects for the public good which were undertaken in Athens brought honor in the eyes of the citizens on him who performed them, still the expenses a citizen incurred in the Olympics made his city famous through all Greece.

My father was not inferior to anyone in ability and strength, but as he thought the situation through, he considered the athletic contests to be beneath him, for he knew that some of the competitors were members of the lower classes, came from small cities, and were not well educated. Consequently, he turned his attention to raising horses, which is the activity of the most wealthy and not one which a poor man should attempt, and he surpassed not only his rivals but also all the earlier victors. For he entered chariots in a larger number than the largest cities could match and of such quality that he came in first and second and third.

Isokrates, *Team of Horses* 32–34

There were two kinds of races: those with horses pulling a chariot and those with a horse ridden by a jockey (Pl 30). The owner of the horses usually did not drive the chariot or ride the horse himself. For an exception, see Chapter 21 on the career of Damonon. The prize was awarded to the owner of the horses, and several women won prizes at the Olympics and elsewhere:

Plate 30 Notice the distortion in the size of the horses and jockeys. Black figure Panathenaic amphora.

Plate 31 Quadriga (=four-horse chariot) rounding turning post. Black figure Panathenaic amphora.

2

My ancestors and my brothers were kings of Sparta; I, Kyniska, won the chariot race with my swift-footed horses and erected this statue. I claim that of all Greeks I am the only woman to have won this crown.

Greek Anthology 13.16

[Kyniska lived near the end of V BC. She won the Olympic chariot race twice. There will be more about this woman owner in Chapter 20.]

In lists of Panathenaic victors, a certain Polykrates, or one of his daughters, was listed as victor in every festival from 190 BC to 178 BC.[1]

There were chariots drawn by four horses (=quadriga; see Pl 31) or by two (=biga; see Pl 32), and there were separate divisions for colts and mature horses. A race for mules drawing a cart was added to the Olympics in 500 BC but was dropped in 444 BC; in the same way, the *kalpe* race for mares was added in 496

Plate 32 Biga (=two-horse chariot) rounding turning post. Red figure oinochoe.

BC and dropped in 444 BC. All horse races in the Olympics were twelve laps in length.

3

For at Olympia he himself won the prize, which at Delphi and at Isthmia the impartial Graces gave his brother, who won the same kind of prize, the victory garland for winning the twelve lap (or course) contests for the four-horse chariots.

Pindar, *Olympian Odes* 2.48–51

At each end of the course was a turning post. The Olympic hippodrome (= racecourse) was 3 or 4 stades long, but it is not clear whether a "lap" was up and back (that is, two lengths, as we could count it) or whether "up" would be one length or "lap" and "back" would be another. For a description of the Olympic hippodrome the reader is referred to Pausanias 6.20.10–19 in Chapter 31. His description of the *husplex* (= starting gate) is confused. At Athens the course was 1600 yards, the longest known. Unlike the Romans, the Greeks did not have a barrier in the center, and, consequently, crashes were frequent and injuries more serious. Pindar says that in one race at Delphi forty chariots crashed:

4

For among the forty drivers who crashed, you ⟨alone⟩ with fearless heart guided your chariot unharmed, and now you have returned from the glorious games ⟨at Delphi⟩ to the plains of Libya and the city of your ancestors.

Pindar, *Pythian Odes* 5.49–54

(a) Why did Alkibiades not compete in the track and field events?
(b) What was the record of Alkibiades in chariot racing? Did he drive the horses himself?
(c) Who was the woman who competed at Olympia? What was her station in life? Do we assume that she drove the horses herself?
(d) How many laps were the chariot races at Delphi and at Isthmia?
(e) Pindar refers to a race with many accidents. How many chariots crashed?

In the play *Elektra,* written by Sophocles (V BC), the ancient *paidagogos* (= tutor) of the play's hero Orestes appears at the palace and recites a fictitious account of Orestes' presumed death:

5

I was sent for this purpose and so I will tell all. When Orestes had gone to the famous festival, the honor of Hellas, for the Delphic games, hearing the herald's clear summons to the footrace, which was the first contest, he stepped forth a brilliant sight, a wonder to all who were there. His performance in the footrace was equal to his beauty, and when he left, he carried away the glorious prize of victory. To be brief, when there is much to tell, I know of no deeds of strength such as this man won. But mark one thing: of all the contests in the pentathlon which the judges announced, he was blessed in taking all the prizes, and he was announced as a man of Argos, Orestes by name, the son of Agamemnon, once leader of the glorious host of Hellas. Now that is what happened in these events, but when a god sends harm, not even a mighty man can escape.

On the next day, at sunrise, when the contest of swift-footed horses took place, he entered along with many other charioteers. One was an Achaian, one came from Sparta, and two masters of yoked cars were Libyans. Orestes with Thessalian horses was the fifth entry in that group. The sixth was an Aitolian with colts of golden brown, and the seventh was a man from Magnesia. The eighth driver had white horses, a man from the stock of Aineia. The ninth came from god-founded Athens. There was also a Boiotian, making the tenth chariot.

They took the places which the appointed umpires assigned them by lot and drew up their chariots. At the sound of the brazen trumpet they darted forward. And straightway the drivers all shouted to their horses and slapped the reins. The whole course was filled with the crash of rattling chariots, and upward flew the dust. They were all mixed together and did not in any way spare the goad, that each might pass the wheels and snorting horses of his rivals. The horses' breath foamed and fell alike on their backs and the turning wheels.

Now, to this point all the chariots remained upright. Then the Aineian's hard-mouthed colts got the bit between their teeth and bolted, and in the turn of the sixth lap going into the seventh, they crashed their heads against a car from Libya. Thereupon, from this one mishap others smashed and broke upon one another and the whole plain of Krisa was filled with the destruction of chariots like a wreck at sea.

Seeing this, the skillful driver from Athens drew his chariot aside and held it as if at anchor, letting go by the wave of horses seething in the middle of the course. Orestes drove in last place, holding back his horses, trusting in his finish, but when he saw that the Athenian alone was left, he sent a sharp cry whistling into the ears of his swift colts, and the two drivers raced with their teams neck and neck, as first one and then the other moved his chariot team in front by a head.

And now ill-fated Orestes had negotiated all the other laps safely and was unharmed, with his chariot also unharmed. Keeping close to the turning post on every turn, he grazed the pillar with his axle, giving slack to the right-hand trace horse and checking the one on the inner side. But at the last turn as he slackened the left rein as the horse turned in, he misjudged and struck the edge of the turning post. The axle box of the wheel broke in two, and he slid over the chariot rail. He was completely entangled in the reins cut from leather, and as he fell to the ground, his colts bolted around the middle of the course.

When the people saw him fallen from the car, they bewailed the youth who had accomplished such feats and had gained such ills, who was now being smashed to the ground, now tossed feet upward to the sky. At last the charioteers with difficulty checked the flight of the horses and freed him from the reins, so covered with blood that none of his friends seeing the wretched corpse would have recognized him.

They burned him at once on a pyre, and chosen men of Phokis are now bringing his mighty body in a small bronze urn, now pitiable ashes, that they might have burial in his ancestral soil. That is what I have to tell you, grievous, if words can grieve; for those who saw it, it was the most tragic thing we have ever seen.

Sophocles, *Elektra* 680–763

(a) In what events did Orestes compete, according to the paidagogos?
(b) What events did the tutor say that Orestes won?
(c) Based on other ancient evidence, is the accident in the chariot race that Sophocles depicts an unlikely occurrence? Is it exaggerated?
(d) Is the paidagogos completely truthful?

In the classical period the horse was not of great economic or military value. The Greeks and Romans had not discovered four important pieces of equipment for horses: stirrups, saddle, horseshoes, and horse collar. Without stirrups or saddle, cavalry charges would usually not be effective. Without horseshoes a horse could not get a good grip on the ground. A horse can carry a pack four times as heavy as a man can carry; however, a horse eats four times as much as a man. The Greeks used a type of harness that choked the horse when he tried to pull; by use of a horse collar a horse can pull fifteen times the load a man can. (See R.J. Forbes, *Studies in Ancient Technology.*)

In battle scenes described by Homer, the chariot and driver served as a means of transporting the heavily armed warrior chiefs to points where they were needed. In classical times horses were used for scouting, carrying messages, and killing or capturing fleeing enemies. These were useful functions, it is true, but the horsemen were auxiliary troops. Nations like the Parthians, which relied heavily on cavalry, were the exception. In times of peace the horse was used in hunting.

In the social, political, and economic life of Greeks (and Romans) however, the horse was of great importance. Although the use of the chariot in war was obsolete by VII BC, racing chariots was a favorite pastime of rich Greeks. At Athens and other places, mounted soldiers had to furnish their own mounts. At Athens the *hippeis* (= mounted soldiers, or knights) became a census class requiring ownership of property of a certain value. The cavalry then became an elite corps, a conservative group favoring oligarchial government and opposing democracy.

Before Rome conquered the Mediterranean world and built a network of roads, travel by horse was difficult, because roads were scarce, usually not paved, and often single track. The lack of horseshoes would make travel difficult for horses, whose hoofs are subject to injury; consequently, travel was usually by foot. If a wagon was used it would usually be drawn by mules: horses were too fragile and too expensive. Obviously, expensive horses were not used in agriculture; instead, oxen and donkeys pulled heavy farm wagons and ploughs.

(a) What four pieces of equipment now used with horses were unknown to the Greeks?
(b) What was the importance of horses in Greece?

(c) What was the condition of roads in Greece in V BC?

(d) What class of person owned horses in ancient Greece?

Further Readings

Anderson, J.K., *Ancient Greek Horsemanship* (Berkeley 1961).

Drees, pp 70–72.

Forbes, R.J., *Studies in Ancient Technology* II (Leiden 1965), pp 80–88. An analysis of the horse as a power source.

Gardiner AAW, pp 222–229.

———— GASF, pp 451–466.

Harris SpGR, pp 151–192.

Yalouris, pp 232–241; 245–247

14

Ball Playing

The evidence for ball games is contradictory and incomplete. There seem to have been several kinds of balls, of which three were the most common: the *harpastum,* small and hard and stuffed with hair, like a golf ball; the *pila,* a larger ball stuffed with feathers; and the *follis,* a bladder filled with air, like a basketball. Scholars do not agree on how ball games were played or indeed even which games were team sports and which were individual contests. Some games appear to be like our playing catch or keep away.

Our fullest account of ball games in Greece and Rome was written by Galen, a Greek philosopher and student of medicine who was born around 129 AD. In his early years Galen was physician for the gladiators in the city of Pergamon in Asia Minor. For many centuries his influence on the study of medicine was profound. The only complete edition of his works was put out by Kühn in 1821–1833. Here is what Galen has to say about ball games in his treatise, "Exercise with a Small Ball":

1

The best philosophers and the best doctors among the ancients have frequently stated how beneficial exercise is toward health, and that it must precede eating. But no one of the past generations has ever sufficiently explained how much better is exercise with a small ball than other exercises. It is only fitting then that we tell what we know. We will be judged by you who are the best schooled of all in this art, but even others to whom you recommend this book will find what is stated there to be of sufficient use.

Now, I say that the best athletics of all are those which not only exercise the body but are able to please the spirit, and I think that those who discovered hunting with hounds and other forms of hunting, mixing work with pleasure, delight, and love of honor, were wise men and understood human nature well. The spirit is able to be so stirred by hunting that many are cured of diseases by their happiness alone and many who are disheartened are won over. There is no physical condition so strong that it can overcome the condition of the spirit.

Therefore, it is wrong to ignore the emotions of the spirit, whatever they are, but it is far more important to think of them than of movements of the body because, among other reasons, the soul is so much more significant than the body. This is common ground for all pleasurable athletics, but there are some special features of exercise with a small ball, which I will now explain.

(a) According to Galen, is exercise beneficial?
(b) Who supports this opinion?
(c) What exercise does Galen consider most beneficial?
(d) What does the right kind of exercise help besides the body?
(e) Do you agree about the benefit of exercise for the spirit?

First of all, there is its accessibility. If you should consider how much equipment and leisure time hunting with hounds and all other types of hunting pursuits need, you would see clearly that it cannot be undertaken either by men in government or by those performing a trade. For these sports require money more than moderate leisure. But this activity of play with a small ball is so much a people's activity that even the poorest man is able to have the equipment for it. It needs neither nets nor weapons nor horses nor hunting dogs, but only a ball, and a small one at that. It interferes so little with other activities that pursuing it demands no neglect of them. Now indeed, what could be more convenient than this, which embraces every human activity and condition? We do not have the opportunity for the sport of hunting, since it requires money to provide the equipment and ideal leisure to wait for the suitable time. On the other hand, the small ball is accessible to even the poorest, as we stated, and the opportunity to use it is there for even the very busy. This accessibility is a great advantage.

You would especially realize that it is the most helpful of all other sports, if you would examine it item by item to see what it can do and what its nature is. You will find that it can stir the enthusiast or the slacker, and it can exercise the lower portions of the body or the upper, some particular part rather than the whole, like the hips or the head or the hands or the chest, or it can exercise all the parts of the body equally. None of the other activities, only this one—exercise with a small ball—is able to give both the most intense workout and the gentlest relaxation, however you might want to do it and your body appears able to bear it. It is similarly able to move all the parts at once, if this seems suitable, and it can also move some parts rather than others, if this should seem better at times. When people face one another and exert themselves in keeping the man in the middle from snatching the ball, this is a major activity and a very vigorous one, combining many neckholds and many of the wrestler's counterholds, so that it exercises the head and neck with the neckholds, the sides, chest, and stomach with the feints of the face, the attacks, the defenses, the stances, and the other wrestling holds. The hips are vigorously exercised this way as well as the legs, the supports of one's stride. Moreover, the attacks and sideward leaps also offer no small workout for the legs.

(a) How much equipment is necessary for the small ball game?
(b) Does the exercise he mentions involve bodily contact?
(c) The rules of Galen's sport are not clear. What are some of the features?

Now to speak the truth, this kind of exercise is the only one which moves all parts of the body so very equally. When the competitors advance, it works some sinews and muscles; when they retire, it emphasizes other parts more; and similarly when they shift sideways, it exercises still others. Whoever immoderately exercises his legs as runners do, with one kind of motion, is just like one who exercises his limbs unevenly in sideward shifting. The exercise with a small ball, however, is most equitable to both the legs and the hands if people customarily get the ball in all kinds of different ways. This variety of postures necessarily works one muscle more strenuously than another so that all of them by working in turn have as much rest as those people do who rest while others work, and they all work and rest in turn in such a way that the whole does not remain idle nor are only the ones who work when they are tired out. One can recognize that the eyes must get a workout, by noticing that if one does not take careful note of where the ball is thrown, he is certain to miss the catch.

Sufficient strategy is required for this game not to throw the ball to the ground, or to hinder the man in the middle, or on the other hand, for him to snatch the ball. Although anxiety by itself attenuates the body, when mixed with some amount of exercise and rivalry, and ending in pleasure, it achieves the maximum for the body's health and the spirit's alertness. This is no small benefit when the exercise is able to help both the body and the spirit with their appropriate virtues. It is not difficult to see that the small ball is able to give exercise in both of the most important practices in which the royal laws order generals to take part. For it is the duty of good generals to attack at the right time, to escape when attacked, to seize an opportunity at once, to turn the tables in adverse circumstances, whether attacked directly or set upon unexpectedly, and to hold what has been won. To put it in a word, a general must be a guard and a clever thief, and this is the sum total of his art. Surely no other sport is capable of preparing a person in advance to guard what has been taken or to regain what has been captured, or to anticipate the enemies' plan. I would be amazed if anyone could suggest anything of the sort. Many exercises achieve an opposite effect: they make people lazy and drowsy and dull witted. In fact, those who work out at the palestra are prompted toward being muscular rather than toward the pursuit of excellence. Many have become so weighed down that they have difficulty breathing. Such men would not be good generals in war or guardians of royal or state business. One would more likely entrust something to pigs than to such men. Perhaps you will suppose that I recommend running and other exercises that slim down the body. That is not the case.

In all instances, I criticize this lack of balance and I assert that every art should be practiced in moderation, and if anything lacks measure it is ugly. Accordingly, I do not approve of the running with which people slim their bodies and in which they gain no practice or manly spirit. Victory does not go to those who flee quickly but to those able to persevere in confrontation. It was not by this—running the fastest—that the Spartans were so capable, but by standing their ground and cutting down the enemy. If you should ask how healthy running is, the answer is that in the same measure that it un-equally exercises the parts of the body, it is unhealthy. For by definition, it has to overwork some parts and leave others utterly idle. Neither of these is good, but both nourish the seeds of diseases and render one's forces feeble.

(a) What objection does Galen have to running as an exercise?
(b) In what respect does Galen's sport resemble warfare?

Accordingly, I approve of exercise which produces a healthy body and a balance between the various parts of the body, and along with that a fine spirit. This is what arises from exercise with a small ball. Certainly it is always able to aid the spirit, and in particular it exercises all the parts of the body equally and produces a moderate build; it brings neither excessive weight nor slenderness beyond measure. Rather it suffices for activities which require strength and for those needing speed. So also then it is inferior to none in its vigor.

Let us now have a look at its great gentleness. For there are times when we need this because of age: either that age which is not yet able to with-stand strenuous tasks or that which is not longer so capable; also when we wish to relax from labor or are recovering from sickness. It seems to me that in this it surpasses all the rest. Nothing is so gentle if you undertake it gently. In this instance one must be constantly moderate and not go beyond due measure, advancing gently and standing still, not working out too much. After this, have a gentle rubdown with oil and a hot bath. This is the gentlest of all activities so that it is the most useful to those needing a rest, and it is most able to revive flagging strength; it is most suitable to both the old man and the child. Whoever wants to participate correctly at all times must also know what is more strenuous than what I just mentioned and what is gentler than the peak of eagerness. For if due to some necessary business you unevenly strain the upper parts of the body or the lower or the hands alone or the feet, you can in this exercise rest the parts that were working before, and those which were altogether idle before you can bring to motion equal to the others. For throwing energetically from a considerable distance makes little or no use of the legs and rests what is below while it moves vigorously the upper part of the body. On the other hand, one who runs more and swiftly from a considerable distance and rarely throws the ball exercises the lower parts of the body. Hustle and speed apart from balanced strength give more exercise to the breathing, while the exercise in recovery, throws, and seizure does not contribute to speed but works and strengthens the body. If the sport is strenuous and fast at the same time, this will greatly exercise the body and the lungs and will be the most vigorous of sports.

I am not able to write concerning how much exertion and relaxation there should be for each particular need, for the amount of each of these cannot be stated, but it is possible to discover and to demonstrate this in the activity itself, in which surely there is complete control. For there is no use in quality if the amount causes destruction. Let this be the concern of the trainer who is to lead the exercises.

(a) How could this game be played "gently"?
(b) What are some additional "rules" that are alluded to in this chapter?
(c) Who should determine how strenuous the game shall be?
(d) Is any official needed for Galen's game?

Let the remainder of this discourse be completed. I want to add to the good things that I have said about this sport and not to neglect the dangers from which it is free, but which other exercises fall into. Sprinting has already destroyed many by rupturing a main blood vessel. Just so, great and vehement shouting, let loose at one time, is a cause of damage to not a few, and vigorous horseback riding has often broken organs around the kidneys and the chest, and many have harmed their seminal ducts, to pass over the mistakes of the horses, who often kill riders who have fallen from their seats. So also for jumping, for the diskos, and for exercises involving bending. Of those who exercise in the palestra, who needs to speak? They are all no less maimed than the Prayers of Sorrow of Homer, just as the poet says [*Iliad* 9.503], "crippled, wrinkled, squinting." You can see them coming from the palestra, the crippled, bent, crushed, or altogether maimed. If then this is added to the good things I have said about the exercises with a small ball, that it entails no danger, then it should appear to be of all activities the best suited for one's benefit.

Galen (Kühn 5.899–910)

(a) What types of injuries does Galen say occur in running, shouting, and horseback riding?
(b) Do these injuries occur today?
(c) How balanced is Galen's judgment?

The next section is taken from Galen, "On Natural Faculties":

2
Children take the bladders of pigs, fill them with air, and rub them on the ashes near the fire in order to warm them but not injure them. This game is frequent around Ionia and among a number of other nations. While they are rubbing, they chant certain words in a certain measure and rhythm, and

Plate 33 Piggyback ball game, rules unknown. Black figure amphora.

Plate 34 Players dribbling ball; again, rules of game unknown. Red figure pelike (= storage jar resembling amphora).

33

Plate 35 A game resembling field hockey, but whether competition is between individuals or teams is unclear. Marble relief.

all the words bid the bladder to increase in size. When it seems to them to have stretched sufficiently, they blow it up again and stretch it more, and again they rub it; they do this several times until the bladder seems to have expanded sufficiently.

                                                                            Galen (Kühn 1.7)

(a) What would this kind of ball look like?
(b) How heavy would it be?
(c) What kinds of games could be played with this ball?

Plate 36 Another side of the marble relief shown in Plate 35. It clearly depicts a team sport, but the rules are uncertain.

Some ball games were performed by players riding piggyback (Pl 33). Several vases show players dribbling a ball about the size of a modern basketball (Pl 34). There are references to ball games that were team sports, but the evidence is inconclusive. Of great interest is a frieze showing two different kinds of ball games. In one of these ball games (Pl 35), two players are each equipped with an implement that resembles a field hockey stick. On either side of these players are two more pairs (all but one of them also carrying hockey sticks). There are two interpretations of this carving. One is that it is a game involving two players, and the two pairs on the sides are waiting for their turn to play. The other view is that the four athletes waiting on the sides are part of the game but just relaxing in the final moments before the ball is actually in play, like outfielders in baseball. The validity of these opposing theories is about equal, although it must be noted that the pairs on the sides are just a little too casual about the action only seconds away that would involve them. Elsewhere on the frieze is another ball game (Pl 36), which is clearly a team sport.

Further Readings

Gardiner AAW, pp 230–238.
Harper's, under *Follis*.
————under *Pila (episcyrus, harpastum, trigon)*.
Harris SpGR, pp 75–111.
Miller, *Arete* 57.
OCD, under *Ball games*.
Robinson, pp 182–184.
Yalouris, pp 255–258.

15

Weight Lifting

Weight lifting played a part in training, but how big a part is not clear. Half a dozen "lifting stones" have been discovered in Greece; one, found at Olympia with lettering of VI BC, has the shape and size of a medium-large suitcase: 0.33 by 0.68 by 0.39 meter, weight 143 kilograms (13 by 27 by 15 inches, weight 288 pounds). It is unusual in having a recessed handle. A spiral inscription reads as follows:

1
Bybon, son of Ph . . . , threw me over his head with one hand.

Syll³ 1071

Whether it is possible to lift this stone has been the subject of much debate. Apparently, no modern athlete has gone to Olympia to try to lift it. Moretti (IAG, pp 4–6) says that the task of lifting a stone of this weight is impossible because it would exceed modern records (as of 1952). Nigel B. Crowther, in an excellent article, "Weightlifting in Antiquity," points out that Moretti's conclusions are wrong because he misunderstood the sport of weight lifting. There are two insoluble difficulties in trying to compare an ancient lift with a modern one. First, the ancient lifting stones, round or square, are obviously much harder to lift than a modern barbell, with weight at each end of a rod which the lifter grasps. For example, it would seem to be harder to lift a round rock of, say, 100 kilograms (220 pounds) than a barbell of the same weight. But, as Crowther says (p 112), "Modern competition involves a strict set of rules and a panel of judges." Without such restriction, the simple way to lift the Bybon stone would be to kneel and raise the stone off the ground, then, with two hands and using the recessed handle, lift the stone to the shoulders, then shifting all the weight to one arm, lift and throw. The inscription on this stone is ambiguous: it can mean either lift with one hand and then throw, or when the stone has been raised to the shoulders, then throw with one arm. Still another difficulty is to know what is meant by the word "lift." When Bybon lifted and threw the stone, did he raise the stone above him with the arm straight or did he raise the stone just above his head? Harris (SpGR, pp 142–146) has an implausible explanation that the stone was a joke at the expense of a braggart named Bybon; the recess, according to Harris, is an unfinished hole to tether a mule. Crowther says that a lift of 140 kilograms by a one-arm jerk or press, though not part of modern weight lifting, "is perfectly possible and has often been performed in exhibition."

Another lifting stone was found on the island of Thera. Its weight is 480 kilograms (1056 pounds), and it varies in circumference from 2.81 to 1.90 meters (7 to 6½ feet). It bears this inscription:

2
Eumastas, son of Kritobolos, lifted me from the ground.

IG 12.3.449

Because of the size of the stone, the lifter could not have reached around it. He must have raised one side off the ground, with the further edge of the stone being the fulcrum in a second-class lever. The lift would have been a dead lift. Crowther says the modern official records for the dead lifts are in excess of 400 kilograms, explaining that, considering the different styles (ie, restrictions in modern lifting), the ancient and modern lifts are reasonably close. Harris (SpGR, p 142) thinks this stone, like the Bybon stone, is a joke.

The editors of *Sports Illustrated,* in answer (November 26, 1979) to mail from readers about their story on a search for lifting stones in Scotland, cite several other examples of famous lifting stones besides Bybon's:

> [One example is] Switzerland's 185-pound Unspunnen Stone, which is brought out from Unspunnen Castle every 10 years so that men may see how far it can be thrown. In Bavaria, there is the 560-pound Steyrer Stone, named for Hans Steyrer, who lifted it with one finger, thanks to an iron ring anchored in the stone. In Basque settlements, contests are held to see how many times in succession a man can lift a stone up to 350 pounds from the ground to his shoulders. And more examples of this ancient sport exist in such places as India, Iran and French Canada.

Some of the ancient contests were extemporaneous. Such is the contest in an account in Aelian's *Varia Historia* (12.22), in which the noted athlete Milo challenged a shepherd to lift a stone. The shepherd not only lifted the stone, but carried it some 45 feet before throwing it.

Similar to weight lifting is weight training, which employs lighter weights and repeated exercises (Pl 37). A weight found near Olympia seems to have been used for weight training. As with the Bybon stone, the lettering is from VI BC:

3
I am the throwing stone of Xenareus.

Inscriptiones Olympicae 718

[The weight is estimated at about 100 pounds. It is obviously one of the lighter stones used in exercises to build up muscle.]

The following anecdote about Milo's weight training is well known:

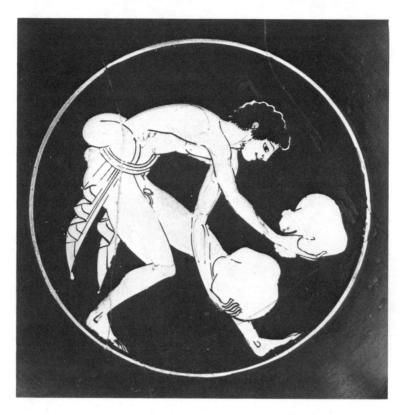

Plate 37 Athlete lifting stones, probably for weight training, although his tucked-up garment suggests manual labor. Interior of red figure kylix.

4

Milo carried the bull which he had been accustomed to carry when it was a calf.

Quintilian, *Institutio Oratoria* 1.9.5

[A modern farm boy tried to duplicate this training routine, and a photographer from *Life* made a pictorial record. Unfortunately, the weight of the calf increased beyond the boy's strength.]

Philostratos (55) tells us that athletes used *halteres* (= jumping weights) to exercise, and vase paintings in this book corroborate this [Pl 13].

Further Readings

Crowther, N.B., "Weightlifting in Antiquity: Achievement and Training," *Greece and Rome*, 24 (1977), pp 111–120.
Gardiner AAW, pp 54–55.
———GASF, p 83.

Harris SpGR, pp 142–150.

Todd, T., "A Legend in the Making," *Sports Illustrated* (5 November 1979), pp 414–454.

Yalouris, pp 252–255.

16

Miscellaneous Activities
and Games

The athletic events of the Crown Games were of the greatest importance, sanctified by religion, and held in honor of gods like Zeus and demigods like Herakles. The Greeks also held other games and diversions of a humbler sort. The suitors of Penelope were said to play at *pessoi* (= a game something like checkers) in the house of Odysseus (*Odyssey* 1.107), but the rules are not known. The game seems to have been played in different ways in both Greece and Rome.

The game of knucklebones was played mainly by girls and women. Each playing piece was made of bone and had four long sides: flat, irregular, concave, and convex, which has the value of one, six, three, and four. The game was one of skill in catching the bones on the back of the hand, as in modern jacks. Knucklebone pieces were also used as throwing dice in gambling. The player threw four of these dice; with four sides there were thirty-five possible throws. The highest score, called the Venus Throw, seems to have been one in which each die showed a different value. The worst throw was the Dog Throw, but its nature is not known. Players used a cup to prevent manipulation of the dice when throwing, making the game one of luck. Six-sided square dice like ours were also in use.

Another gambling game was Odd-or-Even (= Latin *par/impar*). One player held coins, nuts, or other objects in his hand, and the opposing player had to guess whether he held an odd or an even number.

Among the various other activities were walking on stilts, blindman's bluff, hoop rolling (Pl 38), juggling (Pl 39), and spinning yo-yos (Pl 40).

The drinking game called *kottabos* is explained in Chapter 28 on dining.

Plate 38 Boy rolling hoop while carrying
food on tray. Interior of red figure kylix.

Plate 39 Woman juggling balls. Red figure
lekythos (= small vase for oil).

Plate 40 Youth with yo-yo. Interior of red figure kylix.

Further Readings

Chess and Checkers
Harper's, under *Latrunculi*.
OCD, under *Games*.

Dice and Knucklebones
Harper's, under *Talus, Alea*.
OCD, under *Astragalus, Dicing, Ludi*.

Hoops
Harris SpGR, pp 133–141.

17

Palestra and Training

A prominent feature in all Greek cities was a sports center called a gymnasium, from Greek *gymnos* (= naked, or lightly clad). The part of the gymnasium devoted to wrestling was called the *palestra* from Greek *palē* (= wrestling). However, this term palestra was often used for the entire sports complex. We know of

Plate 41 Scene in palestra: one athlete having injured leg examined, another putting on oil, another dressing or undressing. Red figure krater (= mixing bowl for wine and water).

140 such sports centers (Pl 41). Here is a description of one center by Vitruvius Pollio, who lived at the time of Augustus, that is to say at the beginning of the Christian era. His work, *On Architecture,* is the only one of its kind to have come down from ancient times. Although Vitruvius was a Roman and wrote in Latin, the types of buildings he talks about are Greek:

1

About Running Tracks and the Construction of a Palestra

It appears to me that at this point I should discuss in detail the construction of palestras, even though they are not common in Italy, and should show how the Greeks built them.

To have a palestra you must build a *peristyle,*[1] either square or oblong, which will furnish a walk around it of two stades, a distance which the Greeks call a *diaulos.* Three sides of this peristyle should have a portico with a single row of columns, but the south side should be two rows deep, so that when the wind blows in bad weather the rain will not drive in.

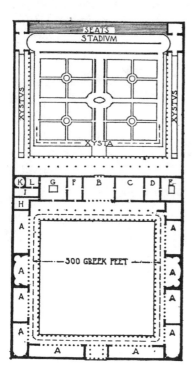

Diagram of a palestra. From M. H. Morgan, *Vitruvius* (Cambridge 1926), p. 161.

In the three porticoes with single rows there should be large *exedrae* (A)[2] in which philosophers, professors, and others who are intellectually inclined may sit and discourse. In the double portico you should build the following rooms. In the center should be the lounge (B). This should be a large exedra with rows of seats, and it should be a third wider than it is deep. On the right of this should be a room equipped with punching bags (C), and beyond that a room for putting on the wrestling dust (D). Off this dusting room, in the corner of the building, should be a room for washing in cold water (E), which the Greeks call a *loutron*. To the left of the lounge (B) should be the room for the athletes to oil themselves (F); beyond this a cold plunge (G), from which is an entrance to the furnace room (H) in the other corner of the building. Next to the cold plunge but further within the complex should be a hot room (I) with a vaulted ceiling, twice as long as it is wide, and it should have in one of the corners a *Laconicum* (K),[3] built as we have described earlier,[4] and in the other part of this corner a warm bath.

Inside the palestra the peristyle should be arranged as we have just described. Outside there should be three porticoes, one of which is directly off the peristyle, with a second to the right and a third to the left, all having running tracks.[5] Of these the one which faces north should be a double portico of ample width, while the other two should be of single width and so constructed that the parts which are next to the walls and those which are next to the columns should have a space at least ten feet wide to serve as walks; the track between these walks should be 18 inches lower than the walks, with steps down to it. The track itself should be not less than 12 feet wide. In this way those who are walking in the portico fully dressed will not be bothered by the oiled athletes who are running.

This kind of portico is called a *xystos* by the Greeks, and their athletes practice in the winter on such tracks covered by a roof. Next to this xystos and the double portico, open-air walks should be planned, which the Greeks called *paradromides* and the Romans *xysta*. In the winter, when it is good weather, the athletes can come out from the covered track to practice here. In my opinion the xysta should be so constructed that there should be a group of trees or perhaps a grove of plane trees between the two porticoes. There should be paths through these trees, with frequent resting places built of concrete. Behind the xystos a stadium should be so designed that the large crowds can comfortably watch the athletes compete.

Vitruvius, *On Architecture* 5.11

(a) What did the Greeks mean by a xystos? What did the Romans mean?
(b) The paradromides served a double function. What was it?
(c) What arrangements were made for warming the palestra in winter and cooling it in summer?

The next selection is taken from a play by Plautus, who lived in II BC and wrote in Latin, although the setting here is Greek. The speaker is a *paidagogos*, a slave who conducted a Greek boy to and from school and also looked after his deportment:

2
"I say that in the first 20 years of your life you never got more than a finger's width from the house without your paidagogos. Unless you got to the pales-

tra before the sun was up, the gymnasiarch laid a pretty heavy penalty on you. When this occurred, there was this additional difficulty: both student and teacher were in disgrace. Here in the palestra the students worked more at running, wrestling, throwing the javelin and diskos, boxing, playing ball, and jumping than at kissing *hetairai*.[6] They spent time there, not in shady spots. When you came back home from the stables and the palestra, you sat down beside your teacher in a chair, with your clothes nicely tucked in, and read. As you read, if you missed a single syllable, your back became as dirtied as a nursemaid's apron."

Plautus, Two Girls named Bacchis 421–434

(a) What is a paidagogos?
(b) How old was the young man addressed in this conversation?
(c) When did this young man have to report to the palestra?
(d) What is a hetaira?
(e) Did the paidagogos ever use corporal punishment?
(f) The paidagogos was usually a slave. How much authority did this slave hold over the freeborn youth he was looking after?

3

When we arrived at the gymnasium, we removed our clothing, then one of our party practiced holds at arm's length, another neck holds and upright wrestling; one of our group after rubbing himself with oil practiced slipping out of his opponent's grasp by twisting; another battered away at the sandbag; still another shadowboxed with lead weights in his bands.

Lucian, Lexiphanes 5

4

When *paidotribes* [= trainers] enroll students, they teach those who attend their classes the techniques which have been discovered for competition.

Isokrates, Antidosis 183

5

You say, "I want to win at Olympia." Hold on a minute. Look at what is involved both before and after, and only then, if it is to your advantage, begin the task. If you do, you will have to obey instructions, eat according to regulations, keep away from desserts, exercise on a fixed schedule at definite hours, in both heat and cold; you must not drink cold water nor can you have a drink of wine whenever you want. You must hand yourself over to your coach exactly as you would to a doctor. Then in the contest itself you must gouge and be gouged; there will be times when you will sprain a wrist, turn your ankle, swallow mouthfuls of sand, and be flogged. And after all that there are times when you lose.

Epictetus, Discourses 15.2–5

The Greeks believed that athletes should abstain from sexual activity. Plato expresses this point of view:

6

Have we not heard reports about Ikkos, citizen of Tarentum, because of his victory at Olympia in the pentathlon in 444 BC and other games? As the story goes, because of his desire to win, his ability, and courage in his heart along with self-control, he never touched a woman, or a boy either, in the entire course of his training. The same story exists about Krison, Astylos, Diopompos, and many others. These men, moreover, had characters much less trained than the citizens of my country or yours, Klinias, and they also possessed much stronger sexual drives.

                                        Plato, *Laws* 8.839E–840A

Here is what Diogenes Laertius, author of the *Lives of the Philosophers*, has to say about sex. His date is uncertain, perhaps III AD. The two quotations that follow are from his life of Pythagoras, a noted philosopher who lived in VI BC (about 582–500 BC). This Pythagoras may have discovered the geometrical theorem that bears his name:

7

Indulge in sex in the winter, not in the summer. It is less harmful in fall and spring than in summer, but it is always injurious and unhealthy. And once when asked when a person should indulge in sex he answered, "When you want to lose your strength."

                                        Diogenes Laertius, *Lives of the Philosophers* 8.9

8

He [= Pythagoras] is said to have been the first to train athletes on a meat diet. The first athlete he did this with was Eurymenes. Formerly they had trained on dried figs, moist cheese, and wheat. Some say that it was a trainer named Pythagoras and not the philosopher who was responsible for this innovative diet. For our Pythagoras prohibited killing, not to mention eating, life which possessed souls like our own.

                                        Diogenes Laertius, *Lives of the Philosophers* 8.12

(a) How do these training rules compare with modern views?
(b) What are modern views on sex for athletes?

The next two sections are from Galen's treatise to Thrasyboulos, "Is Health the Concern of Medicine or Athletics?":

9

There are two divisions concerning the good condition of athletes. One we simply call "good condition," but the athletic condition that is not natural we do not simply call "good condition" but always it is with additional modification, just as somewhere Hippokrates [= Greek physician V BC] says something like "A healthy condition is better than the unnatural state of athletes." Or again, "Among those who do sports, peak conditioning is dangerous, that is to say, in the bodies of athletes and those who participate in sports." But you must understand now that in saying "athletic" and "sporting" he refers not to the activities of those who exercise randomly, doing something like digging, rowing, mowing, or something else that is natural for men, but rather to exercising against the athletic strength of opponents.

Galen (Kühn 5.819–20)

(a) Which does Galen say is better, to be in good shape or to be trained to the finest condition?

(b) What activities does Galen consider "natural"?

10

In Homer's time there was not yet a name for the art of athletics, nor was anyone at all referred to as a *gymnastes* as people referred to doctors as doctors. In the same way the name "athletics" is rarely found in Plato's writing, but he refers to the *paidotribes* rather than the gymnastes as the practitioner of the skill. For the science of athletics arose a little before the time of Plato, when indeed the pursuit of athletics arose. In the old days, a single man who performed the tasks that nature dictated, a man truly in good health, entered the contest and competed not only in wrestling, but also in racing, and one person often won both these events and the javelin, diskos, and chariot races as well. But later things changed and all became like Epeios, whom Homer depicted the worst suited of all in every natural task, but the first in boxing, an art he employed in athletics alone [see *Iliad* 23.664–675]. Athletes became incapable of playing, digging, making a road, or any other peacetime activity, and even less capable of performing well in war.

Galen (Kühn 5.870–871)

(a) When does Galen say that the science of athletics arose?

(b) Were the men of old, according to Galen, all-around athletes or specialists?

(c) Which do we admire more, the all-around athlete or the specialist?

This next section is from Galen's treatise, "On the Preservation of Health, Book II":

11

The gladiator executes the rapid drills with proper timing if that is the regimen, exercises which are strenuous and heavy at the same time, but he by no means knows that such drills build up the body yet also slim it down; he is equally ignorant of the fact that the slower exercises both fill out the body and rarify it. . . . In the same way, the ball player knows all the throws and catches of the ball, but not what effect each has on the body. Thus the paidotribes is an expert on all the activities of the palestra, but he does not know what each activity is capable of doing for the body. . . . But if the gymnastes should see even now for the very first time any of the activities of which I started to speak, he would know their efficacy. . . . What I said a little earlier has now been demonstrated, that the paidotribes is the assistant of the gymnastes, in the same way that the cook is the helper of the physician. For the cook prepares beets or lentils or barley in different ways at different times and does not know what efficacy the preparation has or which recipe is best. The physician is not as capable as the cook in preparing the food, but understands the effect of every preparation.

Galen (Kühn 6.154 f.)

(a) How much does the athlete know about the theory of training the body?
(b) Which has theoretical knowledge of the effects of exercise on the body, the gymnastes or the paidotribes?
(c) The relationship of paidotribes to gymnastes is like the relationship between _____ and _____ .

This next section is from Galen's treatise, "On the Action of Foods, Book I":

12
Each day the gladiators under my charge have a large helping of beans, filling out their frames with flesh that is not tight or dense like swine's flesh, but more supple. This food gives rise to flatulence, but if it is boiled for a long time or similarly prepared, all the gassiness of the bean is removed by the length of the cooking.

Galen (Kühn 6.529)

(a) What is the food value of beans?
(b) Do beans cause gas?
(c) Does Galen recommend beans?

Further Readings

Activities
Gardiner AAW, pp 82–85.

Training
Drees, pp 43–51.
Gardiner AAW, pp 90–93.
Yalouris, pp 114–121.

18

Attitudes toward Athletics

A common modern myth about the ancient Greeks is that they were "moderate," that is, they did not go to extremes. This is demonstrably false: the ancient Greeks were in fact very immoderate, even impulsive. The modern misrepresentation still receives wide publicity through the often-quoted remarks of Baron Pierre de Coubertin, founder of the modern Olympic Games: "The important thing in the Olympic Games is not to win but to take part, just as the most important thing in life is not the triumph but the struggle. The essential thing is not to have conquered but to have fought well." It is unfortunate that this hypocritical statement should be prominently displayed at the modern Olympics. Compare it with the following epitaph for a Greek boxer, Agathos Daimon, who was killed in the ancient Olympic Games and buried at Olympia:

1

Here [= in Olympia] he died, boxing in the Stadium, having prayed to Zeus for either the crown or death, aged 35. Farewell.

Found at Olympia; quoted by Finley-Pleket, p 124

Compare it with this inscription from III BC found at Elis:

2

There you stood, Chaeronides, among the front-line fighters, praying, "O Zeus, give me death or victory in battle."

Also quoted by Finley-Pleket, p 124

Taking part *and* winning were the ancient goal. To lose, even to get second place, was a disgrace in most contests.

3

With cruel purpose you fell from above on the bodies of four opponents, and in these Pythian Games no happy homecoming was decreed for them as there was for you. As they returned to their mothers no sweet laughter brought them pleasure, but they crept along the back roads, avoiding their enemies, bitten by misfortune.

Pindar, *Pythian Odes* 8.81–87

4

In the Olympic Games you cannot just be beaten and then depart, but first of all, you will be disgraced not only before the people of Athens or Sparta or Nikopolis but before the whole world. In the second place, if you withdraw without sufficient reason you will be whipped. And this whipping comes after your training, which involves thirst and broiling heat and swallowing handfuls of sand.

Epictetus, *Discourses* 3.22.52

[However, second places were given prizes in some games, for example in the Panathenaic Games at Athens.]

Another example of immoderation is shown in drinking contests like the one cited below, from Plutarch's *Lives:*

5

Returning from the cremation ⟨of Kalanos, a mystic⟩, Alexander invited many of his friends and officers to a banquet, where he proposed a contest in drinking unmixed wine and offered a crown as a prize. Promoachos drank the most and made way with four pitchers. He got the prize, a crown worth a talent, and died two days later. As for the rest, as Chares says, 41 died from a strong chill caused by this drinking.

Plutarch, *Life of Alexander* 70.1

[It should be mentioned that Macedonian soldiers of Alexander the Great were hard drinkers.]

(a) A Greek pitcher held 3 quarts; how many quarts did the victor drink?

A second myth about the Greeks is that in ancient Greece the athletes were "pure" amateurs. The only prize, say those who hold this opinion, was a wreath of leaves, worthless in itself but a symbol of sport for sport's sake. This myth is as false as that about moderation. The victorious Greek athletes were given enormous rewards. It is true that there were four festivals at which the only prizes were wreaths, also called "crowns"; for this reason the games at Olympia, Delphi, Nemea, and Isthmia were called "Crown Games." At other games (and there were several hundred), money or articles of value were given.

But although the prize at the Crown Games was only leaves, the other rewards given to the victors when they returned home were substantial. For example, there is an inscription listing the prizes in different events in the Panathenaic Games in the late fifth century in Athens (IG II^2 2311). The prizes were amphorae of olive oil, and the victor in the men's stade received 100 of them. In his article "Professionalism in Archaic and Classical Greek Athletics," David C. Young reckons that the lowest value of an amphora of oil [almost 9 gallons] was 12 drachmas. The value of the prize, says Young, was therefore at least 1200 drachmas:

If we take the *highest* possible wage for the period of the inscription, 1.417 drachmas a day, we find that the stade prize equals a *minimum* of 847 days wages for a skilled worker of that time. If the worker, such as a carpenter, were fully employed a year round, it would take him almost three years of work to earn as much as the successful sprinter won in about 24 seconds on the track. For a modern equivalent, I calculate the stade prize as equal to *at least* $67,000 U.S. 1980 . . . and the Panathenaic prize was tax free.

Young based his figures on the wages paid (in 1979) to a carpenter in California, namely $80.00 a day. The current rate (in 1984) in Michigan is $126.56 for a journeyman carpenter. Young again (p 47): "What could the winning sprinter buy with his 1,200 drachmas in Plato's Athens? . . . He could buy six or seven medium-priced slaves, people; or a nice house or two in town; or several houses in the country. $67,000 begins to seem a not wholly unreasonable figure for comparison."

Prizes of money were also awarded. In his *Life of Solon* (23.2), Plutarch tells us that the payment made at Athens in VII BC to a victor at Olympia or at Isthmia was set at 500 drachmas. We are told in the same passage that the value of a sheep at that time was 1 drachma. In 1983 a sheep in Michigan cost $40.00. How many sheep could the victor buy with 500 drachmas? Finley-Pleket (p 70) refer to an inscription which says that an Olympic victor was paid 30,000 drachmas just to enter some local games, and they note that a Roman soldier of that time received between 225 and 300 drachmas a year. The athlete then would get as much for showing up at the games as a soldier would earn in 100 years! An inscription of II AD found at Aphrodisias in Asia Minor shows how large the prizes were, even in this comparatively small city. At that time the Roman coin *denarius* was a day's wages for an unskilled workman:

6

Dolichos	750 denarii
Stade	1250 denarii
Diaulos	1000 denarii
Hoplitodromos	500 denarii
Pentathlon	500 denarii
Wrestling	2000 denarii
Boxing	2000 denarii
Pankration	3000 denarii

CIG 2758

[Note that the prize for the pankration was six times that for either the pentathlon or the hoplitodromos.]

At Athens in V BC victors in the Crown Games received free board:

7

And all those who have won an athletic event at the Olympic, Pythian, Isthmian, or Nemean Games shall have the right to eat free of charge in the city hall and also have other honors in addition to the free meals. Whoever has won or will win the four-horse chariot race or the two-horse chariot race or the race with rider in the Olympic, Pythian, Isthmian, or Nemean Games shall also have the right of free meals in the city hall and they will also get the other honors engraved on the stele.

IG I² 77

It is exceedingly difficult to compare the value of money across cultures, but one thing is clear: the successful Greek athlete was very well reimbursed. The modern concept of an ''amateur'' did not exist; the idea that a winner in athletics should not profit in a material way from his ability was unthinkable. It seems likely that in the fifth century the games were not reserved for the rich and the noble, and that there were some who resented this, just as in modern times the upper classes resisted the entrance of the laboring man into sports. In Chapter 13 on horse racing, the son of Alkibiades presented the point of view held by the upper class, whom we may justly call snobs. It is this view—that the proper contestants are those of good families and financial resources—which motivated E.N. Gardiner, H.A. Harris, and Avery Brundage (president of the U.S. Olympic Committee 1929–1972) in their attacks on professionals.

The evidence from ancient Greece contradicts the viewpoint held by Gardiner and Harris that athletics should be moderate. When the subject of excessive emphasis of Greek sports arises, two passages are usually quoted. The first is by the philosopher Xenophanes, born about 570 BC:

8

But if a man should rise to greatness by being swift of foot or by skill in the pentathlon, in the sacred precinct of Zeus near the streams of Pisa in Olympia, either wrestling or engaging in the painful sport of boxing or the fearful contest men call the pankration, he would be an honored citizen and would take the seat of honor at the games and would feast at the expense of the state and receive expensive gifts from his country to be passed on to his children, or if he gains all these honors through his horses, he would not be as worthy as I, for my wisdom is superior to the strength of men or horses. For these athletic abilities are honored without thought, and it is not right to put physical might ahead of noble wisdom. For if an athlete were one of the citizens, a man good at boxing or good in the pentathlon or in wrestling or in swiftness of foot, which is the most honored of all events in which men compete in the games, his city would not be better governed because of his ability, and little happiness would the city gain if one of her athletes should win beside the banks of the Pisa River, for such achievements do not increase the resources of the state.

Quoted by Athenaeus *Doctors at Dinner* 10.414

(a) Does Xenophanes approve of athletics?
(b) Which does he consider more useful to the state, a person who is a good athlete or one who has the wisdom necessary to help govern his city?

The second often-quoted passage is by the playwright Euripides, who lived in Athens in V BC, the period known as the Golden Age, a century after Xenophanes. This fragment is from a lost play:

9

For of all the many thousands of evils which now beset Greece, nothing is worse than the breed of athletes. First of all, they do not learn to live a good life, nor can they do so. For how could a man who is slave to his jaws and belly increase the wealth which his father had left him? Such people are not able to make an effort to endure poverty, nor can they exert themselves, but not being accustomed to prosperity they cannot help sliding into help-lessness. Glorying in their youth, they parade through the city and are or-naments to it. But when bitter old age falls upon them, they are discarded like a threadbare cloak. And I also blame the Greek custom of calling a meeting for these people and honoring these worthless citizens with the gift of free meals. For what does it benefit the state if a man wins a crown by wrestling well, or by being swift of foot or good at throwing the diskos or skillfully smashing someone's jaw? Will they fight better in battle with a diskos in both hands or will they drive out their country's enemies by striking them with their bare hands instead of using their shields? No one acts so foolishly when facing the enemy's steel. We should crown with leaves our wise and good citizens and whoever guides the city the best and is self-controlled and just, and whoever rids us of evils through his words and eliminates quarrels and civil strife. For such things are good for the whole city and all Greece.

Quoted by Athenaeus, *Doctors at Dinner* 10.413

(a) Is this Euripides' view, or is it the view of someone in the play?
(b) What exaggeration occurs at the beginning of this fragment?
(c) Rephrase the arguments of Xenophanes and Euripides to compare the value of modern intercollegiate athletics and the academic curriculum.
(d) If we take these two passages at face value, what kind of people were the athletes in VI and V BC??

Further Readings

Attitudes
Segal, E., " 'To Win or Die': A Taxonomy of Sporting Attitudes," *Journal of Sport History* 11 (1984), pp 25–31.

Professionalism
Finley-Pleket, pp 70–82.
Gardiner AAW, pp 99–116.
Harris GAA, pp 187–197.
———— SpGR, pp 39–43.
Miller, *Arete* 28, 45, and 73.
Pleket, H.W., "Games, Prizes, Athletes, and Ideology", *Arena* (=*Stadion*) 1.1), pp 49–89. An important article, completely refuting Gardiner et al on "professionalism."

Young, D.C., *The Myth of Greek Amateur Athletics* (Chicago 1984). The most comprehensive treatment of the ''professional'' athlete.
———— ''Professionalism in Archaic and Classical Greek Athletics,'' *Ancient World* 7 (1983), pp 45–51.

Adverse Criticism
Finley-Pleket, pp 113–127.
Miller, *Arete* 70.

19

Nudity in
Greek Athletics

One of the unusual features of Greek athletics is that the participants are almost always shown nude in vase paintings and statues. Many modern Americans find it difficult to believe that the Greeks would not have used some kind of protection for the genitals, like the modern athletic supporter.

One explanation could be that the athletes did wear shorts or an athletic supporter of some kind, but the artist preferred to paint or sculpt the entire body. In Greek vase paintings there are many artistic conventions, for instance showing the head in profile but the body in frontal position, or a head in profile with eyes full face. There is seldom any body hair represented; the fingers may be straight and inflexible, and the toes are often extra long. During some periods athletes were portrayed with extra large thighs. Not depicting apparel seems plausible as an artistic convention. Secondly, the ideal male of many vase painters was the prepubescent boy rather than the mature male. Consequently artists commonly "youthened" the figures, to employ a modern scholar's felicitous phrase. Even mature males were shown with immature genitals, which would not need protection.

Homer represents his heroes as putting on a loincloth before competing in boxing or wrestling (*Iliad* 23.683; 23.685; 23.710). In the *Odyssey* (18.67) the hero "tucked up his rags around his middle" before boxing with the beggar Iros. Several vases show a type of athletic supporter that might possibly have been used by Homeric heroes (Pl 42); however, these vases pose a problem. There are only about a dozen of them, all by the same potter or by a member of his Athenian workshop. Furthermore, on all of these vases, a white loincloth has been painted over the incised outline of the genitals. None of these vases was discovered in Greece proper. It looks as though the vases may have been painted over for a modest clientele.

The modern generally accepted explanation for the use of loincloths in ancient Greece runs as follows. The Homeric heroes wore loincloths while competing in athletics, but in the fifteenth Olympics (720 BC) Orsippos of Megara, a competitor

Plate 42 Vase dated late VI BC, several hundred years after Orsippos, shows runners wearing athletic supporters. Black figure amphora.

in the stade, decided he could run faster without a loincloth. He boldly discarded it and stepped bare-bottomed into history. This view is based chiefly on an inscription found at Megara. It is a poem, generally thought to have been written by Semonides, who lived in VII–VI BC:

1

The Megarians, obeying the word of Delphi, set me up, a magnificent memorial to brave Orrhippos [= Orsippos], who recovered the farthest boundaries of his country where the enemy [= Corinthians] had cut off large amounts of territory. And he was the first of all the Greeks to be crowned *gymnos* [= naked or lightly clothed] at Olympia, since before everyone had competed in the stade wearing loincloths.

E.L. Hicks and Hill, *A Manual of Greek Historical Inscriptions* (Oxford, 1901) 1.1;
CIG 1060 and IG 7.52

[The word *gymnos* means either "naked" or "wearing light clothing" such as a modern runner with shorts and jersey.]

(a) What is the name here of the innovative athlete?
(b) What was his city?
(c) What was the date when he ran without a loincloth?

In describing Megara, Pausanias seems to have seen the inscription, for the resemblance in his text is very close:

2

Nearby is buried Orsippos. At a time when it was the ancient custom of the athletes to compete in the games with a loincloth, he won at Olympia in the stade running *gymnos*. They say that later, when he was a general, he cut off some territory from neighboring people. I think that his loincloth slipped off with his consent, since he knew that a man who is *gymnos* can run more easily than one wearing a loincloth.

Pausanias 1.44.1

[If Semonides wrote this, he wrote it two centuries after the alleged event. We must consider whether Semonides was piously perpetuating an unsubstantiated legend. In fact, we must regard with caution *all* data from the days of the early Olympics.]

(a) What was the name of the athlete?
(b) Why did he drop his loincloth?
(c) Whose opinion was this?

Here is what the *Victor List* of Sextus Julius Africanus (which covers 776 BC through 217 AD) has to say about the incident:

3

In the 15th Olympics Orsippos of Megara won the stade. The dolichos was added, and they ran *gymnoi;* Akanthos of Sparta won.

(a) Who does the *Victor List* say ran *gymnoi?* In what event?

[This *Victor List* seems to be reliable for the most part, presumably going back to official records, but again caution must be employed in evaluating the reliability of the early years of the Olympics.]

The reputation of the historian Thucydides (late V BC) is such that we would expect him to be clear and accurate, but he is not. He says the following:

4

The Spartans were the first to exercise *gymnoi* and to disrobe in public and rub themselves with olive oil after they had exercised while *gymnoi*. Formerly, even in the Olympics, athletes competed with a loincloth around their genitals, and it is not many years since they stopped. People who hold contests in boxing and wrestling and are not Greek, especially those in Asia Minor, do wear loincloths when they compete.

Thucydides 1.6

(a) How long after the alleged events of 720 BC did Thucydides write?

Plato (V–IV BC) represents Sokrates as also saying that the custom of exercising nude was fairly recent:

5

We remind these people that it was not very long ago that the Greeks thought, as the barbarian nations still think, that it was shameful and ridiculous for men to be seen *gymnoi*. And when first the Cretans and then the Spartans began to engage in athletics, it was possible for wits to make fun of the whole business.

Plato, *Republic* 452C

(a) Can the interval between 720 BC and Plato be considered "not very long"?

So far, the testimonia could be interpreted to mean that *gymnos* is not "naked" but rather "lightly clad"; that is, the athletes could have been wearing shorts or loincloths. The following passage from Dionysius of Halicarnassus (I BC) describes a religious procession in Rome:

6

After the chariots came the competitors in both the light and heavy events, *gymnoi* for the rest of their bodies but with their genitals covered. This custom was still observed in my time in Rome, just as it had been originally by the Greeks. It is now ended in Greece, and the Spartans ended it. The person who first removed his clothing and ran *gymnos* in the Olympics was Akanthos, a Spartan, in the 15th Olympics. Before that time all the Greeks considered it shameful to appear in the games with their bodies entirely *gymna,* as Homer testifies, the oldest and most trustworthy authority, when he presents his heroes wearing loincloths.

Dionysius of Halicarnassus, *Roman Antiquities* 7.72.2–3

(a) What is the name of the athlete who removed his clothing?

[Note that the author specifically says the athletes' bodies were *gymna* except for the genitals, which were covered, just as the Greeks used to do before Akanthos. It is clear that *gymnos* here means "totally naked."]

The other testimonia are all late. Here is Isidore of Seville (VI–VII AD):

7

On Athletics

Athletics are the glorification of speed and strength. The place where the athletes work out and where their speed in running is tested is called a "gymnasium." From this fact it happens that the practice of almost all studies is called a "gymnasium." For earlier, when the contestants were covered so that they should not be *nudi* [= *gymnoi*], a certain runner was suddenly thrown and killed when his loincloth slipped. Therefore the archon Hippomenes permitted the competitors to exercise *nudi* from then on. Therefore the location was called a "gymnasium," because the young men practiced *nudi* on the field where they were covered only by their own modesty.

Isidore, *Etymologiae* 18.17.2

(a) What new information do we see here about the reason for discarding the loincloth?
(b) In what game did the accident presumably occur?
(c) When did Isidore live?

Here is another version, this time from the late anonymous *Etymologicum Magnum:*

8

Gymnasia

Places where people exercise. Properly applied to athletes, since they compete *gymnoi,* since Orsippos first ran *gymnos* at Olympia. As Oros says, "It was the custom for the ancients to wear loinclothes over their genitals." But in the 32nd Olympics [=652 BC], when Orsippos the Spartan was competing, the fact that his loincloth fell off was responsible for his victory. From this accident arose the custom of competing *gymnos.*

(a) What is the nationality of Orsippos here?
(b) What is the date of the loincloth drop?
(c) Was the incident planned or accidental?

There are three testimonia from the scholia on Homer. Here is *Scholia* A (Dindorf) on *Iliad* 23.683:

9

It was originally the custom among the ancients to wear loinclothes over the genitals and to compete in this way. In the 14th Olympics [=724 BC] the loincloth of Orsippos the Spartan fell off and was the reason for his defeat, from which the custom was established of running *gymnos.*

(a) What nationality is Orsippos?
(b) When did his loincloth fall off?
(c) Why did it fall?

Here is *Scholia* B (Bekker) on *Iliad* 23.683:

10

They wore a loincloth reaching to their feet so that they would not be easily injured. Later, when there was a contest in Athens in the chief archonship[1] of Hippomenes, it happened that one of the competitors, being tripped, fell, and died because of the loincloth. In the 14th Olympics [=724 BC] in the archonship of Hippomenes while they were running the stade in loincloths, Ersippos [=Orsippos] tripped on his loincloth, fell, and was killed. From this accident it was decreed that they should compete *gymnoi,* as they do to the present day.

(a) Describe the loincloth.
(b) Does it seem a practical garment for competition?
(c) What was the athlete's name?
(d) What was the date when Ersippos tripped?

The Townley *Scholia* on *Iliad* 23.683, is almost identical with Testimonium 10:

11

In the 14th Olympics [=724 BC] in the archonship of Hippomenes at Athens, when they were running the stade, one of the competitors, Orsippos, tripping on his loincloth, fell, and was killed. Consequently it was decreed that they should compete *gymnoi.*

Finally, an author of IV AD (?), Quintus of Smyrna, who wrote an epic called the *Posthomerica* in imitation of Homer, has this passage describing preparations for a footrace:

12

Most eager for victory stood up these two, first Teuker, son of Telamon, and then Aias stood up, the Aias who was leader of the Lokrian archers. And around their genitals each quickly wrapped a cloth and concealed everything beneath it as was proper, out of respect for the bride of great Peleus and the other sea nymphs who had come to see the mighty games of the Argives.

Posthomerica 4.185–192

(a) In what important respect does he differ from Homer?
(b) Now for a decision. Which of these versions is the true account of the custom of running nude?

There seems to be no way of deciding which of these versions, if any, is true. There is no agreement about who dropped his loincloth, or in what event, or in what games. The date of 720 BC is contradicted. We do not know whether dropping the loincloth was seen as an advantage or a hindrance. There are only two points on which there is agreement (except for Quintus):

1. In Homeric times the athletes wore loincloths.
2. In the classical period athletes competed nude.

Value of the testimonia is minimal except for the fact that in only one testimonium (10) is the loincloth used for protection against injury. Neither visual nor literary references give us any reason to believe that Greek athletes in classical times wore any kind of athletic supporter. It is true that there are a few scattered examples of athletes wearing a sort of boxer shorts, but this cannot be considered as showing that wearing shorts was common in classical times.

If the loincloth was not used, perhaps protection was furnished by infibulation, which was the practice of tying a thong around the foreskin of the penis (Pl 43). We are not told the purpose of infibulation, but it is seen on three types of people: athletes, revelers, and the mythological creatures called satyrs. There are many examples of infibulation in vase painting and statues, mostly from the period between 600 BC and 300 BC. Here is what Phrynichos, a lexicographer of II AD, says:

13

Kynodesmai [= dog's leash]: The cords with which the inhabitants of Attica roll back and tie up the penis. They call the penis a *kyon* [= dog] ⟨and the word *desmos* means a leash⟩.

Another lexicographer of II AD has much the same definition:

Plate 43 Scene in palestra, left to right; athlete tying foreskin for protection; slave; diskos thrower; judge/coach; athlete changing clothes. Red figure krater.

14
The cord with which they tie up the foreskin, they call the dog leash.

Pollux, Onomastikon 2.4.171

The fact that the most common use of infibulation is among athletes suggests that it may have been used as a protection for the genitals. But to modern athletes who are accustomed to wearing a jockstrap in almost all forms of athletics, the amount of protection that infibulation would give seems quite inadequate. At best it gives protection to the glans of the penis, but none to the testicles, one of the most vulnerable areas of the body. At best, infibulation would keep the penis from uncomfortably slapping against the body while doing an activity such as jumping jacks.

At this point we had found that the theory of athletes wearing shorts was surely untenable, and that infibulation would give no protection to the testicles. First, how much protection do modern athletes need? A short questionnaire was distributed to members of the athletics staff and the Department of Classical Studies of The University of Michigan, asking among other things what events in the ancient Olympics would necessitate wearing equipment like a jockstrap. Of forty respondents, only six thought no protection would be needed. We have also talked with about a dozen nudists. While conceding the need for protection in a sport like football, they do not believe that most other sports require such support.

One dedicated nudist reported in a letter that he and his friends found that "during vigorous physical activity the scrotum and penis retract into a tight, compact bundle, close to the body and removed from ⟨danger of⟩ injury." He went on to say that his son was required to wear a jockstrap while playing soccer. It was his opinion that this "almost universal requirement" was followed in order to avoid criticism if injury occurred: "The coach can then maintain that all the usual steps were taken to prevent injury." The muscle that lifts or drops the testicles is called the cremaster muscle. The Greek physician Galen, in describing it ("Usefulness of the Parts" 15.336), says it has voluntary motion. Sumo wrestlers in Japan strengthen this muscle by exercise, often beginning in childhood. Female impersonators are also said to use this muscle.

Personal experience in running nude proved to this writer that absolutely no discomfort occurred and the genitals did in fact retract. It is quite likely that many or even most Greeks did without any protection for the genitals. Modern opinion on how much protection the ancient Greeks would need may not be valid. For example, most modern runners would need the protection of shoes in running long distance, but in August 1960 in Rome, the Olympic marathon was won by the barefoot Abebe Pikila from Ethiopia.

It may well be that because in combat sports the athletes had no jockstraps to protect them, the ancient judges were alert to prevent injury to the genitals. This is suggested by a passage from the *Birds* of Aristophanes, in which it is clear that attacking the genitals was a foul:

15

Speaker A: "By Apollo, I will not ⟨address the assembly of birds⟩ unless they make an agreement with me that they won't bite me or pull my balls or stick things . . ."
Speaker B: "You don't mean into your ass?"
Speaker A: "No, I mean into my eyes."
Leader of birds: "I agree."

Aristophanes, Birds 442–444

Although this next passage, from the life of Divus Claudius (III AD), describes Romans, not Greeks, it shows that among the Romans it was a breach of rules to attack the genitals:

16

Claudius became angry at his opponent who had grabbed his private parts instead of his belt, and knocked out all his teeth with one blow.

Historiae Augustae Scriptores, Life of Divus Claudius

Two other groups besides athletes employed infibulation: revelers and satyrs. In plate 44 a pair of revelers is seen en route to a party: it is likely that the infibulated young man is an athlete in training, and his infibulation is a signal to warn suitors that sexual advances would not be welcome. The mythological satyrs are also often shown infibulated. Since their two main interests are wine and sex, the portrayal of an infibulated satyr proclaiming his desire for abstinence is comical.

Plate 44 Revelers. Young man at left is infibulated, probably indicating he is in training. Interior of red figure kylix.

The practice of infibulation makes clear one puzzling feature about nude Greek athletes: in vase paintings the foreskin is often extremely long, in some cases half the total length of the penis, which is then bottle-shaped. This may be explained by assuming that the penis has been tied up daily in the palestra. Doctors agree that permanent elongation would be the result, and they have pointed out that similar modification of tissue occurs in some primitive tribes who extend the lips or the earlobes. It may be that with some athletes the foreskin became so long that infibulation was no longer necessary to cover the glans.

Although the Greeks exercised in the nude, they avoided exposing the glans of the penis. In vase paintings the foreskin almost always covers the glans, even when erect. A child with a congenitally short foreskin might have to submit to special treatment called "epispasm." There were two forms of epispasm. One is described by Soranus (II AD), who recommends (2.34) that if a baby has been circumcised and the parents wish to restore the foreskin, the nurse should constantly tug at what skin remains. Doctors say that such a procedure would in fact work. The second form of epispasm, used with adult males, was much more drastic, requiring surgery, and it is described in detail in Celsus (*De Med* 7.25, 1–2). This is the operation to which St. Paul refers in *I Corinthians* 7.18:

17

"Is any man called being circumcised? Let him not become uncircumcised."

Hellenizing Jews seem not to have been permitted to participate in athletics if they were circumcised. A sharp division therefore existed: there were those for whom removal of the foreskin was a religious duty (the Jews), and those for whom inadequate covering of the glans was unacceptable (the Greeks). Here is an account by Josephus of the voluntary measures taken by a certain Hellenizing Jew named Menelaos in II BC:

18

"And so they [= Menelaos and other Hellenizing Jews] asked him [= King Antiochus Epiphanes] to let them build a gymnasium in Jerusalem. When he had granted their request, they concealed the circumcision of their genitals in order to be Greeks even when they had taken off their clothing."

Josephus (I AD), Antiquitates Judaicae 12.241

In the Jerusalem *Talmud* we have further evidence of continued use in II AD of an operation to remove circumcision:

19

"In the days of Bar Coziba, many people employed epiplasm [sic]."

Talmud (Shabbath 19.2)

It is tempting to say that the Hellenizing Jews underwent this operation in order to protect the penis. But in view of the fact that apparently only a few athletes used infibulation, we cannot believe that protection was the goal. The operation would apparently be as painful as any blow would be. We can only conclude that the action was symbolic. These Jews were renouncing their religion, symbolized by circumcision, and turning to Hellenism, symbolized by concealing the glans and practicing infibulation.

Further Readings

Nudity
Arieti, A.J., "Nudity in Greek Athletics," *Classical World* 68 (1975), pp 431–436.
Gardiner AAW, pp 57–58, 191.
———— GASF pp 86–88.
Sweet, W.E., "Protection of the Genitals in Greek Athletics," *Ancient World* 11, nos 1&2 (1985), pp 43–52.

Participation of Jews in Greek Life
Harris, H.A., *Greek Athletics and the Jews* (Cardiff 1976).
Poliakoff, M., "Jacob, Job, and Other Wrestlers," *Journal of Sports History* 11, no 2 (1984), pp 48–55.
Smallwood, E.M., "The Legislation of Hadrian and Antoninus Pius against Circumcision," *Latomus* 18 (1959), pp 334–347.

20

Women in
Greek Athletics

The evidence for women's participation in Greek athletics is not extensive; some of it is firm, and some is dubious. There are mythological tales about a girl named Atalanta, who appears on vases in a wrestling contest with a mythical hero (Pl 45). She also took part in the famous hunt for the Kalydonian boar. Atalanta was unmarried and required her suitors to compete against her in a footrace. All of them were defeated until one suitor brought three golden apples to the contest. Whenever Atalanta began to catch up, he dropped an apple, which she then stopped to retrieve, and with this stratagem he won the race.

We have several pieces of solid evidence proving that some women competed in some form of athletics at some times and some places. The first is an inscription found at Patrae on the south shore of the Gulf of Corinth, date unknown:

1

I, Nikophilos, set up this statue of Parian marble to honor my lovely sister Nikegora, winner in the girls' race.

IAG, p 168

(a) How much does this inscription tell us? What is missing?
(b) Does the fact that marble from the island of Paros was the best quality tell us anything?

Pausanias (3.17.6) mentions the victory of a woman named Euryleonis in a two-horse chariot race. Chapter 13 on horse racing includes an inscription commemorating victory in a chariot race by a Spartan woman named Kyniska, but the following passage from Plutarch manages to belittle her accomplishment:

2

But Agesilaos, seeing that some of the citizens thought well of themselves and were puffed up, persuaded his sister Kyniska to enter the Olympic chariot

Plate 45 Atalanta wrestling with Peleus. Black figure amphora.

race, wishing to show the Greeks that victory here required no *aretē* [= excellence] but was a victory of money and expense.

Plutarch, *Agesilaos* 20.1

(a) Evaluate this antifeminist statement by Plutarch.

The next testimonium comes from Pausanias (see also Pl 46):

3

Every four years ⟨at Olympia⟩ 16 women weave a *peplos* [= robe] for Hera, and they also put on the Heraia [= Games for Hera]. This contest is a running event for unmarried girls. They are not all the same age, but the first to run are the youngest, after them the next older, and the last to run are the oldest of the girls. Here is their method of running. They let down their hair, let the tunic hang down a little above the knee, and uncover the right shoulder as far as the breast. They use the stadium for this event, although the length of the track is reduced by a sixth. To the victors they give crowns of olive leaves and a share of the cow which they sacrifice to Hera, and the

Plate 46 Girl runner dressed as described by Pausanias. Bronze statuette.

victors may set up statues with their names inscribed. Those who assist the 16 who put on the games are also women.

Pausanias 5.16.2–3

(a) What additional information do we get here?
(b) Do the sixteen women take part in the race?

The next two testimonia are also from Pausanias; in the first he is describing Argos, where at one period the Nemean Games were held:

4
Next is the Stadium, in which they hold the games for Nemean Zeus as well as the games for Hera.

Pausanias 2.24.2

[It is possible that the games for Zeus were for men and the games for Hera were for women, as was the case at Olympia.]

Next, Pausanias is describing a temple in Lakonia, a district in which the city of Sparta was located, whose local hero was the god Dionysos:

5
The other 11 priestesses are also called "daughters of Dionysos," and they put on a running competition, a custom which they took from Delphi.

Pausanias 3.13.7

(a) What additional evidence does this give?

The next testimonium is an interesting inscription from Delphi, dated around 45 AD:

6

Hermesianax, son of Dionysios, a citizen of Caesarean Tralles [=city in Asia Minor] and of Corinth, put up these statues of his daughters, who held the same citizenships, in honor of Pythian Apollo.

His daughter Tryphosa was winner of the girls' stade race at Delphi in the year when Antigonos was director of the games and again when Kleomachides was director, and then at the next Isthmian Games when Juventius Proclus was director, the first girl to accomplish this.

His daughter Hedea was winner of the race of war chariots at Isthmia when Cornelius Pulcher was director, winner of the stade at Nemea when Antigonos was director, and at Sicyon when Menoetas was director. She also won the girls' lyre contest at Athens in honor of the Emperor when Novius son of Phileinus was director. She was the first girl in a long time to become a citizen of [name of city lost].

His daughter Dionysia won the stade at [name of festival lost] when Antigonos was director and at the Asklepian Games in sacred Epidauros, when Nikoteles was director.

IAG 63 and Syll³ 802

(a) What is the approximate date of this inscription?
(b) What honor had Hermesianax and his three daughters received from the town of Tralles?
(c) What event had each of the girls competed in successfully?
(d) Besides the stade, what two events had Hedea won?

The fact that Hedea and her sisters were made honorary citizens shows that by 45 AD women had made some progress toward equality. This is borne out by several inscriptions. One comes from Asia Minor:

7

The council and the people and the senate honored Tatia, who was the daughter of Glykon, who was the son of Glykon, who twice received the honor of wearing a crown. He was director of the gymnasium and a priest of Herakles and head of the council. They thought Tatia worthy of this honor because she was a faithful wife, was directress of the gymnasium, and was honorable in all aspects of her life.

CIG XVII, 3953c

The next inscription is similar but more detailed:

8

The council and the people and the senate honored with highest honors Tata, daughter of Diodoros, who was himself the true son of Diodoros, who was born the son of Leon. She was the virtuous priestess of Hera all her life, mother of her city, who became the wife and remained the wife of Attalos, son of the Pytheos who received the honor of wearing the crown. She herself came from a leading family, one that was illustrious. When she was priestess of the emperor Augustus for the second time, she twice supplied flasks of oil for the baths in great abundance and great expense, even through most of the night.

CIG 2820

[The inscription goes on to list further examples of her piety and generosity in financing plays and concerts.]

Vase paintings show that, in some localities at least, women were admitted to the palestra (Pl 47). From the two previous inscriptions (and others like them) it is clear that the position of *gymnasiarch* (= director of a gymnasium) could be held by a woman. It was not a salaried position but, on the contrary, involved considerable expense. Furthermore there is no indication that a woman gymnasiarch was concerned primarily with girls and women. It is not clear how much the girls who went to the gymnasium participated in athletics. There is an inscription (CIG 3185.19) where mention is made of a man who is in charge of the *eukosmia* of the unmarried girls. This word means both "orderly behavior" and "attractive appearance" (Pl 48).

The city-state of Sparta lived in a perpetual state of readiness for war. Consequently athletes received much attention. Spartan men first won Olympic victories in 720 BC, and for about 150 years the Spartans were supreme. After 580 BC, however, the name of Sparta is less common in the Olympic victories. We must be cautious about accepting information about Sparta; none of the information about this strange military state comes from Spartan sources. However, it is clear that Spartan girls participated in athletics. Here is an angry speech from a character in a play by the Athenian Euripides, the *Andromache* (about 425 BC), when Sparta and Athens were at war. The speaker, Peleus, father of Achilleus, is criticizing Menelaos, husband of Helen, who deserted him for Paris.

9

Peleus: you wish to be considered a man, O most cowardly of all cowards? Is there a place for you in converse with men? You, who relinquished your bed to a person from Troy, leaving the sacred hearth of your great hall unguarded, untended by slaves! But I speak as if the cursed woman you had there was a chaste wife. But even if a Spartan maiden wanted to be chaste she could not be in your Sparta, where the girls leave their houses and, in the company of young men, lay aside their clothing and display their naked thighs, sharing with them their races and wrestling as well as other activities which I cannot endure. Should we wonder then if you do not teach your women chastity?

Euripides, *Andromache* 590–601

(a) How much solid evidence is in this quotation?

The next piece of evidence about women in Sparta is also suspect. The author was a Roman poet named Propertius, born between 54 and 47 BC. We have no reason to believe that he even visited Sparta, but perhaps this poem reflects some truth:

Plate 47 Woman in shorts talks with athlete who is scraping oil from his body. Interior of red figure kylix.

Plate 48 Girl with pickaxe wearing track clothes. Name Atalanta at top. Interior of red figure kylix.

10

O Sparta, while we admire the many rules which govern your palestra, we praise even more the excellent ones of the girls' exercise grounds. We are impressed that a naked [or "lightly clad"] girl may take part in games in the midst of men wrestlers without incurring criticism. The ball she swiftly throws eludes the hands of her opponent; her curved stick clatters against the hoop; although a woman, she stands there at the distant turning post covered with dust from her race, and she bears up under the wounds she receives in the cruel pankration.

At one time she joyfully wraps the *cestus* [= Roman boxing glove] around her forearms; at another she whirls in a circle to throw the heavy diskos; now she follows her father's dogs over the long ridge of Mount Taygetos, her hair starred with frost. Again, she tramples the riding ring with her horses, fastens a sword to her snow-white thigh, and covers her maidenly head with a helmet of bronze, like the warlike crowd of Amazons washing in the waters of the Thermodon River with breasts bare or like Kastor and Polydeukes on the sands of the Eurotas [= river in Sparta], the first fated to be victorious with his fists, the other with his horses. In their presence Helen is said to have put on armor, leaving her breasts exposed, and her actions did not make her brothers blush.

For these reasons, Spartan law forbids lovers from separating, and they are permitted to be at one another's side in the public streets. There is no fear for a young girl's safety, nor is she shut up and watched carefully; there is no jealous husband whose vengeance one must avoid. With a Spartan girl you need not send a messenger; you may speak to her yourself, and you are not repulsed by a long wait. A Spartan girl does not deceive your wandering eye with clothes of Tyrian purple, nor do you lose patience as your sweetheart has her perfumed hair arranged.

But here in Rome my loved one goes surrounded by a great crowd, and the way is so narrow I cannot touch her even with my fingers. You cannot find what she looks like nor can you find an opportunity to talk. The lover follows a blind path. But if, O Rome, you were to imitate the laws and wrestling matches of the Spartans, you would be all the dearer to me for this benefit.

Propertius 3.14

(a) How reliable a source would Propertius be on the customs of the Spartans?
(b) List the sports in which Propertius says the Spartan girls competed. Are any of these supported by separate evidence?
(c) What seems to have been the status of women in Rome at this time? How much freedom did they have?
(d) What was said to be the characteristic dress of Amazons?
(e) The cestus was the Roman boxing glove, with protruding nails to be damaging to the recipient of the blow. It was unlike the Greek "sharp glove." Does this give any evidence on the value of Propertius' testimony?

So scanty is the literary evidence about women athletes that scholars quote the following from Athenaeus (about 200 AD), who wrote a curious book called "The Feast of the Professors," where the guests discuss various topics, quoting copiously from Greek authors. Here is one:

11

It is extremely pleasant to stroll to the gymnasium and running track on the island of Chios and see the young men wrestling with the girls.

Athenaeus, *Doctors at Dinner* 13.566e

[The trouble with this evidence is that "wrestling" is frequently used in Greek and Latin as a metaphor for sexual intercourse.]

12

Herakleitos, in *The Guest,* says there was a woman named Helen, who was an enormous eater.

Athenaeus, *Doctors at Dinner* 10.414d

[This sentence follows a discussion of the gluttonous life that athletes led. Some scholars think this means that Helen had been an athlete. Perhaps. At least it shows how limited our evidence is.]

Here is another type of evidence that should be viewed with caution. In the next two selections the philosopher Plato presents his ideas on what kind of training in athletics girls should receive. Plato was a student of Sokrates and the teacher of Aristotle, and he lived from about 429 to 347 BC. In the dialogue called *Laws* he describes what he believes the ideal city should be. In using this material as evidence, we must constantly keep in mind that Plato is describing things as he thinks they *should be.* However, it is clear that this ideal has some basis in reality, just as science fiction reflects the culture of the authors. An "Athenian Stranger" puts forth what seem to be Plato's own views:

13

Athenian Stranger: To continue, we have talked about building public gymnasiums and schools in the three divisions inside the city, as well as facilities in the three divisions outside the city for riding horses along with gymnasiums and open spaces arranged for archery and other types of shooting long distances as well as for the young people to learn and to practice. If I did not explain these properly, I shall describe them systematically so that they can be set up by laws.

In all these facilities teachers hired from abroad for each subject shall live to give instruction in all kinds of military science and music to the students who come to them. No student will take this instruction because his father wants him to nor omit it because of his father's orders, but everyone, "man and boy," as they say, shall be compelled to receive as much instruction as possible, since they are more the children of the state than of their parents.

As for women, my laws will require the same training for them as for men.

I set forth with confidence the proposition that instruction in riding and athletics is as fitting for women as it is for men.

Plato, *Laws* 7.804C–E

(a) From what class would the teachers be chosen? Why?
(b) Besides the bow, what other means of long-distance shooting would there be?
(c) Would instruction in military science include athletics?

Next, the Athenian Stranger is describing the kind of athletic games he would like to initiate in his ideal city:

14

Athenian Stranger: The first competitors whom the herald shall summon shall be the runners in the stade, as it is now. They shall present themselves in armor; we will offer no prize to those without armor. The first entrants will compete in armor for a stade; the next group will run the diaulos, the third the *ephippios* [= 800 meters?], and the fourth the dolichos. In the fifth group we shall first start those with heavy equipment, called hoplites, to run to a temple of Ares and back, a course of 60 stades over even ground. The second group will have full equipment for an archer and will run a distance of 100 stades, to a temple of Apollo and Artemis ⟨and back⟩; the course will be held through mountains and varied terrain. When we have started the races we will wait until their return and we will award the prizes in all events.

Klinias: Good idea.

Athenian Stranger: We will divide these contests into three divisions, one for boys, one for beardless youths, and one for full-grown men. We will make the distance of the archers' race and the hoplite race two-thirds of the regular course for the youths and one-half for the boys. As for the women, girls who have not reached puberty will compete on the race course in the stade, the diaulos, the ephippios, and the dolichos, and they will compete without clothing. Those over 13 will continue to participate until married or until they reach 20 or at least until they are 18. When these present themselves for competition in these races they must be dressed in appropriate clothing. These are to be my regulations for men's and women's races.

As for events which require strength, in place of wrestling and other "heavy" events which we now have, we should set up contests in fighting armor, one against one, two against two, and so on through ten against ten. We will have experts determine what one has to do on both defense and offense and how much it takes to win. Just as we now have experts in wrestling who have decided what is good form and what is not, so we will have to convene experts in armed fighting to set down rules by which we can determine who deserves the victory in such contests, whether on defense or offense and also a method of determining the loser. There should be similar rules set up for women until they are married.

We must replace the pankration by a general competition for peltasts.[1] They shall compete in handling bows and shields, in hurling javelins and in throwing stones, whether by hand or with a sling. We shall also establish rules for these events to reward the person giving the most skillful performance.

Plato, Laws 8.833A–8.834A

(a) What major differences do you notice between Plato's proposed games and the Olympic program?

(b) What evidence does this passage give us about the position of the stade in the Olympic sequence? Does it seem reasonable that the stade would come first at Olympia? Does it seem reasonable that the Panathenaic Games (which is probably what the Athenian Stranger means by ''as it is now'') would keep the same order as the Olympic Games?

(c) The length of the ephippios is not known. How long would you assume it was from its place in this list? How long were the hoplite and archer races?

(d) We have added ''and back'' to the description of the archers' race because of what follows in the text. What is this?

(e) In what running events do the women not compete?

(f) Do the women wear armor in the races?

(g) Besides the wrestling, what were the other two ''heavy'' events in the Olympics and similar games?

(h) What is unusual about the fighting contests that Plato suggests? What great difference is there in determining the victor? Were wrestling matches decided on points?

(i) What is the single greatest difference between these games and the customary schedule of events? Where does Plato (or the Athenian Stranger, if you will) put the emphasis?

It is essential to keep in mind that the Greek (and Roman) world was male dominated. Women gained some freedom but never came close to equality. Here is the point of view as expressed by Perikles (about 495–429 BC) in his ''Funeral Oration'' for those who died in battle:

15

If it is necessary for me to remind those who from now on will be widows of the feminine virtues, I will do so in one short piece of advice. It is your great glory not to be inferior to the nature which was given you and not to be talked about by men at all, neither for praise nor for blame.

Thucydides 2.45

[It is easy to see that in V BC Athens, there would be no reason for a girl to try to excel in sports.]

In trying to discover the facts about the position of Greek women, we must bear in mind the *time*, the *place*, and the *social class* of the women concerned. That is, when did the action take place? It may be dangerous to introduce evidence from Homer for V BC in Athens. Even so, a Spartan girl seems to have had more freedom than a girl living in Athens. Finally, a girl of high social class would have restrictions on her conduct that a girl of poor parents would not. For example, Nausikaa, a daughter of Alkinous, King of the Phaeacians, went with a group of girls to the sea to do the family wash. Such activity would be unheard of in V BC Athens. Races for young girls, perhaps 10–15 years old, were held at Brauron. The position of women in the Greek world has been well summed up by Susan B. Pomeroy: "Athenian men and women lived separate lives, and most of our information is about men's lives. It is almost easier to describe the activities of men and simply say, 'Women did not do most of these things.' "

Further Readings

Forbes, C.A., *Greek Physical Education* (New York and London 1929; reprinted 1970), pp 9, 200–201, 227, 231, 251.

Harris GAA, pp 179–186. Excellent survey of the evidence.

Lefkowitz, M.R., and Fant, M.B., *Women's Life in Greece and Rome* (Baltimore 1982).

Perlman, P., "Plato 833C–834D and the Bears of Brauron," *Greek, Roman, and Byzantine Studies* 24 (1983), pp 115–130.

Pomeroy, S.B., *Goddesses, Whores, Wives, and Slaves* (New York 1975).

Spears, B., "A Perspective of the History of Women's Sport in Ancient Greece," *Journal of Sport History* 11 (1984), pp 32–47.

21

Individual Athletes

Much important information about individual athletes comes from inscriptions carved in their honor. The following inscription was found near Sparta, dated 440–435 BC. The games mentioned all took place in the Peloponnesos.

1
Damonon set this up to Athena, Guardian of the City, after he had won such victories as no man of the present has done.

Damonon won the following victories in four-horse chariots, driving the chariots himself and using his own horses: four times in the sanctuary of the Earth Shaker [= Poseidon], four times at the festival of Athena, and four 5 times at the festival of Eleusis.

And Damonon won at the festival of Poseidon in Elis, at the same time winning the race on horseback, and seven times the same Damonon won the race for full-grown mares, using horses which were bred from his own stallion and his own mares. 10

And Damonon eight times won the race for full-grown mares in the sanctuary of Ariontia, driving the chariot himself, using horses bred from his own stallion and his own mares, and at the same time he won the race on horseback.

And Damonon won the race for full-grown mares four times at the festival 15 of Eleusis, driving the chariot himself.

Enymakratidas [= son of Damonon] won the following victories. First, at the festival of Apollo Lithesios he won the boys' dolichos and the race on horseback on the same day. And Enymakratidas in the sanctuary of Ariontia won the dolichos for young men and the race on horseback on the same 20 day. And Enymakratidas at the Parparonia festival won in one day the boys' stade, the diaulos, the dolichos, and the race on horseback.

As a boy Damonon won the stade and the diaulos in the sanctuary of the

Earth Shaker. And Damonon as a boy won the stade and the diaulos at the
25   festival of Apollo Lithesios. And Damonon as a boy won the stade and the
diaulos at the festival of Apollo Maleatas. And Damonon as a boy won the
stade and the diaulos at the festival of Apollo Lithesios. And Damonon as
a boy won the stade and the diaulos at the Parparonia festival, and at the
festival of Athena he won the stade.
30   The year Echemenes was ephor [= Spartan official elected annually], Damonon won the following victories. At the festival of Athena he won the race
for full-grown mares, driving the chariot himself, and on the same day won
the race on horseback and at the same time his son won the stade.
        The year Euhippos was ephor, Damonon won the following victories. In
35   the sanctuary of the Earth Shaker he won the race for full-grown mares,
driving the chariot himself, and on the same day he won the race on horseback, and at the same time his son won the stade and diaulos and dolichos
in one day, beating all opponents.
        The year Echemenes was ephor, Damonon won the following victories.
40   In the sanctuary of the Earth Shaker he won the race for full-grown mares,
driving the chariot himself and his son won the stade, the diaulos, and the
dolichos on the same day.

                                                          IAG 16; IG V.1.213

(a) The order is somewhat confused. What victories are mentioned in lines 1–16?
    In 17–22? In 23–29? In 30–42?
(b) Where did this talented father and son win their victories?
(c) How did they do in the Crown Games?
(d) Although Sparta had dominated the Olympic Games in the earliest years, the
    Spartans at this time were participating less and less in festivals outside their
    own territory. The question is, how good was the local competition against
    which Damonon and son competed?
(e) Harris (SpGR, p 161) says that this pair "obviously belong" to the "not very
    admirable class" of those who "contrive to shine by carefully avoiding com-
    petition with their equals or superiors in skill." How fair is this criticism?

    The next inscription was found at Rome, though written in Greek, about 200
AD:

2
I, Marcus Aurelius Asclepiades, also named Hermodoros, am the son of
Marcus Aurelius Demetrios. He was high priest of the World Track Association, president of the Association for life, and manager of the Augustan
Baths. He was a citizen both of Alexandria and Hermopolis, champion in all
5   four Crown Games, and a famous wrestler.
    I myself am the senior warden of Sarapis [= Egyptian god] the Great,
high priest of the World Track Association, president of the Association for
life, and manager of the Augustan Baths. I am a citizen of Alexandria, Hermopolis, Puteoli, and Naples, senator of Elis and Athens, and citizen and

senator of many other cities, a pankratiast, champion in all four games,   10
undefeated, immovable and unchallenged.[1]

I won all the contests in which my name was entered, defeating everyone. I issued no challenge nor was there anyone who dared issue a challenge to me.[2] I was never in a tie match, never forfeited a bout, never
protested a decision, never walked out of a contest nor entered a contest   15
in order to please a king,[3] nor did I ever win a fight that was started again,[4]
but in all the contests which I entered I won the crown right there in that
skamma, and I always qualified in the preliminaries.[5]

I competed in three parts of the world, in Italy, Greece, and Asia, and
won the following victories, all in the pankration: the Olympic Games in the   20
district of Pisa in the 240th Olympiad [= 181 AD], the Pythian Games at
Delphi, twice in the Isthmian Games, and twice in the Nemean Games. In
the second of these contests ⟨at Nemea⟩ I stopped my opponents.[6]

⟨And I won⟩ the shield of Hera Games at Argos, the Capitoline Games in
Rome twice. In the second of these contests I stopped my opponents after   25
the first round. ⟨And I won⟩ the Games in Honor of Antoninus Pius at Puteoli
twice, and in the second I stopped my opponents after the second round,
and the Augustan Games at Naples twice, and in the second I stopped my
opponents after the second round, and the Actian in Nikopolis twice, and in
the second I stopped my opponents.   30

I won at Athens five times: ⟨once⟩ in the Panathenaic Games, ⟨once⟩ in
the Games for Olympian Zeus,[7] ⟨once⟩ in the Panhellenic Games, and twice
in the Hadrian Games.

I won at Smyrna five times: twice in the General Asian Games, in the
second of which I stopped my opponents, and also at Smyrna the same   35
number in the Olympic Games and the Hadrian Olympic Games.

I won the Augustan Games at Pergamon three times, in the second games
I stopped my opponents before the contest began and in the third I stopped
my opponents after the first round.

I won at Ephesos three times, namely in the Hadrian, the Olympic, and   40
Balbillan Games, stopping my opponents after the first round.

I won the Asklepeian Games at Epidauros, the Games of the Sun at
Rhodes, and the Chrysanthinian Games at Sardis, and at other thematic
games,[8] among them the Eurykleian Games in Lakedaimon, the Mantinean
Games, and others.   45

Having competed for six years, I retired from competition at the age of 25
because of the risks and the jealousies involved. A long time after my retirement I yielded to pressure and won the pankration in the Sixth Alexandrian Olympic Games, held at my native city.

IAG 79; IG XIV 1102

(a) The fixed date in this inscription is the 240th Olympic Games, which were
held in 181 AD. Moretti (IAG, p 231) then reconstructs the dates of the victories in major games as follows:

Date, AD	Games
178	Capitolian, Nemean, Actian
179	Isthmian, Pythian
180	Nemean
181	Olympics, Isthmian
182	Capitolian, Actian

Judging from this record, just how good was this athlete?

(b) How successful was he after he retired?

(c) In how many contests did his opponent withdraw?

(d) There is something strange about his retirement. Can you suggest a possible answer?

(e) In what games did he compete when he came out of retirement?

The following inscription was found in the theater at Miletos in Asia Minor, dated about 20 AD. The names of the athlete and his father, which must have occurred at the beginning, are lost:

3

⟨This inscription honors X, son of Y,⟩ who won the diaulos in the 190th Olympiad [= 20 AD];

⟨won⟩ the Pythian men's stade, diaulos, and hoplitodromos on the same day;

⟨won⟩ the Nemean men's stade, diaulos, and hoplitodromos in succession in the same year,[9] the first of all to accomplish this;

in the Freedom Games set up at Plataia by the Greek states jointly, ⟨won⟩ the men's stade and hoplitodromos, beginning at the Victory Monument, gaining the title "Best of the Greeks," the first and only from Asia Minor to win this honor;

in the Great Caesarean Games at Actium, ⟨won⟩ the men's stade, diaulos, and hoplitodromos on the same day, the first of all to do this;

⟨won⟩ the Nemean diaulos and hoplitodromos again;

in the Roman Augustan Games set up by the states of Asia Minor jointly, ⟨won⟩ the hoplitodromos, first of the Ionians [= Greek inhabitants of Asia Minor] to do this;

⟨won⟩ the Isthmian hoplitodromos, first of any from Miletus to do this;

⟨won⟩ the Pythian stade and hoplitodromos for the second time, first of the Ionians to do this [illegible letters here];

in the games set up by the Sacred Victors and Crown Winners of the World, ⟨won⟩ the stade, diaulos, and hoplitodromos, first of all to do this;

in the Games at Argos ⟨won⟩ the stade, first of any from Miletos, and the hoplitodromos;

⟨won⟩ the Nemean stade, diaulos, and hoplitodromos again, first of the Ionians to do this;

in the Halieian Games on Rhodes, ⟨won⟩ the stade and hoplitodromos;

in the Freedom Games set up by the Greek states jointly at Plataia, again ⟨won⟩ the stade, diaulos, and hoplitodromos, and the special hoplitodromos beginning at the Victory Monument, gaining for the second time the title of "Best of the Greeks," the first and only to receive this, honored by the Greek states jointly with a gold victory crown;

⟨won⟩ the Isthmian hoplitodromos for the second time;

and in the Great Eleusinian, which the people of Athens set up, ⟨won⟩ the diaulos and hoplitodromos, and was honored for his accomplishments by the people of Athens with citizenship and a statue and a wreath of leaves.

IAG 59

(a) Near Plataia in 479 BC the Persian general Mardonios was defeated. What bearing does this have on the importance of the hoplitodromos? For unique rules governing the hoplitodromos at Plataia, see Philostratos, *On Athletics* 8.
(b) In what running event was this athlete not proficient?
(c) Which "first of all" records seem particularly important?

The following two inscriptions were dedicated at Delphi in 337 BC to commemorate the athletic feats of a family from Thessaly in northern Greece. The statues under which these inscriptions are written are on display in the museum at Delphi. Five epigrams have been preserved, of which we give you the first two:

4

O Hagias from Pharsalos, son of Aknonios, first from the land of Thessaly to win the pankration in the Olympic Games: you won the Nemean Games five times, the Pythian Games three times, and the Isthmian Games five times. And no one ever erected a trophy for a victory over your hands.

Syll³ 274

(a) What three notable achievements does this inscription mention?
(b) What does the word "trophy" mean in this connection? Use a dictionary if necessary.
(c) Who is addressed in this poem? Who is supposed to be speaking?

5

And I was the brother of the preceding; I carried off the same number of crowns in the same number of days that he did, but I won in plain wrestling. I killed a powerful man from T———, but I did not intend to do it.[10] My name is Telemachos.

Syll³ 274

(a) Who is addressed in this poem? Who is supposed to be speaking?
(b) How many victories did Telemachos win?
(c) What unusual bit of information do we learn here?

Pausanias, in 6.11, gives a lot of attention to Theagenes of Thasos; the name is also spelled Theogenes. There is a feeling of romantic adventure in finding an inscription that supports Pausanias. The following inscription was found at Delphi:

6

Your mother, the island of Thasos, is blessed, O son of Timoxenos [=Theagenes], because of all the Greeks you have the greatest reputation for strength. For no other man was crowned victor at Olympia, as you were, for both boxing and pankration. Of the three crowns you won at Delphi, one was gained akoniti [=without opposition], for no other mortal sought it. In nine Isthmian Games you won ten victories, for in the assembly the herald announced you alone of all mortals twice in the same day as victor, in the boxing and in the pankration. Nine times you won at Nemea, O Theagenes. Your personal victories were one thousand plus three times a hundred, and I attest that you were not beaten in boxing in 22 years.

Theagenes, son of Timoxenos, citizen of Thasos, won the following:

Boxing at Olympia	Boxing at Isthmia
Pankration at Olympia	Boxing at Isthmia
Boxing at Delphi	Boxing at Isthmia
Boxing at Delphi	Boxing at Isthmia
Boxing at Delphi, akoniti	Boxing at Isthmia and
Boxing at Nemea	pankration at same
Boxing at Nemea	Isthmian Games
Boxing at Nemea	Boxing at Nemea
Boxing at Nemea	Long-distance run in
Boxing at Nemea	Hecatombian
Boxing at Nemea	Games
Boxing at Nemea	at Argos
Boxing at Nemea	

Syll³ 64A

[The inscription is also quoted in Moretti IAG, p 21; its date is around 370–365 BC. Theagenes won his victories about a century earlier. The reading of the first part is difficult, and I have relied heavily on Moretti.]

Here is an inscription on the base of a victory statue, which was erected in the time of the Emperor Augustus (who ruled from 27 BC to 14 AD) in Pergamon in Asia Minor:

7

The people honor Hippolochos, son of Aesclepiades, victor in the boys' boxing and pankration, in the young men's boxing and pankration, and in the men's wrestling and pankration. He was twice commanded to go to Rome for the special purpose of the contests of the rulers [=the Romans], for the honor of his country.

Staatliche Museen zu Berlin (DDR), P536

(a) Where did Hippolochos probably win these victories?
(b) From what the inscription does *not* say, how would you assume Hippolochos did in the games at Rome?

For the last hundred years the sands of Egypt have been yielding papyri, preserved by the dry, hot climate. They include tax rolls, literary texts, and personal letters written on a kind of paper made from a water plant. Since papyri are almost always illegible in certain parts, they are difficult to read. The editor must usually restore missing parts.

The following papyrus is in the National Museum at Berlin (number 6222). It is a letter from an athlete named Dios to his sister Sophrone, telling how he competed before the Emperor:

8

Dios greets his sister Sophrone. I pray to God first of all for good health for you and after that that the best things in life happen to you.

I have been wondering why you have not written us so far, although every day friends have been coming here. So at least write us, please, and tell us how you and father are. We are all in good spirits here after our arrival. I will tell you everything that happened to me in Alexandria.

When we got here, we didn't find the person we were looking for; we found our leader, the Emperor, on his official visit.[11] And he ordered the athletes to be brought out on the field, and as a favor, five others.[12] And when I went in, I was placed in the first bout of the pankration, and this was bad because I understand nothing about the pankration. I performed badly for a long time and was (finally?) thrown. And since God wanted to help me, I challenged the other five to fight with me individually, since the Emperor wanted to see whether I would be lucky or whether I would be beaten again, and he wanted me to fight them, one after the other. As I know of course that anyone who withdrew from the contest would take a lot of shit,[13] I challenged them to fight.

The prize was a linen garment and a money prize the value of 100 *aurei*[14]; the garment has no embroidery on it. And I got my reputation back and made them my debtors,[15] and I got a gold coin in addition to the silver coins, and the other five got a garment apiece. This happened on the . . . day of Choiak.[16] And on the 26th day of the same month he led the holy procession in the Lagaion [=hippodrome in Alexandria], and we made for there, and I received a tunic embroidered with silver and another tunic and money. So, don't feel badly because we didn't find our man, for Fortune gave us something else. We send our respects to ———'s sister. We are looking forward to meeting you, God willing, after Mechir. So-and-so sends you warm greetings. My regards to father and all whom my heart loves. I wish you health, esteemed sister, for many years.

[On the reverse]

Take this to my sister Sophrone in D———, for her house is there; from her brother Dios.

(a) Why were six athletes (five plus Dios) entered secretly in the contest?

(b) Was the group of six composed entirely of pankratiasts?

(c) Is it likely that an athlete would be put in an event in which he was entirely unskilled?

(d) How much did Dios win in gold and silver?

Further Readings

Finley-Pleket, pp 68–82.
Harris GAA, pp 220–223. A series of maps showing home cities of Olympic victors.
Miller, *Arete* 66 and 67.
Yalouris, pp 264–271.

22

Walking and Mountaineering

Without automobiles or public transportation, the ancient Greeks had to walk more than most Americans. Walking was in fact a means of travel and virtually the only way over mountainous terrain. Most of the citizens of V BC Athens had no desire to leave the comfort and safety of the city, except for short walks. Outside the walls was the unknown, with few roads until the Romans came (II BC). Most of these roads were impassable for wheeled vehicles. This does not mean the Greeks did not walk for pleasure. For example, the scene of the Platonic dialogue, the *Phaidros,* takes place as Phaidros and Sokrates go for a walk "outside the walls." According to Xenophon, Sokrates thought it no great difficulty to walk from Athens to Olympia:

1

Someone expressed to Sokrates a fear of the trip to Olympia.[1] Sokrates said, "Why are you afraid of the journey? Don't you walk about the whole day here in Athens? When you go to Olympia, you will walk a ways and after that have lunch; then you will take another walk and have dinner and then rest. Don't you see that if you put together the distance you walk here over a period of five or six days, you would easily make it from Athens to Olympia? It is better to start a day early than a day late, for to be forced to go further than one wants in a day is tiring, but to travel with a day to spare makes the trip easy. Therefore it is better to hurry up the start rather than hurry on the road."

Someone else said that he was tired from having made a long journey, and Sokrates asked him if he carried a pack.

"By Zeus, no; just my cloak," said he.

"Did you go by yourself or did you have an attendant with you?"

"I had an attendant."

"Did he carry a pack or not?"

"Yes, by Zeus," the man replied, "he had the blankets and the rest of the gear."

"And what kind of shape was he in after this journey?" asked Sokrates.

"In my opinion, in better shape than I was."

"Well now," said Sokrates, "if it had been necessary for you to have carried his pack, how do you think you would have felt?"

"By Zeus, terrible," said the other, "or more accurately, I couldn't have done it."

"Do you think that a man in good physical shape should be able to do less than his slave?"

Xenophon, Memorabilia 3.13.5–6

(a) How many miles a day did Sokrates say his friend walked in Athens?
(b) Where did the travelers seem to have passed the nights? Was there an alternative?
(c) In some cultures a gentleman is not supposed to be able to do heavy labor. What are the views of Sokrates?

Pausanias tells us of an annual pilgrimage made by women:

2

The Thyiades are women from Athens, who go every year to Mt. Parnassos with the women from Delphi, and there they celebrate the sacred rites of Dionysos. These Thyiades are accustomed to dance at various places on the way from Athens, and one of these places is Panopeus.

Pausanias 10.4.2

Pausanias describes the road to Delphi:

3

The path from here to Delphi becomes steeper and hard even for an active man.

Pausanias 10.3

Pausanias has numerous other remarks about the poor condition of roads. Most routes were mere footpaths. The modern highway from Athens to Delphi is about 100 miles, but a path through rough terrain, such as the ancient road between Athens and Delphi, would probably add 50% to the distance. We are now presented with the fact that a group of women walked this distance through the mountains, stopping at villages like Panopeus for ritual dancing. What, then, becomes of our picture of the Greek female, married or unmarried, confined to her house?

Walking and mountaineering were necessary for travel and for hunting and fishing. Here is Oppian, Greek author of *On Hunting:*

4

But after them [= mythological figures like Orion] the fierce desire for hunting seized many. For no one once captured by the attractions of the lovely hunt would willingly give it up; sweet bonds hold him fast. How pleasant is sleep upon the flowers in the springtime! Again, how wonderful is a bed spread in a cove on a summer's day! How delightful for hunters is a repast among the rocks! What pleasure for them in gathering honey-sweet fruit! Cool clear water flowing from a cave, what glorious drink or bath does it furnish! And in the forest, what welcome gifts the herdsmen who watch over the goats bring in pleasing baskets!

Oppian 2.31–44

(a) How does this kind of recreation resemble a modern picnic?
(b) How does it differ?
(c) What is the main purpose of this person being out in the mountains?

It should be pointed out that many Romans were happy in the country. Wealthy Romans had several villas in which they seem to have spent much time when their duties in the city would permit. One might say that there is a sharp division between the Greeks and the Romans: the Greeks loved competition, which centered around the palestra; many Romans looked down on these typically Greek activities but liked the relaxing life in the country. But one thing they had in common: they considered the mountains an abominable mistake of nature. There was steady traffic over the Alps, but no one was inspired to comment on the beauty of the mountains. Very few ancients climbed a mountain "because it was there," as the modern cliché has it. If one did climb a peak, it was by the easiest route. There is no evidence that there were ascents where the climber deliberately chose the most difficult route. Both Greeks and Romans, however, did go into the mountains for various reasons, for example to hunt, as in Testimonium 4.

Here is an ambitious climb, made in 183 BC by Philip V of Macedonia, as described by the Roman historian Livy. The mountain, Mt. Haimos, is in modern Bulgaria and is 8,060 feet high.

5
Philip developed a desire to climb to the top of Mt. Haimos, because it was commonly believed that from there one could see the Pontus [=Black Sea], the Adriatic, the Ister [=lower Danube], and the Alps. It would be of great importance for strategy in the war against the Romans if he could have this panorama before his eyes. But on questioning those who were acquainted with the ascent of Haimos, he found that there was no path fit for an army to pass, but there was a way for a few experienced men. In order to console his younger son [=Demetrios], whom he had decided not to take with him, Philip asked him whether, considering the difficulties of this expedition, Philip should persevere in the attempt or give it up. If he decided to press on, he said, he should not forget the example of Antigonos in a similar situation, who when overwhelmed by a dreadful storm with all his family in one boat, was said to have advised his sons that they should remember themselves and should pass on to their children the advice that no one should run a risk in a dangerous situation with his whole family. He went on to say that, mindful of this advice, he was not going to expose both his sons to chance in the danger which threatened and, since he was taking his older son with him, he was going to send the younger son back to Macedonia to support

his ambitions and to guard his position as king. It did not escape the notice of Demetrios that he was being banished so that he would not be present in the council when they decided what route led most directly to the Adriatic and Italy, and what the strategy of the war would be . . . Philip, first crossing the territory of Maedica and next the wilderness between Maedica and Mt. Haimos, came at last on the seventh day to the base of the mountain. He stayed there one day to choose the men to go with him and began the ascent on the third day. At first they had moderate difficulties in the foothills, but the higher they climbed the more they ran into wooded terrain and many places where there was no path at all. Finally they came to a path in which the shade was so dense that because of the thickness of the trees and the interlacing of branches they could scarcely see the sky. But when they reached the ridges, they were so covered with fog, which is unusual at high altitudes, that they were as much hampered by the poor visibility as they would have been had it been night. On the third day they reached the summit. When they had descended they did not contradict the common belief about the view, more, I think, so that the failure of their expedition might not cause them to be a laughing stock.

Livy 40.21–22

(a) What was the main purpose of the ascent? Was it successful?
(b) What does this passage tell us about mountain climbing in antiquity? Is there evidence that the participants enjoyed the climb?

Of course the climbers in Philip's venture were under military discipline and may not have had an opportunity to enjoy the underbrush and bad weather.

In the next testimonium Plutarch describes the high jinks of the Germans crossing the Alps in 101 BC:

6
These barbarians [= Germans] were contemptuous of the Romans and so eager to harass them that they faced snowstorms dressed in light clothing, more to show their endurance and fortitude than because it was necessary; more than this, they forced their way through deep snow and ice to the summit of mountains and, putting their wide shield beneath them and pushing off, slid down the steep and slippery slopes covered with deep cracks.

Plutarch, *Marius* 23

(a) Why did the Germans climb the mountains?
(b) What does mention of cracks tell about the terrain? Was it dangerous?

Here is an account taken from the *Anabasis* (= The March Inland), written by Arrian, a well-regarded Greek historian of II AD on the military expedition of Alexander. What follows is perhaps the most important passage we have on ancient rock climbing. In this passage the Greeks have been prevented in January, 327 BC, from going further east by a stronghold called the Rock of Sogdiana:

7

Alexander announced that a prize of 12 talents would go to the soldier who first reached the top of the Rock; the next would get 11 talents, the third would get 10, and so on to the twelfth man, who would receive 300 gold darics.[2] The morale of the Macedonians was already high, and this offer made them even keener. When 300 who had practiced assault climbing in earlier sieges had gathered at the stronghold called the Rock of Sogdiana, they gathered the small iron tent pegs which they used to drive into the snow when it was firm and also into stretches of bare rock, and fastened to them ropes made of linen. When night fell, they started to climb the steeper route because they knew this would be unguarded. They drove their pitons into bare ground when this appeared and into the snow where they seemed most likely to hold, and they assisted one another as best they could up the sheer face. Thirty of the climbers died in this climb, and their bodies could not be recovered for burial since they fell into the snow at inaccessible places. The survivors seized the peak about dawn and signaled to those below, by waving linen flags, as Alexander had ordered them to do.

Arrian, *Anabasis* 4.18–19

(a) Were the assault climbers experienced?
(b) Do the losses seem "acceptable," to use the military term?
(c) What equipment did the climbers use?
(d) What was the state of morale in the Greek army?
(e) Was the failure to recover the bodies for burial serious to the Greeks?
(f) Was the climb a competition?

Here follow three testimonia from Strabo, a Greek geographer of I AD:

8

Mt. Argaios is the highest mountain in Asia Minor (almost 13,000 feet) and on its summit is perpetual snow, and those who have climbed it—and these are very few—say that when the visibility is good, one can see both the Pontos [= Black Sea] and the Bay of Issos [= in Asia Minor, opposite the island of Cyprus].

Strabo 12.2.7

(a) If Strabo says "few have climbed this mountain," does this illustrate interest in climbing?

9

Above Sardis [= a city in Asia Minor] is Mt. Tmolos (about 6,000 feet), a sacred mountain, with a lookout on the summit, an arcade with seats of white marble, erected by the Persians, and from it one has a view of the plains.

Strabo 13.4.5

(a) What reason would people have to climb this mountain? Compare the biblical mountain Mt. Sinai (*Exodus* 19) and the Pisgah (*Deuteronomy* 34.1), as well as the unnamed mountains which Jesus climbed with three disciples.
(b) What accommodations were made for climbers? What does this tell us about the number of people who climbed this sacred mountain?

There was one mountain, however, which even had accommodations where climbers could spend the night before going to the summit. This was Mt. Etna in Sicily.

10

Near the town of Centoripa is a small village called Etna, which takes in climbers and sends them on their way, for the ridge of the mountain begins here. Those who had recently climbed the summit told me that at the top was a level plain, some 20 stades in circumference, around which was a pile of ashes as high as the wall of a house, so that if anyone wished to get down into this plain he had to jump down from this wall. . . . Two of their party were courageous enough to venture into the plain of this crater, but since the sand on which they were walking was becoming hotter and deeper, they turned back and could not tell their friends who were watching anything more than these friends could see for themselves. They went on to say that as far as they could observe, many of the accounts about the crater are just stories, especially the tale about Empedokles, who is alleged to have leaped into the crater and as a clue to his fate left behind one of the brass sandals he wore. This sandal, my informants told me, was found a little way from the rim of the crater, as if it had been propelled by the force of the fire. But as a matter of fact this place cannot be approached or even seen, nor could anything be thrown into the crater because of the blast of air from the interior.

Strabo 6.2.8

(a) What seems to have been the purpose of climbing Mt. Etna?
(b) What facilities, if any, were provided for the climbers?
(c) What evidence did the climbers bring down the mountain about the supposed suicide of Empedokles?

Here is an annual climb of a mountain in northern Greece:

11

On the highest peak of Mt. Pelion is the cave of Cheironion and a shrine to Zeus Akraios; when it is the season of the Dog Star [=Dog Days], when the heat is most extreme, the chief young men, citizens of the state, chosen by the head priest for this, dress in coats made of the finest fleece because of the extreme cold of the top of the mountain.

Dikaiarchos 8, *Geographi Graeci Minores*

(a) What was the main purpose of climbing this mountain?
(b) What were some of the additional benefits for making the climb?

Ascents were made of the sacred Mt. Olympos.

12

The mountain in Macedonia which is called Olympos is said to be so high that at its summit no wind is felt nor do clouds gather there. It rises so much above the damp air in which birds fly that it is said that birds do not fly there. This is said to be borne out by those who make a yearly ascent to perform some kind of sacrifice, who say that they make marks in the dust, which they find unchanged from one year to the next, which could not happen if the spot permitted wind or rain. Finally, because the air which is so thin cannot sustain their breathing, they could not stay there if they did not put wet sponges in their nostrils by which they breathe in air which is heavier and more like what they are used to.

St. Augustine, *On the Book of Genesis against the Manicheans* 1.24

(a) The height of Mt. Olympos is 9570 feet. Is this high enough to cause the phenomena that St. Augustine described?

(b) The Greek volume of the *Blue Guide* says that Mt. Olympos is usually covered with clouds at midday hours in hot weather. What does St. Augustine say?

St. Augustine seems to have followed the tradition of Homer:

13

With these words Athena of the flashing eyes left for Olympos, where, they say, is the eternal home of the gods. It is not shaken by the winds nor yet wet with rain nor yet covered with snows.

Homer, *Odyssey* 6.41–44

(a) How do we reconcile these different accounts of this sacred mountain?

Finally, here is a man who knew why he was climbing his mountain, the Emperor Hadrian (II AD):

14

He [= Hadrian] then sailed to Sicily, where he climbed Mt. Etna to see the sunrise of different colors, it is said, like a rainbow.

Historiae Augustae Scriptores, *Life of Hadrian* 13

We have seen that the Greeks (and Romans) went into the mountains for several "practical" reasons: military expeditions, religious ceremonies, hunting, and scientific investigations. In Testimonium 6 we have the lighthearted Germans sliding down steep slopes, and Hadrian wished to see the sunrise from Etna (Testimonium 14), a mountain that attracted others who had no practical reasons to climb it (Testimonium 10). It is clear, however, that the most common reason for going into the mountains was that they lay on the great trade routes. Roman coins have been found in the Julier and Theodule passes of the Alps, and bronze tablets of thanksgiving were found in the Great St. Bernard Pass.

Finally, we should not overlook the occasional use of beacons to signal important news. Such beacons would naturally seek the highest points for the fires. The best-known example, though legendary, occurs in the *Agamemnon* of Aeschylus

(281–316), where beacons on eight mountains carried the news of the fall of Troy in Asia Minor to Mycenae in Greece.

Further Readings

Casson, L., *Travel in the Ancient World* (Toronto 1974), pp 65–94.

Forbes, R.J., *Studies in Ancient Technology* II (Leiden 1965), pp 140–145. Use of horses.

Pease, A.S., "Notes on Mountain Climbing in Antiquity," *Appalachia* 132 (1961), pp 289–297.

23

Swimming and Boating

One activity enjoyed by both Greeks and Romans, at least by the educated upper class, was swimming. A collection of Greek proverbs has the following comment on a cliché:

1

"Not knowing how to swim or to write." For among the Athenians they learn these skills from childhood.

Diogenianos, Paroemiographi 6.56 (date unknown)

(a) Does this indicate that *all* Athenians learned to swim and read?

The proverb is also quoted by Plato:

2

These stupid people are called wise although, as the proverb goes, they do not know how to read or to swim.

Plato, Laws 689D

Herodotus explains why the Persians had more casualties than the Greeks at the naval battle of Salamis in 480 BC:

3

Many Medes and Persians died but only a few Greeks. For since the Greeks knew how to swim, when their ships were destroyed, those who were not killed in hand-to-hand combat swam into the harbor of Salamis. But many barbarians perished in the water since they did not know how to swim.

Herodotus 8.89

Pausanias describes a monument at Delphi set up to honor a man whose profession was probably gathering sponges:

4

Next . . . is a memorial set up by the League of Skione to honor Skyllis, who was famous for diving to the deepest part of the sea, and he taught his daughter Hydne how to dive. When a great tempest came down on the fleet of Xerxes when it was anchored off Mt. Pelion [in 479 BC], these two added to the destruction by pulling up the anchors and other means of mooring the triremes [=fighting ships]. As a reward the League set up a memorial to Skyllis and his daughter. The statue of Hydne was among the statues taken by Nero from Delphi. The only women who do deep-sea diving are virgins.

Pausanias 10.19.1

Children used aids in learning to swim:

5

They act like boys who are learning to swim; they lie on a raft of bullrushes so that they don't have to work so hard to keep afloat but can easily float and use their hands.

Plautus, Pot of Gold 595–6

The only mention of formal competitive swimming is found in the following passage from Pausanias:

6

Nearby is the Temple of Dionysos of the Black Goat; they have annual contests here in music and offer prizes for competition in swimming and racing boats.

Pausanias 2.35.1

Here are two descriptions of swimming. The first was written by a Latin poet in I AD:

7

For just as the dolphin glides through the water on swift fins, now rising above the surface and now sinking to the depths, and piles up moving waves and sends them off in circles, just so will each person born under the sign of the Dolphin fly through the waves, raising one arm and then the other in slow arcs. At one moment one can hear the sound of the water as he strikes it, at another moment he will separate his arms under water, like an oar concealed by the water, and at another time he will enter the water in a vertical position and will pretend to swim when he is walking and pretending to have found a shallow place he will imitate a field on top of the water. Or he will rest his motionless limbs by bringing them to his back and sides; he does not depress the water but will float on top of the waves and will hang there, an entire boat without a rower.

Manilius, On Astronomy 5.419–430

(a) Identify the different types of swimming and playing in the water which Manilius described.

The next author was a Greek poet in IV or V AD who described an informal contest between the god Dionysos and a mortal, Ampelos:

8

With these words Dionysos dove into the water. And Ampelos rose from where he sat and joined him. Pleasant was their course from one side of the gold-bearing river to the other. The god took the lead and as he went through the water, he opposed his naked breast to the current, and thrusting with his feet and using his arm like oars, he marred the previously undisturbed calm of the wealthy river. At one time he held his course right beside that of his young friend, at another he pulled ahead in an attempt at leaving the youthful Ampelos behind. Then Dionysos of the swift knees let his tired hands go in circles and willingly yielded the victory to his friend.

Nonnus, *Dionysica* 11.400–426

(a) Nonnus was not a good poet. What completely unsuitable phrase does he use to describe Dionysos?
(b) What stroke does Dionysos use?

Philostratos mentions swimming once, as a training exercise for a boxer:

9

The boxer Telsander from Naxos used to swim around the headlands of his island and went far out to sea, using his arms, which in exercising the rest of his body, also received exercise themselves.

Philostratos, *On Athletics* 43

A vase in the Louvre Museum in Paris (Pl 49) shows a woman swimming with alternate strokes of the arms. It is not clear how she is using her legs. Another woman is about to dive. A third woman is putting on oil. A bronze statuette (Pl 50) is an athlete about to dive. Plate 51 shows what seems to be an informal place to swim, where the girls hang their clothes on trees, but there is a substantial diving platform at the right.

(a) Considering literary and visual evidence, what kinds of swimming strokes did the Greeks use?
(b) What kinds of dives?

No city in the loose association of city-states that we call Greece is very far from the sea. There are said to be 1425 islands in the Ionian and Aegean seas. It is obvious that much travel was by boat. Literary evidence on boating is scanty. There is the evidence of inscriptions that mention prizes awarded to boats. In a list of the prizes in the Panathenaic Games (Syll³ 1055), sometime in IV BC, there was a boat race in which the prize for first place was three bulls, 300 drachmae, and 200 free meals.

Alexander, on his return from India, held games in Persia:

10

At this time he set up frequent races for boats, and there were frequent contests for triremes [=boats with three ranks of oars] and quadriremes

Plate 49   Column at right and diving platform suggest artificial pool; presence of fish indicates water. Red figure amphora.

[= boats with four ranks of oars], with contests for rowers and captains and crowns for the victors.

Arrian, *Anabasis* 7.23.5

(a) What sizes of boats are mentioned?

Plautus has a scene where two girls are left on a sinking vessel and escape through their own efforts, as seen from the shore and described thus:

11

Speaker 1: What do I see?
Speaker 2: Two girls sitting in a dinghy all alone. How the poor things are thrown about! Good, good, hurrah! A breaker carried them away from the rock to the shore; no helmsman could ever have steered a straighter course. I don't believe I have ever seen larger waves! They are safe now, if they can just avoid those waves that are coming! Now, it's do or die!

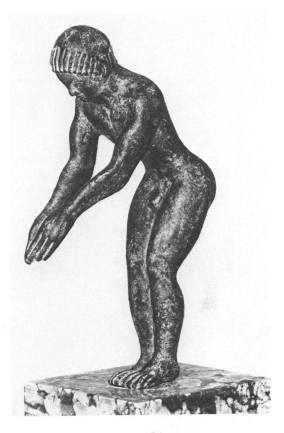

Plate 50 Does this small bronze statue (14.5 cm) have any connection with the aquatic contests mentioned in Testimonium 6?

Plate 51 Girls swimming. Much damaged figure, upper right, is girl poised to dive. Black figure amphora.

Plate 52 Since boats rigged like this could not beat into wind, travel by sea was hazardous. Note twin rudders. Interior of black figure kylix.

There goes one of them! No, she's in shallow water; she can easily swim to shore. O, good! She's safe. But the other girl has also jumped out of the dinghy. She is so frightened that she just fell on her knees in the water. She's safe, she's out of the water. Now she has reached the shore.

Plautus, Rudens 164–174

(a) How well can these girls handle a small boat?
(b) Can they swim?

There is visual evidence for boats. In many pictures, however, the artist has chosen to make the figures of the people in the boat much larger than they actually are. In Plate 52 the large figure sailing the boat is Dionysos [= god of wine]; he has caused grapevines to grow up the mast and has turned his mutinous crew into dolphins. In Plate 53 three men are either beaching their boat or preparing to dive. Plate 54 is a good example of artistic distortion; there was not enough room to

Plate 53 Large eye on bow helps boat to find its way. Black figure oinochoe.

Plate 54 Victorious crew in boat steered by single rudder. Replica of marble relief.

Plate 55   Accident in harbor; scene on sarcophagus made for victim. Replica of marble relief.

show all the victorious crew, so the artist put in just three figures, one carrying a wreath and the palm of victory. Finally, Plate 55 is a graphic representation of an accident where three sailing ships are trying to rescue someone who has fallen from his small boat. For a detailed description of this attempted rescue, see Lionel Casson.

Further Readings

Casson, L., *The Ancient Mariner* (New York 1959), pp 220–222.
Gardiner, AAW, pp 93–95.
Harris SpGR, pp 112–132.
Sanders, H.A., "Swimming among the Greeks and Romans," *Classical Journal* 20 (1924), pp 566–568.

24

Hunting and Fishing

There is considerable evidence about hunting and fishing in the Greek world. One of our literary sources is the poet Oppian (III AD), who has this to say in general about hunting, fishing, and fowling (hunting birds):

1

God has given mankind three types of hunting, in the air, on the ground, and in the lovely sea. But the contests are not the same. How could they be the same, to pull the twisting fish from the deep water, to snatch the winged birds from the air, or to attack deadly animals in the mountains? Yet the fisherman's task is not without effort, and neither is that of the hunter of birds. Yet pleasure alone accompanies the fisherman's labor, and his sport is without bloodshed; both kinds are unstained by blood. The fisher sits in comfort on the rocks of the seashore, and with curving rod and deadly hooks catches fish of different colors. What pleasure is his when he pierces the jaw of his prey with hook of bronze and sweeps the twisting dancer from the depths high into the air. Yes, but sweet also is the toil of the hunter of birds. For to his chase he carries no knife, no sword, no spear with tip of bronze. The companion who follows him to the woods is the falcon, and besides the bird he takes his nets with long cords and sticky bird lime,[1] and the hunter makes a path in the air from which the birds have no escape.

Oppian, *On Hunting* 1.47–66

(a) What type of hunting does Oppian first discuss?
(b) What three types of implements does this bird hunter use?

Here is Oppian again, describing the qualities a hunter should have:

2

The young men who wish to hunt should not be overweight. For it will be necessary for them to leap upon the back of a lofty steed in the middle of a rocky field, and they will also have to jump over ditches. And also they will often have to run down a wild beast in the woods with nimble feet and graceful limbs. Therefore those who are heavy should not come to the contest of the hunt. But they should not be overly thin either, for now and then it is necessary for the bold hunter to fight with fierce beasts. Therefore our hunter should be swift at running and strong at fighting. And in his right hand he should brandish two long spears and at the middle of his belt he should have his hunting knife. For he should be prepared to inflict bitter death on the animals and to defend himself against lawless men. If he is on foot he should hold the leash for his dogs with his left hand. But if he is on horseback he should control the bridle which guides his horse. He should wear a tunic well pulled up above the knee and fastened with cords. His cloak should hang on either side of his neck over his sturdy shoulders so that his hands will be free to make his task easy. He who goes on foot to follow the tracks of wild animals should do so with bare feet so that the noise of his sandals under his graceful feet may not expel sleep from the eyes of the wild animals. Better to wear no cloak, since often a garment moved by the breath of the breeze arouses the animals, and they turn to flight.

Oppian, *On Hunting* 1.81–107

(a) What physical abilities should the hunter have?
(b) What is the greatest single difference between the hunting that Oppian describes and modern hunting?
(c) What weapons does Oppian's hunter carry if he is on foot?
(d) Under what circumstances should the hunter go on foot?

Oppian turns to the matter of techniques:

3

Later we will tell the special tricks and snares which the deadly hunter uses in the mountains for each animal, but now we will sing in one song the techniques common to all types. Hunting with nets is the same for all animals and so are traps and so is the pursuit of all swiftfooted animals by horses and dogs, or sometimes we pursue them with just horses, using those born in the land of the Moors or Libya, which are not directed by the bridle and strength of the rider's hands but obey the whip and go where the master wishes. Therefore riders who are mounted on such horses leave their beloved dogs behind and, without other assistants, ride trusting in their horse and the rays of the sun. Hunting with the javelin is the same for all animals, and so is shooting a bow at close quarters with fierce animals who fight boldly with men.

Oppian, *On Hunting* 4.39–55

Here are testimonia about four different types of animals hunted by the Greeks. First is a common animal, the hare; rabbits were not found in ancient Greece:

4

In hunting the swift race of hares, the hunter should run ahead and turn them aside from any height of land or rock, and with his craft of hunting should drive them downhill. For when the hares see the men and dogs they dash uphill since they know that their front legs are shorter than their rear ones. Therefore hares do well on hills, but a man on horseback has trouble.

Oppian, On Hunting 4.425–432

(a) In what direction does a hare (or rabbit) run when it wishes to escape a hunter?

Here is the fox:

5

The Sly One [=the fox] you cannot catch with ambush or by lasso or by net. For she is fearfully clever at discovering them, clever at gnawing through ropes or loosening the knots and by her clever tricks avoiding death. A pack of dogs can seize her, but strong as they are, they do not subdue her without bloodshed.

Oppian, On Hunting 4.449–453

(a) Foxes are not hunted for their meat. What reason do modern hunters give for killing them?

Deer are difficult to catch because of their speed. Here, Xenophon describes how they may be caught by use of a trap that slows the deer so it cannot escape the dogs:

6

If the trap catches the front leg of a deer, he will be taken quickly, for the trap will strike every part of his body and head as he tries to run. But if the trap catches a hind leg, the drag of the trap will also interfere with the whole body. Sometimes the clog[2] is caught in the fork of a tree, and unless the cord breaks, the deer is captured then and there. But whether you overtake the deer in this way or wear the animal down, do not approach it, for if it is a stag it will gore you with its antlers or kick you. If it is a doe, it will kick. So you should throw javelins at it from a safe distance. Deer are also taken without the use of a leg breaker in the summer. For they become so exhausted by running that they stand still and are killed by javelins. They also jump into the sea and pools if they are worn out. Sometimes they collapse from lack of breath.

Xenophon, On Hunting 9.19–20

(a) What purpose do dogs have in this type of hunting?
(b) Compare the danger of hunting deer in antiquity and today.

The boar is one of the most dangerous of all wild animals, as we see in this testimonium from Homer:

7

Helios [=sun god] was now striking the fields as he rose from deep-running, softly-flowing Okeanos. The beaters came to a ravine; before them went the dogs following the scents and behind them came the sons of Autolykos and with them was Odysseus the godlike, close to the hounds, brandishing his long spear. Now, in a dense thicket, which the powerful damp clouds could not penetrate nor could the bright rays of Helios enter it nor could the rain come through, so thick it was, and dried leaves were there in plenty— here lay a mighty boar. To his ears from round about came the uproar of dogs and men as they pushed eagerly on. And from his den he burst out against them; his thick back bristled and his eyes flashed fire, and he took his stand, up close. Odysseus was the first to close with him, holding a long spear high in his sturdy hand, all keen to strike the beast. But the boar struck first and hit him above the knee, slashing from the side, and with his tusk tore a long gash, but did not reach the man's bone. But Odysseus was able to strike him on the right shoulder, and all the way through went the blade of the shining spear, and with a cry the boar fell in the dust and his life went out.

Homer, Odyssey 19.433–454

(a) What important weapon did this hunting party apparently not have?

In ancient Greece it was customary to dedicate objects to a god. In a collection of poems called the *Greek Anthology* there are several that describe hunting and fishing implements dedicated in this way. Here is an example:

8
Therimachos of Crete dedicated to Lykeian Pan near the Arkadian cliffs these throwing sticks for hares [see Pl 56]. In return for his gift, O god of the countryside, guide his bow hand in battle, and in the mountain glens stand at his right hand, giving him mastery in the hunt, mastery against his foes.

Leonidas, Greek Anthology 6.188

(a) What is significant about the nationality of Therimachos?
(b) What advantage in hunting hares would a throwing stick have in bushy terrain?
(c) What do we call the curved throwing sticks used in Australia?

Plato recommends that the young men in military service should show skill in using the sling:

9
In place of the pankration contest, we should have a general contest for peltasts [= lightly armed foot soldiers] who will compete with bow, shield, javelin, stones thrown by hand, and stones thrown by slings.

Plato, Laws 7.834

(a) Which weapons were regularly used by Athenian soldiers in Plato's time?

Vergil refers to farmers using the sling:

10
Winter, when the snow lies deep, is the time to pick acorns from the oaks and blood-red berries from the myrtle, a time to set traps for cranes and

Plate 56   Hunter returning with game on hare stick. Interior of polychrome kylix.

nets for deer, to chase the long-eared hares and to lay low the does by whirling the straps of a sling from the Balearic Islands.

Vergil, Georgics 1.305–309

(a) Was the sling powerful enough to kill a grown deer?

One of the attractive features of hunting, hinted by Xenophon, was that some women (probably very few!) went hunting with their menfolk:

11

Not only have all the men who loved hunting been good people, but also the women to whom the goddess [=Artemis] has given the love of the chase, like Atalanta, Prokris, and others.

Xenophon, On Hunting 13.18

[When women rode on horseback, as in hunting, they seem to have ridden sidesaddle; evidence that they rode astride is scanty and unclear.]

We now turn to the sport of fishing. The sport of hunting was mainly a rich man's sport, requiring dogs, horses, and beaters; fishing, on the other hand, required little capital investment. Commercial fishing was a way to earn a living, albeit a hard one. Here is a chorus of fishermen in a comedy by the Roman writer Plautus, singing about the difficulties in their life:

12

The life which men lead who are poor is a miserable one in every way, especially for those who never had a steady job or learned a trade. They are forced to make do with what they have at home. You can just about figure out what our economic status is from this equipment we are carrying. These hooks here and these rods tell you what our job and training are. Every day we come here from the city to get food. This is what we do for physical education and wrestling. We hunt for sea urchins, limpets, oysters, shellfish, snails, sea nettles, mussels, and grooved scallops. After we gather these, we turn to fishing with hooks from the rocks. We get our food from the sea. If it turns out that we don't get anything in the way of fish, well, we are the ones who are nicely washed and salted, and we sneak back home and go to bed without supper. And now that the sea is running so high we have no hope of getting anything. Unless we get some shellfish, we are sure going to go hungry. Now let us go and worship Venus [=goddess of the sea] so that she may graciously help us out of this difficulty.

Plautus, *Rudens* 290–305

(a) What kinds of seafood are described here?
(b) The chorus who sing this song are commercial fishermen. Can the activities they described be done for sport?

Plutarch (and Plato) did not approve of fishing:

13

Plato in his *Laws* (823E) advised, or rather prayed, that young men would not be overcome by a love for hunting in the sea. For in contests with sea bass or conger eels or parrot fish, there is no need to show traits of bravery or examples of wisdom, strength, speed, or agility, whereas brave animals build up the qualities of courage and manliness in those who fight with them. Clever animals improve the powers of reasoning and deduction of those who pit themselves against them, and those animals which are fleet of foot increase the strength and endurance of those who pursue them. This is what makes hunting a noble sport.

Plutarch, "On the Cleverness of Animals; 9, *Moralia* 965F–966A

(a) Why does Plutarch (and Plato) disapprove of hunting?
(b) Can fishing be dangerous under certain conditions?

Here are two more epigrams listing fishing equipment, and ostensibly dedicated by a fisherman (Pl 57):

14

Diophantos the fisherman has piously dedicated to the gods these implements, reminders of his former trade: bent hook, long poles, fish line, creels to hold fish, trap designed to catch fish as they swim, an invention of fishermen who sail the sea, sturdy trident, which is Poseidon's weapon, and the two matching oars of his boat.

Leonidas, *Greek Anthology* 6.4

Plate 57 Boy fishing, with basket of chum (= cut up fish) as lure. Interior of red figure kylix.

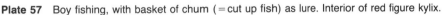

(a) What fishing aids mentioned here were not listed before?

15

Peison the fisherman, weakened by years of toil, whose right hand has already begun to shake, dedicated to Hermes the following: his cane poles wrapped at the tips, his oar which swam through the sea, curved hooks with barbs which bite the gullet of fish, his net with lead weights, the cork which shows where the fish trap lies, his two creels woven from rushes, the stone pregnant with fire,[3] and the anchor, the trap which restrains ships wishing to wander.

Philippos, Greek Anthology 6.5

(a) What implements listed here were not in previous testimonia?
(b) What was used for night fishing?
(c) Peison seems to have "sculled" his boat, using one oar over the stern. What statement suggests this?

Two weapons, the sling and the bow, both used in hunting and warfare, need some explanation. At the start it should be made clear that the ancient sling was unlike our modern slingshot. The modern weapon projects a missile from a small pouch by the power of elastic bands or strips of rubber. The ancient sling consisted of a pouch to which was fastened two cords each about 18 inches long (Pl 58). Placing a missile (often made of lead) in the pouch, the slinger whirled it

Plate 58   Four men fishing from boat; man on bank using a sling to hunt birds. Etruscan wall painting.

once rapidly around his head and released one of the two cords smartly. Vegetius, a Roman writer of IV AD, describes the training of Roman soldiers in using the sling:

16
The slingers and the archers used to set out targets, which were bundles of twigs or straw, as a mark to aim at, and the result was that even when they were 600 feet away they used to hit the mark more often than not, with arrows or at least with stones thrown from a two-handed sling[4] . . . They were trained before to twirl the sling over their head only once.

Vegetius, On Military Matters 2.23

(a) What was the range of the sling?
(b) What was the range of the archers?
(c) What was the range of the two-handed sling?

In Homer the evidence for archery is confusing. Among the nobles only a few, like Teukros, Paris, Pandaros, and Odysseus, seem to have used the bow, although plain soldiers were archers. Odysseus boasts of his skill with a bow:

17
For I am not unskilled in any of the sports in which men compete with one another. I know well how to shoot a shining bow, and I was the first to loose an arrow and strike the man I aimed at in the crowd of enemies, even though my friends stood beside me and were shooting at the foe. Only

Philoktetes bested me with the bow in the land of the Trojans where we Achaians shot our arrows.

Homer, *Odyssey* 8.214–220

The contest in archery in the funeral games for Patroklos was conducted under ridiculous rules. In the *Odyssey,* Penelope sets up a contest that still puzzles scholars:

18
But come now, you suitors, since your prize [= Penelope herself] is now set before you. I will put before you the great bow of Odysseus the godlike, and whichever one of you most easily takes the bow in his hands and strings it and shoots an arrow through all twelve axes, with him will I go and leave this home where I have spent my married life, a beautiful home full of lovely furnishings, and I think I will remember it even in my dreams.

Homer, *Odyssey* 21.73–79

Odysseus' son Telemachos sets up the twelve axes:

19
First he set the axes upright after he had dug a trench, one long enough for all the axes, straight in line, and he tramped down the earth. And astonishment seized all who saw him, so accurately did he set the axes, although he had never seen them before.

Homer, *Odyssey* 21.120–123

(a) Do you gather from these testimonia that shooting the bow was a skill that all the suitors had mastered?
(b) Can you devise a way in which the shooting at the axes could be done?
(c) Here is a hint for one solution: the axes may have had a blade on one side and a ring of some sort on the other.

Whatever may have been the popularity of the bow in Homeric times, it was not much used by Greeks in classical times, except in backward areas like Crete and Arkadia. The feeling seemed to be that it was a cowardly weapon, with which a weak man could kill a brave warrior at a distance. However, by V BC the military value of skilled archers who could harass the enemy became obvious. Because the bow and the arrows were light, the archers could move very quickly. The main source of archers was the island of Crete.

But if archery ceased to be a universal weapon, the use of the bow was part of the Greek heritage, much as in our own culture when children play at Robin Hood or Cowboys and Indians. Plato recommends in several places in his *Laws* that children of both sexes learn to shoot. And we should not forget that two of the twelve Olympic gods were archers: Apollo and his sister Artemis.

There are numerous questions about the shape and material of the ancient bow, as well as the technique of shooting. In general we may say that most common shape of the bow was the Scythian bow, familiar to us as the bow carried by Cupid on Valentine's Day cards (Pl 59). The doubly convex bow is shown on a vase (Pl 60), where Apollo and Artemis are shooting Niobe and her children.

Plate 59   Marble statue of Cupid (= Eros) stringing Scythian bow.

Ancient bows were constructed in several different ways: (1) simple bow, made of wood, (2) reinforced bow of wood with backing of a sinew, and (3) composite bow, with whole layer of sinew and a belly of incompressible material, usually horn, plus a third layer, usually wood.

That there were competitions in archery is shown by several inscriptions. The following was found at Olbia, a colony from Miletos on the Black Sea at the mouth of the River Bug:

20

I say that Anaxagoras, the glorious son of Demagoras, shot 282 fathoms [= 564 yards].

IAG 32, pp 82–84

The distance of 564 yards does not match modern performances. Modern distance contests, however, often employ a ''foot bow,'' where the archer lies on his back with his feet in a stirrup on the bow and pulls the bowstring with both hands.

Plate 60 Artemis and Apollo shooting bows. Red figure krater.

There is no evidence that the ancient Greeks used a foot bow. *Sports Illustrated* (November 8, 1976) reported a record flight of 1077 yards, 3 inches, with a hand-held bow, far beyond any recorded mark in ancient Greece. This introduces another variable in trying to make comparisons: the material out of which the bow is made. In a 1977 advertisement in *Sports Illustrated,* Owens–Corning stated that before the use of fiberglass the record for flight shooting (= distance shooting) was about the length of five football fields, but in 1970 with a fiberglass bow Harry Drake shot the length of nineteen football fields. With such disparity in materials, comparison of records is meaningless. Wallace McLeod says that authorities use the term "bowshot" as if it were an appropriate measurement. Modern estimates of "bowshot" run from 64 meters to 600 meters.

The ancient technique of shooting the bow is not clear. For example, some visual evidence shows the arrow placed on the right-hand side of the bow, whereas other pictures show it on the left. Modern archers in the United States and Europe put the arrow on the left. The Greeks seem to have used both techniques, if (and this is a big "if") the artists actually drew what they saw. The main trouble with the arrow on the right is that it may fall away from the bow. The advantage of shooting with the arrow on the left of the bow is that then the arrow is held snugly in place. There are two disadvantages. The first one is hypothetical: the arrow in this position is pointing not at the target but to the left of it. Actually this is no practical problem; because the arrow straightens out immediately on release, or rather, the arrow bends around the bow to straighten out, as shown in high-speed photography. The other difficulty is that in this position the bowstring often strikes the inside of the wrist, to the great discomfort of the shooter. One solution is to protect the arm with a "bracer." It is interesting that there is no evidence of Greek archers having used such protection.

The last problem is how the bowstring is drawn and released. The simplest release is the "primary." This is the method that a person with no knowledge of archery would employ. The arrow and string are pinched between the thumb and forefinger, with the arrow on the right of the bow. The obvious disadvantage is that in this way one can shoot only a weak bow. This draw is used by people who hunt in the forest and jungles, where the need is rapidity of shooting at short range, and where long flights would lead to loss of arrows. The "secondary" release is like the primary except the middle finger is over the string and beneath the arrow. This is rare, confined to a few American Indian tribes. In the "Mongol draw," the right thumb grasps the string from the left. The index finger locks the thumb to the right side of string, and the rear end of the arrow is held between thumb and upper joint of index finger. This is the draw used by most Asiatic peoples, and by most Moslems in Africa. The last draw we will describe is the "Mediterranean," in which the index, middle, and ring fingers are over the string, with arrow between index and middle fingers. This is the draw used by all people of classical antiquity except the Persians. It is also widely used throughout the world today. There are still other draws that we will pass over.

The Athenians in the period 530–490 BC had an opportunity to learn archery from the Scythians, who served as a police force. The bows were short Cupid types. The arrows were most unusual: they were short, 18 inches; and the arrowheads were only about 1 inch in length. Quivers have been found in Scythian graves with 200 or 300 arrows. The emphasis was on rapid delivery of arrows; the effect on the opposing forces must have been like walking through a colony of angry wasps, and it must have been difficult to maintain order.

Here is a curious observation by Plato in discussing the value of being ambidextrous:

21

It is the Scythian usage not only to use the left hand to draw the bow and the right hand to fit the arrow to the string, but also to use either hand for either action.

Plato, Laws 795A

(a) Under what circumstances, if any, would the ability to shoot with either hand be an advantage?

Further Readings

Butler, A. J., *Sport in Classic Times* (Los Altos CA 1975), pp 34–35; pp 195–198.
Gardiner AAW, p 27.

Harper's under *Arcus*.

McLeod, W., "The Range of the Ancient Bow," *Phoenix* 19 (1965), pp 1–14.

Rousing, G., *The Bow* (Bonn, Lund 1967).

Snodgrass, A.M., *Arms and Armour of the Greeks* (Ithaca 1967).

Wace, A.J.B., and Stubbings, F.H., *A Companion to Homer* (London 1963), pp 534–535 (archery contest); pp 518–520 (Homeric bow).

25

Music

Those who see Greek plays today find them comparatively easy to understand. There is an appealing universality about the problems that confront the characters on the stage. But two important ingredients that the Greeks enjoyed are often missing for modern audiences: dancing and music. What evidence has come down to us about these two key features of Greek drama is too scanty for accurate reconstruction. Consequently, our treatment here of these two forms of artistic expression will be brief.

We can tell something about what the Greek instruments looked like from studying vase paintings, statues, partial remains of instruments, and ancient treatises. But none of these tells us how the instruments were played or what the music sounded like. Fragments of music scores have survived, but musicologists are unable to decipher the ancient system of notation.

Listening to the modern harp or oboe will perhaps give us some idea of the ancient *lyre* or the *aulos,* but it will be on the whole misleading. The pipes played by shepherds in rural Greece today offer at best a slight hint of the sounds of ancient Greek music. The *Oxford Classical Dictionary* says, "It is very probable that if we should hear a piece of ancient Greek music accurately performed, we should regard it as bizarre, uncouth, and possibly barbaric." Some authorities suggest that the nearest parallel might be the raga music of India.

Although so much is unknown about Greek music, certain facts emerge. First, music was held in high regard by Greeks. This fact is dramatized by a passage in the *Iliad,* where Achilleus has refused to leave his tent after a quarrel with Agamemnon, and the ambassadors find him singing and accompanying himself on a lyre:

1
They found him delighting his heart with his handsome clear-toned lyre, beautiful and carefully wrought, and the crosspiece was made of silver. He had taken this from the spoils when the Greeks destroyed the city of Eetion.

With this he was pleasing his spirit, and he was singing of the fair deeds of
men.

Homer, *Iliad* 9.186–189

Contests in music were held at all the Crown Games except the Olympics, and at
the Panathenaic Festival in Athens. Pindar's *Twelfth Pythian Ode* was written in
honor of Midas of Akragas, winner of the aulos contest in 490 BC; Pindar regarded
this victory by an aulos player as seriously as he did those of the victorious athletes.

The only two types of instruments used in serious Greek music were stringed
instruments and woodwinds. The string instruments were the lyre (Pl 61) and its
more elaborate form, the *cithara* (Pl 62). Each instrument had strings of equal
length but different pitches. Usually there were seven strings, but some instru-

Plate 61   Strolling musician carrying lyre and playing diaulos. Red figure amphora.

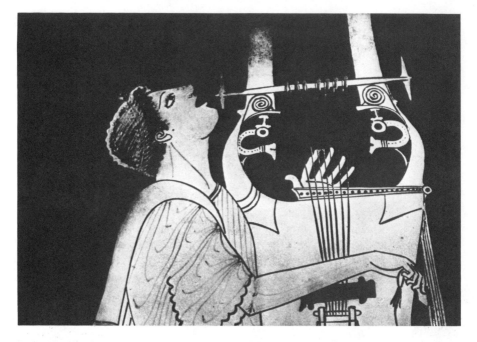

Plate 62   Youth playing cithara and singing. Red figure amphora, detail.

ments had as many as twelve and others as few as five. The soundbox on some was made from tortoise shell; others were of wood with leather across the hollow like a modern banjo. The instrument was held against the body and supported by a strap, like a modern guitar. Since there was no fret board, each string had just one pitch, which could be adjusted. The strings were plucked, sometimes with a plectrum. It may have been possible to vary the pitch by some sort of stopping.

The chief wind instrument was the aulos, somewhat like the modern oboe or clarinet, with an interior reed that produced vibrations. The aulos was sometimes a single pipe, but the common form had two pipes and was called a *diaulos* (Pl 63), which was also the name used for the 2 stade, up-and-back footrace. The pipes were usually held together by a strap called a *phorbeia,* a device that assisted the player in blowing evenly. The number of holes in the pipes varied from six to sixteen holes, which the player covered and uncovered with his fingers to produce different notes. It is not clear whether the notes of the second pipe were sounded separately in order to extend the scale or to serve as a bass drone like bagpipes. Techniques included overblowing and partial stopping of holes.

The simplest of the wind instruments was the *syrinx* or Pan pipe, which commonly had seven pipes with graduated inside stops, and was played by blowing across the tops of these pipes. However, the syrinx was not used by the Greeks for serious music.

In discussing ancient woodwinds, modern scholars tend to use the word "flute" as a translation for aulos. This is misleading, because few ancient reed instruments were played like the modern flute, which is held horizontally as the player blows across a hole.

Singing and playing musical instruments were part of every citizen's education. Singing could be solo or accompanied by an instrument or in chorus. Part singing was unknown.

Perhaps the greatest difference between ancient and modern music is that, whereas conventional modern music has only two scales (major and minor), Greek music had seven scales (also called modes). These modes were assumed to have inherent values. For example, Plato disapproved of the Ionian and Lydian modes as being effeminate; he praised the Dorian and Phrygian modes as representing bravery and moderation; and he rejected two others for being melancholy, as he indicates in the following dialogue:

2
"What are the mournful modes? Tell me, for you are a musician."

"The Mixolydian and the Syntonolydian."

"Then these should be banned, for they are useless even to women, who would use them most."

Plato, *Republic* 398F

Plato did not approve of music for recreation; on the other hand, Aristotle approved of all seven modes for recreation. For serious music, however, he would

Plate 63 Youth playing diaulos with phorbeia, hetaira dancing with castanets. Interior of red figure kylix.

permit only Dorian. If we bear in mind the awesome reputation of these two philosophers, Plato and Aristotle, we are puzzled by these evaluations, particularly since they contradict each other.

(a) What instruments were used to produce serious music?
(b) What is the difference between the lyre and the cithara?
(c) What were the differences between the aulos and the diaulos?
(d) What instruments were used in recreational music?

The most important role of music was its occurrence in plays, particularly the passages where the chorus sang and danced. However, such poems as those of Pindar were accompanied by music of aulos or of lyre. One puzzling feature of Greek music is that an aulos player commonly performed during the long jump; how this would help the jumpers is not clear.

There were other instruments besides the lyre and aulos, but they were not used in serious music. Brass instruments were used for military purposes. Finally, there were percussion instruments—tambourines, cymbals, and castanets. And in Roman times there was a hydraulic organ.

Further Readings

Harpers, under *Musica, Tibia, Cithara, Lyra.*
OCD, under *Music.*
Whibley, pp 370–374, 603–604.

26

Dance

Dancing was popular with the Greeks. Like music, it was a part of drama and was also a popular pastime. Although we have both visual and literary evidence (Pl 64–66), we usually do not know what the dance figures were, since the ancients had no good way of recording the patterns. We can say that the dances varied from stately and solemn to wild and erotic (Pl 67). There was dancing for males, females, and mixed groups, but our ballroom style of pair dancing was unknown. Here is a testimonium from Lucian's essay on dance:

1

The Spartans, considered the bravest of all the Greeks, learned from Kastor and Polydeukes to do the *Karyatik,* a form of dance taught at Karyai in Sparta, and they do everything with the help of the Muses, even to going into battle with the aulos and rhythm and disciplined step; and for the Spartans the first signal for battle is the aulos. In fact, this is how they conquered everyone, led by music and rhythm. And even today you can see that their young men spend as much time learning to dance as learning to fight. And when they have finished sparring and trading blows in turn, their contests end in dancing, and an aulos player sits in the middle, playing a tune and beating time with his foot, and the young men follow one another in single file, keeping in time and presenting all the different figures, now the warlike moves and then the figures of the chorus, dear to Aphrodite and Dionysos. This is why the song which they sing along with the dance is an invitation to Aphrodite and the Cupids to join in the party and dance with them. The second of all these songs (for they sing too) has instructions on how to do the dance. "Swing your foot forward, men, and liven up the party," meaning "Dance better." Those who dance the so-called Necklace Dance do the same sort of thing. The Necklace is a dance of boys and girls mixed, who move in single file and really do resemble a necklace. The young man goes ahead, dancing with abandon and using movements which he will someday

187

Plate 64 Girl dancing in flowing gown. Terra-cotta statuette.

use in battle, and the girl follows, demonstrating how to dance the feminine role with restraint, and so the Necklace alternates modesty with manliness.

Lucian, *The Dance* 10–12

(a) How specific are the descriptions?
(b) What practical use would this dancing be after workouts?
(c) Who are the participants in the dance?
(d) How does the girls' role differ from the boys' role?

Greek dances included animal dances, dances in plays, in celebration of religious rites, in orgiastic and mystery celebrations, in dances at shrines and festivals, and in informal dancing at such occasions as weddings, harvest time, naming-day for babies, and banquets (Pl 68). The names of some of the dances and *schemata* (= figures or patterns) have been preserved. A random sampling produces such colorful names as "Knocking at the Door," "The Itch," "The Beggar," "Scattering the Barley," "The Piglet," "Setting the World on Fire," "The Messenger," "The Snort," "Stealing the Meat," "The Little Basket," "The Split," "The Tongs," "Going past the Four," etc. Colorful these names certainly are, but they give little real evidence of what the dancing was like.

Plate 65 Topless dancer; headdress is drinking cup. Terra-cotta statuette.

Plate 66 Women dancing (or running?). Black figure hydria (=vase for carrying water).

Plate 67   Wild dance. Red figure psykter (= vase for cooling wine).

Plate 68   Bird dance, part of a religious ritual. Black figure amphora.

Plate 69 Dancing lesson.
Case for flute hanging on wall.
Red figure krater.

Here Plato speaks of the value of music and dance:

2
So the well-educated man should be able to both sing and dance well.

Plato, Laws 654B

(a) How big a role do dance and music have in modern education?
(b) In modern education do boys receive the same training as girls?

Girls who were being trained as hetairai received instruction in dancing (Pl 69).

Further Readings

Harper's, under *Saltatio*.
Lawler, L.B., *Dance in Ancient Greece* (London 1964).
Lucian, ''The Dance,'' *Loeb Classical Library*, vol 5.
OCD, under *Dancing*.

27

Theater

We are fortunate in having numerous Greek theaters still preserved, although some are heavily restored. Among the best known are those at Athens, Delphi, and Epidauros. The Greeks built their theaters into the side of a hill, thus reducing the amount of construction needed. The most noticeable feature of these theaters was the orchestra, a curved space between the seats and the stage. The Greek word *orchestra* meant "dancing place," because the chorus danced in this space. Today, of course, the word "orchestra" has a wider use, applying to the area where the musicians perform, and to the area on the main floor where the audience sits. The theater in Athens, built in IV BC, has twenty-five tiers of seats remaining; when intact, the theater held about 17,000 (Pl 70). The theater at Delphi, built in IV BC, and restored in white marble by King Eumenes in 159 BC, has a beautiful natural setting with thirty-five tiers and a capacity for 5000 (Pl 71). In Epidauros, the best preserved of all Greek theaters, built in III BC, held 14,000 (Pl 72).

Like the athletic games, the drama was a religious festival. At Athens dramatic pieces were presented at the Great Dionysia, a festival in the spring lasting for six days, with plays given in the Theater of Dionysos. On three of these days plays were given. Only at this festival could plays by living authors be presented. Another festival at which plays were presented in the Theater of Dionysos was the Lenaea. Prominently displayed in the sacred procession was a large wooden replica of the *phallos* (= erect male organ); strange as it may seem to us, a phallus was a sacred emblem. Plays were also put on at six towns in Attica during the Rural Dionysia, but we know almost nothing about them.

What we know about the plays mainly describes what went on in Athens. In V and IV BC an admission charge was 2 obols. At this time a juryman received 3 obols a day. Some citizens had the honor of free admission with reserved seats; poorer citizens could draw their 2 obols from the state; the purpose of this may have been to check the list of citizens.

Plate 70   Theater at Athens.

Plate 71   Theater at Delphi, with temple columns in background.

Plate 72   Theater at Epidauros.

1

Part of the theater is called the *bouleutikon* [=place reserved for members of the council] and part is called the *ephebikon* [=place reserved for young men].

Pollux 4.122

Because the plays lasted all day, food and wine were brought into the theater. It is not clear whether the audience was often as casual as appears from this testimonium:

2

At the festival to Dionysos, the Athenians, after having eaten their lunch and drunk wine, went to the theater and, wearing wreaths, watched the play, and throughout the play drank and ate snacks [=raisins, nuts, figs, etc.], and when the chorus marched in, they gave them wine and gave the chorus wine again when they marched out.

Athenaeus, *Doctors at Dinner* 11.464F

At the Great Dionysia three days were devoted to drama. Three poets submitted three tragedies apiece, and three writers each submitted a comedy, which was put on in the evening. The three tragedies might be part of the same mythological story. The only trilogy (=three connected plays) that has survived is the *Oresteia* of Aeschylus, made up of the *Agamemnon*, the *Choephorai*, and the *Eumenides*.

There were three (occasionally four) actors who played all the parts, assisted by occasional mutes (= actors with nonspeaking parts). The actors all wore masks, which served to identify the characters (Pl 73 and Pl 74). The speaking parts were performed by mcn, including the women's roles, and the masks would permit a man to appear as a woman with quick change. All the plays had a chorus, usually twelve to fifteen men, who sang the lyric passages and performed the dances. The members of the chorus in comedies wore grotesquely large phalluses.

The expense of putting on these plays was considerable, and wealthy citizens were required to bear this burden in rotation. At each festival there were three days of plays. Prizes were awarded to the poet who wrote the plays, the *protagonist* (= chief actor), and the *choregos,* who was responsible for the expenses.

Some modern dramatic conventions were followed in ancient times. The most striking of these is the lack of action by the modern audience, who usually do nothing to advance the play. In Greece the chorus also followed a course of inaction; they saw disaster coming but, outside of giving advice, did nothing. In Athens, when a character came on stage from the right side, the audience knew he had come from the neighborhood or perhaps from the harbor close by. Coming from the left side signaled that the actor came from far away. Another convention was the *deus ex machina* (= god from the machine), where a mechanism much like a modern cherry picker introduced a deity who solved some difficulty.

Aeschylus, Sophocles, and Euripides are considered to be among the greatest writers of tragedy in the world. A legend that may be true claims that Aeschylus fought in the great victory by the Athenians over the Persians at Salamis in 480

Plate 73   Comic mask on left, tragic mask on right. Mosaic.

Plate 74   Comic actor wearing mask that serves as megaphone. Terra-cotta statuette.

BC, Sophocles was in the chorus that celebrated this victory, and Euripides was born on that same day of victory. We have seven of the tragedies that Aeschylus wrote; the best known of these is the *Agamemnon*. We also have seven tragedies by Sophocles, of which the best known is *Oedipus the King*. We have seventeen tragedies by Euripides, of which one often presented today is the *Medea*.

By far the best known of the writers of comedy is Aristophanes, who produced his first play in 427 BC. Next to Shakespeare he is perhaps the leading writer of comedies in all literature of the Western world. Eleven of his plays have survived; the most popular today is perhaps the *Lysistrata*. A later playwright, Menander (IV–III BC), was a prolific writer and highly regarded in his lifetime, but none of his works were thought to have survived, until in the twentieth century the sands of Egypt yielded substantial fragments of half a dozen of his comedies plus a complete play, *The Ill-natured Man*. However, these recent discoveries do not support the high regard the ancients had for Menander.

It may come as a surprise to modern readers to find that the tragedians did not use original plots but rather took their stories from the rich treasury of Greek mythology. The plots of the comedies, however, were not mythological but were often laid in Athens. The characters were often contemporary Athenians. To judge by Aristophanes, the plays of Old Comedy were hilarious and bawdy. The plays of Menander (IV BC) belong to the era called New Comedy, and they were often called comedies because they were not tragic and had a happy ending. It is interesting to note that in many plays the female characters are admirable; even those like Medea who commit dreadful acts are powerful personalities, a striking exception in the Greek male-dominated society.

The origin and development of tragedy, and even the meaning of the word tragedy, are matters of debate. The next two testimonia show the kind of evidence on which we have to rely:

3

Thespis is said to have discovered the tragic Muse, a type of activity hitherto unknown, and to have carried his plays about in wagons for the players to sing and act with their faces smeared with dregs of wine. After Thespis, Aeschylus invented the mask and attractive clothes and set up a stage made of small planks, teaching the actors to use noble speech and to wear the buskin [= high boot with thick sole used by tragic actors].

Horace, *Ars Poetica* 275–280

(a) What innovations does Horace say were introduced by Aeschylus?
(b) What effect would wearing the buskin achieve?

Horace continues:

4

These poets were followed by Old Comedy, much praised, but its freedom turned to excess and a violence which needed to be ruled by law. Such a law was passed, and the chorus, in disgrace, fell silent with its right to harm now removed.

Horace, *Ars Poetica* 281–284

Many of the extant plays, both tragedy and comedy, have a synopsis of the play and a brief comment called a *didaskalia:*

5

⟨The *Acharnians*⟩ was put on in the archonship of Euthynos [= 425 BC] as part of the festival of Lenaia at the expense of Kallistratos. And he [= Aristophanes] won first prize; Kratinos was second with the *Tempest Tossed;* it has not been preserved. Third place went to Eupolis with his *New Moon.*

Didaskalia for the *Acharnians*

6

⟨The *Frogs*⟩ was put on in the archonship of Kallias, the one after Antigenes [= 405 BC] at the expense of Philonides at the festival of Lenaia and he [= Aristophanes] was first. Phrynichos was second with his *Muses,* and Platon was third with his *Kleophontes.*

Didaskalia for the *Frogs*

7

The *Knights* was put on in the archonship of Stratokles in the Lenaia festival. Aristophanes himself met the expense. He [Aristophanes] won, Kratinos was second with his *Satyrs,* and Aristomenes with his *Wood Carriers* was third.

Didaskalia for the *Knights*

(a) What unusual information does this testimonium give us?

Further Readings

Harper's, under *Theatrum, Tragoedia.*
OCD, under *Tragedy.*
Whibley, pp 414–417.

28

Dining

The Greeks, like ourselves, often entertained their friends by having them to dinner. But there are many differences between their meals and ours, one of which is the kind of food served.

As we have remarked earlier, it is difficult to evaluate information found in Homer. We have little evidence either to support him or refute him. Here are some excerpts from Homer about diet. Meat seems to have been common; the following line occurs several times:

1
They cut the meat into pieces and put them on spits.

Homer, Iliad 1.465

Fish was not popular in Homeric times:

2
But when all the food we had in the ship was exhausted, my men were forced to forage, to hunt for fish and birds and whatever might fall into their hands, fishing with bent hooks, since hunger squeezed their stomachs.

Homer, Odessey 12.329–332

The hungry men of the *Odyssey* killed the cattle of Helios, the sun god, which they had been forbidden to harm:

3
When they had said the prayers and cut the throats of the cattle and skinned them, they cut off the thighs and wrapped them in two layers of fat and placed raw flesh on them. They had no wine to pour as a libation over the blazing sacrifice, but they poured a libation of water and roasted all the entrails. And when the thigh pieces were burned and they had tasted the entrails [= heart, liver, and lungs] then they carved the rest into bits and put them on spits.

Homer, Odyssey 12.359–365

Odysseus, disguised as a beggar, has entered his house accompanied by a swine-herd. His son Telemachos does not recognize him but receives him gracefully:

4

Then Telemachos called the swineherd to him and, taking a whole loaf of bread from the handsome bread basket and as much meat as his two hands could hold, said to him, "Take this to our guest and tell him to go among the suitors and beg."

Homer, Odyssey 17.345–347

Here Kirke (= Circe), an enchantress, feeds the men of Odysseus:

5

She brought them inside and put them on seats and chairs and set before them cheese and barley and yellow honey with Pramnian wine, but in this food she mixed harmful drugs to make them completely forget their native land.

Homer, Odyssey 10.233–236

(a) What similarities do you see between meals Homer describes and our meals?
(b) What differences do you see? What common foods do not appear in these citations?
(c) If you had to base your opinion on these quotations, what seems to have been the most common food of the people in Homer? How did food like birds and fish rate?
(d) Odysseus and his men lived for some time on the stores they had in the ship. Would these stores have included meat?

Contrary to general opinion, both Greeks and Romans were frugal in their diet, which was based on wheat, olive oil, and wine. The main source of carbohydrates was cereals. Fats were supplied chiefly by olive oil. Wine, usually diluted with water, was the standard beverage. Milk would not keep in a warm country, so milk was not drunk much but was made into cheese, a major source of protein. Fish was popular. Meat was expensive, and we hear of it mainly as a food for athletes. Cane sugar was unknown; honey furnished sweetening. In addition to wheat, olive oil, and wine, vegetables were important: peas, beans, onions, rad-ishes, squash, beets, and garlic. The most common fruits were figs and grapes along with apples, pears, and dates. Some vegetables and fruits that are common today were unknown then; potatoes, tomatoes, oranges, and bananas had not yet reached the Mediterranean world. Alexander's troops bought rice back from India, but it did not become an important food in ancient Greece. All in all, the diet of the Greeks seems somewhat lacking in protein.

At formal dinners (= symposia) the guests and host reclined, leaning on the left elbow on couches arranged around the side of a room (Pl 75). They were served food from a low table. There were also public dining rooms, some of considerable size. Here follows a description of a feast given in the town hall of Naukrates on a festival day, as reported by Athenaeus:

Plate 75 Symposium, with hetaira at center. Polychrome krater.

6

Kneeling, each one received a *kotula* of wine [= about half a pint], except
for the priests of Pythian Apollo and of Dionysos, for to each of them is
given a double portion of wine as well as double portions of everything else.
Then each diner gets a flat loaf of pure wheat, and on this is placed another
loaf called "oven bread" and a slice of pork, a small dish of barley gruel or
some vegetable in season, two eggs, some fresh cheese, dried figs, a flat
wheat cake, and a wreath. If any official of the festival serves more than
this, he is fined by the proper officials. More than this, those dining at this
feast in the town hall are not permitted to bring in anything else, but they
eat just this and give anything left over to the slaves. But on ordinary days
of the year any diner who wants can go to the town hall, having prepared
at home some green vegetables or beans, salted or fresh fish, and a small
helping of pork. He shares this food and receives half a pint of wine. No
woman is permitted to go to the town hall except a flute girl. Nor can one
bring his chamber pot into the town hall.

Athenaeus, *Doctors at Dinner* 4.149

(a) Comment on the quantity and quality of the food and drink.

   Wine was important but dangerous (Pl 76):

Plate 76   Party out of control. Exterior of red figure kylix.

7

For those who are temperate I prepare three mixing bowls. The one they drink first is for their health. The second drink is for sex and pleasure, and the third is to make them sleep. When the wise guests have drunk this third cup they go home. But the fourth bowl is not ours but belongs to excess, the fifth is for shouting, the sixth for revelry, the seventh is for black eyes, the eighth is for the police, the ninth is for vomiting, the tenth is for madness and makes one throw furniture.

Athenaeus, *Doctors at Dinner* 2.36

The company is discussing the change in eating habits and consequent effect on the system:

8

The order in which the food is served and its arrangement makes no small difference. For what we used to call the "cold course," consisting of oysters, sea urchins, and raw vegetables has been moved like a company of light-armed soldiers from the rear to the front and now comes first in the dinner and not last. The introduction of the "before dinner drinks," as they are called, has been an important change too. In the old days people did not even drink water until the sweets were served at the end of the dinner. In this day and age people get drunk on empty stomachs before eating a thing; they then seize upon the food when their bodies are heated and soaked with wine. The servants bring in stimulants for their appetite in the form of sharp and sour delicacies, and then they take on the rest of the meal.

Plutarch, Moralia 733F–734A

(a) Compare with modern dinner parties.

Appetizers are mentioned by Athenaeus also:

9
The following ingredients are put into "before dinner drinks": pepper, salad leaves, myrrh, sedge, and Egyptian perfume.

Athenaeus, Doctors at Dinner 2.66C–D

Here is an account of a famous dinner called "The Symposium," written by Xenophon, probably in 422 BC. Most of the account consists of discussion of philosophy by Sokrates and others. We have omitted these discussions, leaving just the setting of the symposium:

10
It was the time of the horse race of the great Panathenaic Festival; Kallias, son of Hipponikas, the lover of the boy Autolykos, who had just won the boys' pankration, had brought him to see the race. When the contest was finished, Kallias brought both Autolykos and his father to his house in the Peiraieus [= main harbor of Athens]. His friend Nikeratos also followed along.   1.2

[The group meets Sokrates and others, whom Kallias invites to supper, and they all go to his home.]

On arriving there, after some of them took exercise and rubbed down with oil while others bathed, they gathered in Kallias' dining room.   1.7

Autolykos of course sat beside his father, and the others, as you would expect, reclined on couches.   1.8

[The beauty of Autolykos impresses them all, Kallias, his lover, most of all. A professional comedian drops in unexpectedly to ask for dinner and lodging in return for his jokes. Kallias accepts his offer. They finish eating.]

When the dining tables were removed and they had poured the libation and sung the hymn to the gods, a certain man from Syracuse came in to furnish entertainment, having as his assistants a girl skilled in playing the flute, a dancing girl marvelously adept at acrobatics, and a boy at the peak of his beauty, skilled in playing the lyre and in dancing. By exhibiting them in their marvelous performance the owner earned a living.   2.1

[The musicians play, to the pleasure of all. The party then starts to discuss philosophy, and the question arises why, if a boy is taught the skills of the pankration, he should not be taught wisdom.]

Then Sokrates said, "Since this is a subject for debate. let us put it off until later; right now let us continue with the entertainment. For I see that the dancing girl has come out and they are giving her some hoops."   2.7

Thereupon one girl played the flute for her, and someone else standing beside the dancer kept giving her hoops until she had 12. As she danced   2.8

she threw them into the air making them spin and judging how high she would have to throw them to catch them in time to the music.

And Sokrates said, "In what this girl is doing and in many other respects   2.9 is proof that woman's nature is not at all inferior to man's, but it needs strength and force. And so those of you who have wives, be encouraged to teach them whatever you would like them to know.

[One of the guests then suggests that Sokrates might start with his own wife Xanthippe, known for her bad temper. Sokrates says that she is good for his self-control.]

After this a hoop was brought in, bristling with sharp swords. The dancer   2.11 did somersaults in and out through these swords, until the spectators were terrified that she might hurt herself, but she coolly completed her performance without accident.

[Sokrates says that this display shows that courage can be taught. The boy then dances. Sokrates comments upon his skill.]

"No part of his body was inactive while he was dancing, but his neck,   2.16 legs, and arms were all being exercised. This is the way someone ought to dance who wants to improve his physique. And I would be very pleased, stranger from Syracuse," said Sokrates, "if I could learn the movements of dancing from you." And he replied, "What will you do with them?"

"Do with them? By Zeus, I will dance." At this they all broke into laughter.   2.17 But Sokrates, with a serious look on his face, said, "You are laughing at me? Is it because I wish to improve my health or enjoy eating or sleeping more by exercise in dancing than if I were to indulge in your kind of exercises? Dancing would not thicken the legs and weaken the shoulders like long-distance running, nor thin down the legs and thicken the shoulders like boxing. But by distributing the strain over the whole body it makes it well proportioned.

"Or are you laughing because it will not be necessary for me to seek a   2.18 partner for exercise nor for me, old man as I am, to strip off my clothes? A room that is big enough for seven couches will be big enough for me, just as it was for the boy just now, and in the winter I can exercise inside and when it is too hot, in the shade. Does this strike you as amusing?

"Or are you laughing because I want to reduce the size of my stomach,   2.19 which is bigger than it should be?"

[The comedian burlesques the feats of the entertainers. He then asks Kallias for a drink. Sokrates thinks that they should all start drinking, and slaves bring on the wine. The conversation then turns to philosophy, and ends with a short ballet put on by the troupe of entertainers about the love between Dionysos and Ariadne.]

Seeing that the ballet was over, those who were unmarried swore that   9.7 they would marry, and those who were married mounted their horses and rode away to their homes.

(a)   In 1.2, comment on the presence of the father of Autolykos.
(b)   What means of transportation do you suppose they used in order to get to the Peiraieus?

(c) In 1.7, comment on their predinner activities. Would we have anything sim-
     ilar?
(d) In 1.8, what position at the table did Autolykos take?
(e) What religious service takes place after the meal?
(f) Whose beauty does Xenophon comment on in 2.1?
(g) In 2.7, is Sokrates more interested in the girl or in philosophy?
(h) In 2.8, does the dancing girl's trick with 12 hoops seem remarkable?
(i) In 2.9, what does Sokrates say about the ability of women?
(j) In 2.16, how does the boy's style of dancing compare with ours?
(k) Do running and boxing have the effects Sokrates describes in 2.17?
(l) Sokrates describes himself as an old man in 2.18. He was born in 469 BC; if
     the party took place in 422 BC, how old was he at this time?
(m) Does drinking occur throughout the party?
(n) How many women are present at this dinner? What is their social position?

At banquets most of the drinking occurred after dinner. The tone of the banquet
was set by one of the banqueters, chosen by throw of the dice, who dictated the
entertainment and how much wine each guest would drink. The wine was diluted
with water in a punchbowl called a *krater*. Sometimes the guests had serious
entertainment, such as the philosophical conversation in the *Symposium* of Xenophon. At other times the party would become boisterous, like the one described
in Testimonium 7.

A popular game was the *kottabos,* shown on numerous vases (Pl 77 and Pl 78).
The players would try to flip the dregs in their drinking cups in such a way as to
hit another cup. Sometimes the target was a cup held by another guest, sometimes
the goal was a platter suspended on a stand, and sometimes they tried to fill and
sink small dishes floating in a bowl.

We see many vase paintings that show women at banquets (Pl 79). They are
professional entertainers called *hetairai*. Here is a famous passage from IV BC,
formerly thought to have been written by the orator Demosthenes:

11

For we have hetairai for our pleasure, *pallakai* [= concubines] for daily care
of our physical needs, and wives to bear us lawful children and take care
of the household faithfully.

                                                    Demosthenes, *Neaira* 122

No upper-class Athenian would ever under any circumstances permit his wife to
dine with men unless they were close relatives. The Romans, in contrast, did
bring their wives to banquets, as we learn from a I BC Roman:

12

For what Roman is ashamed to bring his wife to a banquet? What matron
does not appear in the front room of the house and go about in the throng
of guests? Things are much different in Greece. For women are not brought
to meals except in the presence of close relatives, and they stay in the

Plate 77 Preparing for game of kottabos. Pine cone staff and panther skin identify seated figure as Dionysos, god of wine. Slave mixes wine in krater. Red figure krater.

Plate 78 Guest spinning common cup to throw dregs into kottabos. Exterior of red figure kylix.

Plate 79 Symposium scene with seated hetaira preparing to drink from common cup. Red figure kylix.

interior of the house, which is called Women's Quarters, where no male goes except a close member of the family.

Cornelius Nepos, preface, *Lives*

(a) Does Nepos prefer the Greek or Roman custom?

The meals that we have been describing were formal affairs. The following passage possibly from Lucian shows how a Greek ate at informal gatherings. The speaker is telling about a visit with a stranger to whom he has a letter of introduction:

13
I entered the house, greeted my host, and gave him the letter. He was just beginning dinner and was reclining on a narrow couch, while his wife was seated near him, and beside them was a table still empty . . . I bathed and then went directly to the dining room, where Hipparchos [=the host] greeted me and asked me to recline beside him.

Lucian, *The Ass* 3

(a) What were the arrangements when a man of means dined at home with his wife?
(b) Where did the guest recline?

Plutarch tells us that the hetaira Aspasia (V BC) was an exception. However, his opening phrase, "some writers say," is one that he uses when he wishes to avoid appearing to believe what he records:

Plate 80　Mythological figure of satyr performing sacrifice to Herakles, whose statue is on column. Red figure krater.

14

Some writers say that Perikles [=leader of Athens in V BC] loved Aspasia because she was wise and understood political matters. For there were times when Sokrates visited her with his followers, and his close friends brought their wives to hear her talk, although she was connected with a profession which was neither respectable nor decent, since they say she brought up young girls who were hetairai.

Plutarch, *Life of Perikles* 24.3

(a) How does this information conflict with what you have just read?

In the next scene (Pl 80) a mythological creature called a satyr is preparing a sacrifice of broiled meat. Part of the food was sacrificed to the gods, and the rest of it was eaten by the humans.

Further Readings

Athenaeus, *Doctors at Dinner* (*Loeb Classical Library*, vol 7). All of Book 15 is devoted to dining.
Harper's, under *Symposium* and *Cottabus*.
OCD, under *Symposium* and *Games*.
Vickers, M., Greek Symposia (London n.d.).
Whibley, pp 639–644.

29

Pindar

The remaining chapters of this book will focus on individual authors, beginning with the Greek poet Pindar, who is ranked high among the world's great poets.

Pindar was probably born in 522 BC and therefore lived through the stirring years of the Persian Wars. He was a native of Boiotia but lived for a while in Athens and also in Sicily at the court of the tyrant (=ruler) Heron. Pindar wrote ten types of verses, including those for dancing, processional hymns, and hymns to various gods. The only part of his output that has survived, except for fragments, are his *Epinikia* (=victory odes) in honor of victors in the four Panhellenic Games. It was customary for wealthy patrons to commission poets to write an ode celebrating a victorious athlete. These odes were usually sung in a temple or in front of the athlete's house or during a festival procession. Pindar's odes were gathered into separate books (not a full-sized book, by our standards) for each of the four Crown Games. Pindar wrote fourteen odes celebrating victories at Olympia, twelve for victories in the games at Delphi, eleven for victories at Nemea, and eight for victories at Corinth. In one year alone (476 BC) he was commissioned to write odes for five Olympic victors.

We naturally expect that a victory ode would describe in some detail the contest the athlete won. Not so. The *Victory Odes* praise the athlete's ancestors or his native land or some mythological subject.

Perhaps the main thing we learn from Pindar is how important victory was in athletics. We must never lose sight of the fact that the athletic games were above all a religious ritual.

1

Eleventh Olympian Ode
In Honor of Hagesidamos of Western Lokroi
Winner in Boys' Boxing[1]

1–6   There is a time for men when there is great advantage in winds, a time for heavenly waters, the rain-bringing daughters of the cloud. But when

someone succeeds through toil, then honey-sweet poems are the beginning
of future renown, and a faithful witness to great deeds of courage is created.

Such praise, which is too great to be envied, is reserved for the Olympian   7–12
victors, and my tongue is eager to cherish such things, but a man blooms
forever in the wisdom of his heart through the gift of the god. Know now,
Hagesidamos, son of Archestratos, that because of your victory in the boxing contest

I will cry out a sweet song as a decoration to your crown of golden olive   13–19
to glorify the people of Western Lokroi. Join me now in my song, O Muses.
I promise you a band of men which is hospitable to strangers and experienced in the good, which has achieved both great wisdom and skill in war.
For neither the burning fox nor the loud roaring lion changes his innate
character.

(a) This poem is divided into three parts, as labeled above. What is the subject
matter of each part?
(b) How complete is the description of the event whose victory is celebrated?
(c) What light, if any, does this throw on the Olympic Games?

2

Seventh Pythian Ode
In Honor of Megakles of Athens, Winner in the Quadriga[2]

Fairest opening to a song is the great city of Athens, a foundation of   1–8
songs for the mighty clan of the Alkmanidai[3] to set up in honor of their
horses. What country, what house which you inhabit, can you name to be
better known in Hellas?

For in all the cities is the story told of the citizens of Erechtheus [= leg-   9–16
endary king of early Athens] who made thy home, Apollo, in divine Pytho
[= Delphi] a wondrous sight. ⟨I am inspired to sing of⟩ five victories by you
and your forefathers: one at Isthmia, a distinguished win at Olympia, two at
Krisa,[4] ⟨and now⟩, O Megakles, ⟨another one at Delphi⟩. At this new deed   16–22
of excellence I feel some joy. But I grieve that envy alters glorious deed.
And yet they do say that for man, success which remains in constant bloom
brings now this and now that.[5]

(a) This poem, like the other Epinikian odes, strikes many readers as strange.
What or who does Pindar praise?
(b) Why does Pindar identify the victory at Delphi with the seaport of Krisa?
(Recall the topography of Delphi.)

Further Readings

Lattimore, R., *Odes of Pindar* (Chicago 1947).

30

Philostratos

There were three or perhaps four Greek writers named Philostratos. The Philostratos whose work *On Athletics* you will now read was born around 170 AD. He covered the whole field of the events that occurred in the Crown Games, except horse racing. However, he made a number of serious errors, and we should accept what he says with great caution.

1

On Athletics

1. Athletics as a Science
2. Reasons for the Decline of Athletics
3. The Various Events of Athletics
4. Origin of the Long-Distance Race
5. Origin of the Single-Stade Run
6. Origin of the Double-Stade Run
7. Origin of the Hoplite Race
8. The Hoplite Race at Plataia
9. Origin of Boxing
10. Two Styles of Boxing Gloves
11. Wrestling and Pankration
12–13. Adoption of Events into the Olympic Games
14. The Science of Athletics
15. Specialization in the Science of Athletics
16. Capacity of Man to Perform Athletic Events
17. Clothing at the Olympics
18. The Coach's Strigil
19. Spartan Coaches
20. Anecdotes about Coaches and Athletes: Glaukos
21. Further Anecdotes: Arrichion
22. Further Anecdotes: Promachos

1. Athletics as a Science

We should consider that the following subjects are worthy of scientific study: philosophy, speaking according to the laws of rhetoric, the study of poetry, music, geometry, and yes, by Zeus, astrology, provided it is not carried to excess. I would also include the study of military strategy, as well as the following: all types of medical studies, painting, modeling, making portraits, and engraving on stone and metal. Granted that the practical arts require technical skill by which tools and furniture can be correctly built, the term "science" should be reserved for only the fields I have described. I except navigation from the manual arts since it requires knowledge of stars and winds, and of forces whose nature is not clearly understood. I will proceed to show why. As far as athletics go, we consider this a science not inferior to the others I have named, so much so that instruction books have been written for those who wish to train. The old system of athletics produced great athletes like Milo, Hipposthenes, Poulydamas, Promachos, Glaukos son of Demulos, and also the athletes before them, Peleus for example and Theseus and Herakles himself. Those who have studied the science of athletics recognized that the competitors in the time of our fathers were inferior to those of the earlier periods but were still marvelous and worth remembering. The science of athletics as it exists today has changed so much that most people are repelled by people who are interested in athletics.

(a) Describe Philostratos' distinction between practical and scientific pursuits. Give examples.
(b) What three divisions of time in athletics does Philostratos make?
(c) In what period did Peleus and Theseus compete?

2. Reasons for the Decline of Athletics

It seems to me that I should explain the reason for this decline and tell what I know to both athletes and coaches and to defend Nature, who is criticized because the athletes of today are much inferior to those of an older time. The lions which she now produces are not a bit inferior; dogs, horses, and bulls have the same appearance, and as for botany, her vines are the same and so is the fruit of the fig tree. She has made no change in gold, silver, or precious stones, but she makes everything like the earlier form, just as she planned originally. As for athletes, Nature did not alter whatever virtues they once possessed, for she still produces eager, handsome, intelligent people, for this is the way she operates. But unsound methods of training and practice have deprived Nature of the power. I will show later how this came to happen, but first let us look at the origin of running, boxing, wrestling, and the like and see when and where each began. We shall always quote the authorities of Elis, for our reports about these matters should be as accurate as possible.

(a) What reason does Philostratos give for the decline of athletics? What view does he reject?
(b) What sources does Philostratos say he intends to use? Why?

3. The Various Events of Athletics

The following are the light events in athletic competition: the single-stade dash, the long-distance race, the hoplite race, and the two-stade dash. The heavy events are the pankration, wrestling, and boxing. The pentathlon has both types, for wrestling and the diskos are heavy events, while the javelin, jump, and run are light. Before the time of Iason and Peleus, jumping was a separate event, the diskos was a separate event, and winning the javelin throw was enough for a victory at the time of the voyage of the Argo. Telamon was best at the diskos, Lynkeus best at throwing the javelin, and the sons of the North Wind excelled at running and jumping. Peleus was second in these events but was superior to all in wrestling. Therefore, when they held games in Lemnos, they say that in order to please Peleus, Iason combined the five events and that Peleus won the victory in such fashion that he was considered to be the best soldier of them all, because of his courage in battle and his skill in the pentathlon, which was regarded as a military exercise, because of the competition in the javelin.

4. Origin of the Long-Distance Race

The origin of the long-distance race was as follows. Messengers from Arkadia used to go throughout Greece with military messages, and they were ordered not to ride horseback but to run on foot. This constant running as many laps every day as there are in the long-distance race turned them into runners of messages and trained them for war.

5. Origin of the Single-Stade Run

The single-stade dash competition was invented in this way. When the Eleans sacrificed, they placed offerings on the altar, but they did not light the fire. Runners took their place a stade from the altar and in front of the altar stood a priest with a torch, serving as a judge. The victor in the race set fire to the offerings and went away as an Olympic winner.

6. Origin of the Double-Stade Run

When the Eleans made their sacrifices, all of the ambassadors for the Greeks who were present were required to offer sacrifice. So that their arrival should have some dignity, runners ran from the altar as if to invite the Greek legation and then doubled back as if to announce that the Greeks should approach with rejoicing. This is what we know about the origin of the double-stade.

7. Origin of the Hoplite Race

Hoplite races are very old, especially those at Nemea, which they also called the "armor race" and the "horse race"; they were established to honor Tydeus and the Seven against Thebes. According to the Eleans, the hoplite race was introduced at Olympia for the following reason. The Eleans were fighting continuously with the city of Dyme in a war with no cessation; emotions were so fierce that there was not even an armistice during the Olympic Games. On the day of the games the Eleans were victorious in battle, and a hoplite who had fought in this battle is said to have run into the stadium, bearing the welcome news of the victory. The story is one we can believe, but I hear the same story about the people at Delphi, when they were fighting against some of the cities of Phokis, and about the people of Argos, when they were exhausted by a long war against the Spartans, and about the people of Corinth, when they were fighting in the Peloponnesos and beyond the borders of the Isthmus. I have a different view about the hoplite race. I admit that it was established for some military reason, but I think it was added to the games because a war had begun, and the shield showed that the armistice had ceased and that arms were now necessary. If you listen carefully to the words of the herald, you see that he is announcing to the crowd that the games where prizes are given have come to an end, and that the trumpet is sounding the signal of Enyalios, that is, the god of war, calling the young men to arms. The herald's announcement also orders them to take the oil and carry it away, and not to oil their bodies, indicating that the time for using oil has passed.

8. The Hoplite Race at Plataia

The hoplite race at Plataia in Boiotia had the most prestige because of the length of the run and because of the long armor which reached to the feet and protected the athlete as if he were in battle. It was also instituted to celebrate their accomplishments against the Persians; the Greeks had thought this up to show contempt for the barbarians, but of great importance was the law which the Plataians long ago passed concerning the competitors. For once a man had gained this crown, if he wished to compete again, he had to find people to give security as guarantee that he would not run away, for if he was defeated he was put to death.

9. Origin of Boxing

The Spartans invented boxing, which was adopted by the barbarian tribe of Bebrykians, and Polydeukes was best at the sport; from these facts the poets made up their songs. The early Spartans began to box for the following reasons. They had no helmets, thinking that it was not in keeping with Spartan ways to fight wearing one. But the shield is as good as a helmet for a solder who knows how to use it. To protect themselves from blows in the face and to be able to stand up under these blows when they did land, they worked at boxing and hardened their faces to take punishment. However, with the passage of time they discarded boxing and the pankration with it, thinking it shameful to compete in sports where if one Spartan admitted defeat, the whole country might be accused of being cowards.

10. Two Styles of Boxing Gloves

The early equipment for boxing was like this. The four fingers were thrust into a loop formed by a strap and projected far enough beyond this strap so that when they were doubled over they formed a fist and were held together by a thong which they wrapped around the forearm for support. But this is now changed. Today they knead the hide of the fattest cattle they can get and from it make a sharp boxing glove, one which projects beyond the hand, but the thumb does not then take part in the striking in order to reduce injuries, so that the whole hand does not hit.[1] Because of this same desire for safety, they ban gloves made of pigskin from the matches, since blows from these are painful and slow to heal.

11. Wrestling and Pankration

Wrestling and the pankration were introduced because of their application to war. The usefulness of the first event was made clear by the action at Marathon, where the Athenians fought in such a way as to seem to be almost wrestling. The usefulness of the second was shown at Thermopylae, where the Spartans, after their swords and spears were broken, fought effectively with their bare hands. The pankration is ranked the highest of all the contests in the games, even though it is made up of imperfect wrestling and imperfect boxing. Ranked highest by others, that is, since the Eleans consider wrestling to be the real test of strength and a "grievous event," as the poets call it, not only because of the grappling, which requires a body which is quick and supple, but also because it is necessary to compete at least three times, since this is the number of falls required for victory. Although they think it is a terrible thing for a person to win the prize in the pankration or boxing "without dust,"[2] they do not disqualify a wrestler, since the rules state that they can concede such a victory to "hunched and painful wrestling." The reasons why the regulations permit this is obvious to me. For although the competition at Olympia is fearful, the training for it is still more difficult. In the light events, the distance runner will run eight or ten stades in practice, the pentathlete will practice one of the light events, and the other three types of runners run a stade or a double stade or perhaps both. None of this is difficult; the training program of the light events is the same whether the Eleans are the coaches or someone else. But athletes in the heavy events are trained by the Eleans at the time of year[3] when the sun bakes the mud in this Arkadian valley the hardest; the athletes have to endure dust hotter than the desert of Aithiopia, and to stand up under this, beginning at noon.[4] Of these painful events the most difficult is the wrestling. Only when the hour of competition comes will the boxer stand toe to toe with an opponent and strike and receive damaging blows, but in practice he performs only shadow boxing. The pankratiast in competition will use every move that is known in the event, but in practice he uses first one technique and then another. But wrestling is the same in practice as in the contest. Each workout shows how much the wrestler knows and what he can do. And it is rightly called "hunched," for a wrestler is hunched over, even when he is standing up. Therefore the Eleans give the prize to the best-trained athlete and reward only one who has trained.

(a) List the "heavy" events and the "light" events. What other important events were held at the different games?
(b) After 776 BC, was the diskos a separate event?
(c) How much reliance can we place on Philostratos' account of the origins of different events? What authorities did he use?
(d) Give the origin, as Philostratos explains it, of the pentathlon, the single-stade run, the double-stade run, the distance run, and the hoplite race.
(e) Who invented boxing, according to Philostratos?
(f) In what events did the Spartans not compete at Olympia? Why not?
(g) Describe the two types of gloves. Why did they change from one type to another? Were the officials interested in protecting the boxers?
(h) How persuasive is Philostratos on the relative difficulty of wrestling?
(i) What event usually had the most prestige? What events did the Olympic judges think superior? What is Philostratos' favorite? Give his reasons.
(j) Which event in Greek athletics would you say was the most difficult?

12–13. Adoption of Events
into the Olympic Games

These events did not all appear in the games at the same time, but one after another, as they were discovered and perfected. In the beginning through the 13th Olympics (728 BC), the Olympic Games consisted only of the stade run, and there were three winners from Elis, seven from Messene, one winner from Corinth, one from Dyme, and one from Kleonai. In the 14th Olympics (724 BC), the double stade was introduced, and the winner was Hypenos of Elis. In the next Olympics the distance run was added, and the winner was Akanthos from Sparta. In the 18th Olympics (708 BC) they held the men's pentathlon and the men's wrestling; Eurybatos from Lysoi won the wrestling, and Lampis from Sparta the pentathlon; some authorities, however, say that Eurybatos was a Spartan. The 23rd Olympics (688 BC) summoned men to boxing, and the best boxer proved to be Onomastos of

Smyrna, who won the prize and brought honor to the city of Smyrna with his glorious feat. For by being the first city of Asia Minor to produce an Olympic victor, Smyrna all at once surpassed all the cities of Ionia and Lydia, those along the Hellespont and Phrygia, and all the races of Asia Minor. This athlete from Smyrna wrote the rules for boxing which the Eleans still follow out of respect for his knowledge of the sport, and the Arkadians do not object to the fact that the rules for the event were written for them by someone coming from the effeminate land of Ionia. At the 33rd Olympics (648 BC) the pankration, which had not been an Olympic event, was admitted, and Lygdamis of Syracuse was the winner. This Sicilian was so large that his foot was a cubit in length. He is said to have measured off the length of the Olympic stade with these feet, which is acknowledged to be 400 cubits long.

It is said that the boys' pentathlon was introduced in the 38th Olympics (628 BC), when Eutelides the Spartan was victor, but that no boy ever competed in this event at Olympia again. The winner of the boy's stade in the 46th Olympics (596 BC)—for this was when it was first put in[5]—was Polymestor of Miletos, who tended goats and was fast enough to be able to catch hares. Some say that boys' boxing began in the 41st Olympics (616 BC) and that Philytas of Sybaris was victorious, but others claim that this occurred in the 60th Olympics (540 BC), and the winner was Leokreon of the island of Keos. Damaretos is said to have been the first to win the hoplite race in the 65th Olympics (520 BC), a native, I think, of Heraia. In the 145th Olympics (200 BC) after an unaccountable delay they finally put in the boys' pankration, admitting that it was an event held in good repute elsewhere. It was late in Olympic history when Egypt first won a crown, and the boys' pankration was also won by an Egyptian; the city of Naukratis gained this honor, when the Egyptian Phaidimos was victorious. In my opinion, these events would not have been added to the Olympics one after another nor would the Eleans and all the other Greeks have been so enthusiastic if the science of athletics had not been invented and handed on. For the victories of the athletes belong to the coaches no less than to the athletes.

(a) Are there any discrepancies in the records that Philostratos consulted? What was the source of these records? (See Chapter 2 if necessary.)
(b) What region of Greece dominated the early Olympics?
(c) Were the Olympic officials conservative in adding events to the program? How many that were added were dropped? What is the practice in the modern Olympics?
(d) How important did an Olympic victory appear to have been? Compare with modern sports.
(e) What two groups of people deserve credit for athletic victories?

14. The Science of Athletics

What is one to understand by "athletics?" It is simply a body of knowledge made up from medicine and physical education, more comprehensive than the latter but only a part of the former. I will proceed to show how much it owes to each. The *paidotribes* show their students all the wrestling holds, explaining the proper time to employ them; they tell them how hard to wrestle, how long the workouts should be, and how one can go on the defensive or break down the defenses of his opponent. The *gymnastes* will also teach these things to the athlete who does not yet know them. There comes a time when an athlete is practicing wrestling or the pankration, learning how to fight back against an opponent who has gotten an advantage or how to be able to escape or to throw him back, techniques which a gymnastes does not know, unless he happens to know this part of the paidotribes' profession. So far the two sets of skills are the same. But to know how to clear up humors[6] and check their excessive flow, to soften any part of the body which has become hard, to fatten up some parts or change them or soften them by applying heat, all this is in the area of knowledge of the gymnastes. The paidotribes does not have this knowledge or, if he does have it, he will apply it harmfully to his pupils, preventing the unhampered flow of unmixed blood. So much greater is the knowledge of the gymnastes than that of the paidotribes as I have described it. He has medical knowledge of the following kind: the diseases which we call rhinitis, edema, tuberculosis, and various kinds of epilepsy which doctors cure by hydrotherapy, drinking liquids, or putting on plasters, while the gymnastes restrains them with diet and massage. But if someone suffers a break or wound, loss of vision, or a dislocation, he should go to a physician, since a gymnastes does not have competence in these fields.

(a) Outline the field of competence of (1) the paidotribes, (2) the gymnastes, and (3) the physician. How are the responsibilities divided up in modern athletics?
(b) How many humors did the ancient physicians believe were in the body? What were they? The words ''sanguine'' and ''melancholy'' preserve this tradition. Look them up in a dictionary.
(c) How did Philostratos define the science of athletics?

15. Specialization in the Science of Athletics

In what I have just said I think I have demonstrated how much knowledge is borrowed from each of two fields ⟨that of the doctor and that of the paidotribes⟩, and I think the following opinion is true also. No one learns the whole field of medicine, but one doctor knows about wounds, another understands fevers, a third studies diseases of the eyes, and a fourth successfully treats tuberculosis. While it is important to specialize in just a small field, doctors justly claim to know the whole of their science. But no one would announce that he knew the entire field of athletics. For the man who knows the running events does not know about wrestling or the pankration, nor will the expert in the heavy events be competent in other fields.

16. Capacity of Man to Perform Athletic Events

Such is the definition of the field, but its origin lies in the natural ability of man to wrestle, box, and run in an upright position. For the behavior would not exist if there were not an innate ability to do it. Just as the origin of metal working depends upon the existence of iron and bronze, farming upon the existence of land, and sailing upon the existence of the sea, so let us assume that the ability to do athletics is born and grows in man. A poet tells us that athletics were not yet in existence when Prometheus[7] lived, that Prometheus was the first to practice athletics, that Hermes trained others and was amazed at Prometheus' discovery. The first palestra was started by Hermes and, as for the creation of men from mud by Prometheus, the men practicing wrestling there thought they had been created by Prometheus, since his exercises in the mind made their bodies vigorous and well.

(a) How much of the field of medicine are modern doctors supposed to understand? How much are they supposed to master in order to specialize in it?
(b) The poet whom Philostratos quotes implies that Prometheus did not actually make men out of mud. Why did these first men, according to this story, think that he had? (In answering, remember that wrestlers and pankratiasts frequently practiced in the mud.)

17. Clothing at the Olympics

At Delphi, at Isthmia, and wherever else there are games, the gymnastes, wrapped in a cloak, rubs his athlete with oil, and no one takes this cloak from him against his will, but at Olympia he stands unclothed. The opinion of some is that the Eleans are testing the gymnastes at this season of the year to see if he can take the heat and the stress. The Eleans say, however, that there was a woman from the island of Rhodes named Pherenike, daughter of the boxer Diagoras; her physical appearance was such that the Eleans at first thought she was a man. At Olympia she wrapped herself in her cloak and trained her son Peisidoros, who was a skilled boxer, the equal of his grandfather. When the Eleans learned about the trick, they hesitated to execute Pherenike because of their admiration for Diagoras and his children, since the members of Pherenike's family were all Olympic victors, but they passed a law that the gymnastes must take off his clothes and submit to a physical examination.

18. The Coach's Strigil

The gymnastes at Olympia carries a strigil with him.[8] This may perhaps be explained as follows. It is necessary for the athlete at Olympia to cover himself with dust in the palestra and to oil his body. So that the athlete may not injure his health, the coach's strigil reminds the athlete of olive oil and tells him clearly that it is necessary to apply it liberally so that he may scrape off the oil after he has put it on. There are those who say that a gymnastes at Olympia killed his pupil with a sharp strigil because he did not fight hard enough for the victory. I go along with this story. For it is better that people believe this story than not believe it. Let the strigil be used as a sword against any cowardly athlete and let the gymnastes at Olympia be superior to the Hellanodikai in some respect!

19. Spartan Coaches

Since the Spartans considered the games ·to be a preparation for war, they used to expect their gymnastes to have complete knowledge of military matters. This should cause nobody any surprise, inasmuch as the Spartans have turned even dancing, in times of peace the most relaxed kind of enjoyment, into a military exercise. For they dance as if throwing spears or avoiding them; in their dancing they leap from the ground and show their skill in manipulating their shields.

(a) What was unusual about the coaches' dress at Olympia?
(b) What explanation did the Eleans give?
(c) Did the coaches wear clothes at other athletic contests?
(d) Summarize the information about the strigil and the theory of Philostratos.
(e) How does Philostratos feel about the Olympic officials?

20. Anecdotes about Coaches and Athletes: Glaukos

The different kinds of psychological approaches which the gymnastes have used on their athletes, whether encouraging them or scolding them or through threats or trickery, are numerous and would take too long to relate, but let me tell the most noteworthy. When Glaukos from Karystos was being forced back by his opponent in boxing at Olympia, Tisias, his gymnastes, brought him through to a win by shouting, "Hit him like you did the plow!" By this he meant a right-handed punch against his opponent. For Glaukos' right was so strong that back in Euboia he once straightened a bent plowshare by using his right hand as a hammer.

21. Further Anecdotes: Arrichion

The pankratiast Arrichion had won two Olympic victories and was fighting in the finals trying to win still another, but he was weakening. His gymnastes Eryxias inspired him with a desire for death by shouting from the crowd, "What a wonderful inscription on your grave, 'He did not give up at Olympia!' "

22. Further Anecdotes: Promachos

The gymnastes of Promachos of Pellene noticed that his pupil was in love. The time of the Olympics was drawing near, and the gymnastes said, "Promachos, it seems to me that you are in love." When he saw that his pupil was blushing he went on, "I did not ask you this to embarrass you but with a wish to help you in your love affair. Perhaps I can put in a good word for you with the girl." Later, although he had in fact not said a word to the girl, he returned to the athlete with a message which was false but very welcome to the lover: "She will not refuse you her love if you go all the way to an Olympic victory." Promachos was encouraged by what he heard and not only won but defeated Poulydamas of Skotoussa, who had subdued some lions in a contest in front of King Ochus of Persia.

23. Further Anecdotes: Mandrogenes

I have myself heard Mandrogenes of Magnesia say that the fortitude which he exhibited as a young man in the pankration was due to his gymnastes. He told me that after his father's death the household had come under the control of his mother, who was not only wellborn but had virtues of a man as well. His gymnastes, he said, sent his mother the following letter, "If you hear that your son has been killed, believe it; if you hear that he has been defeated, do not believe it." He said that he was so affected by this letter that his morale was raised to the highest pitch, since he did not want his gymnastes to be proved a liar or his mother to be misled.

24. Further Anecdotes: Optatos

Optatos the Egyptian won the race at Plataia, where, as I have said, anyone who lost this race after having been a victor in it before, was publicly executed. We explained that a former winner cannot practice for it until he has found someone to give security to guarantee that he will not run away if he loses. When no one was found who was willing to offer the large security required, the gymnastes submitted to this requirement and himself helped his pupil to win a second victory. In my opinion, the important thing for those who are intending to undertake something of great importance is to have faith.

(a) What psychological approaches did each coach take with his athlete?
(b) Which anecdote had Philostratos heard first-hand from the athlete himself?

43. Athletic Training in Older Times

In the old days the trainers did not even recognize the existence of these humors but merely trained the body. In the old times "athletics" meant any kind of physical exercise. Some trained by carrying heavy weights, others by chasing hares and horses or by bending and straightening thick rods of wrought iron; others yoked themselves with strong oxen to pull wagons or bent back the neck of bulls; and some did the same with lions. Such activities were the training of men like Polymester, Glaukos, Alesias, and Poulydamas from Skotoussa. The boxer Tisander from Naxos used to swim around the headlands of his island, and went far out to sea, using his arms, which in exercising the rest of his body also received exercise themselves. These men washed in rivers and springs; they learned to sleep on the ground, some of them lying on stretcher beds made of oxhide, others on beds made of straw they gathered from the field. Their food was bread made from barley and unleavened loaves of unsifted wheat. For meat they ate the flesh of oxen, bulls, goats, and deer; they rubbed themselves with the oil of the wild olive and phylia.[9] This style of living made them free from sickness, and they kept their youth a long time. Some of them competed in eight Olympic games, others for nine; they were also excellent soldiers and fought under their city's walls, where they were not defeated, but earned prizes for valor and trophies. They made war a training for athletics, and they made athletics a military activity.

(a) Describe some of the training activities in the "good old days."
(b) What characterized the training of the athletes in the old days?
(c) What connection was there, if any, between athletics and warfare? Have athletics been praised (or criticized) in modern times for their contribution to the military?

44. The Degenerate Nature of Modern Athletics

Then things changed, and men became civilians instead of soldiers, lazy instead of energetic, and soft instead of tough. The Sicilian style of fancy food gained popularity; the guts went out of athletics and, more important, trainers became too easy on their pupils. Doctors took the lead in introducing permissiveness, setting it up as an adjunct to their treatment, a good enough technique on the whole but too soft an approach to use with athletes. From these doctors athletes learned to be lazy and to exercise after sitting around stuffed with enough food fill an Egyptian or African meal sack; they gave us chefs and cooks to please our palates. They turned athletes into gluttons with bottomless stomachs. Doctors fed us white bread made of ground meal sprinkled with poppy seeds and introduced the eating of fish, contrary to previous medical practice. They classified fish according to location in the sea. Big ones they claimed, came from muddy bottoms, tender ones from rocky areas, those with a lot of meat on them from deep waters, slender ones from areas full of seaweed, and those without nourishment from waters full of algae. They also introduced the use of pork with a collection of wonderful theories; they told us that the flesh of herds which had been driven down to the sea should be considered useless because of sea garlic, which the shores and beaches are full of; likewise we should be on guard against pigs raised near rivers, since they may have eaten crabs. The only pork suitable for an athlete's diet, they told us, was from pigs fed on acorns and cornel berries.

(a) What military-political event is Philostratos referring to in the opening sentence of this chapter?
(b) At the present time there is considerable interest in diets, including some that have been clearly shown to be injurious to health. Compare some of these modern diets with what Philostratos describes here.
(c) Is there any truth in the classification of fish that Philostratos ridicules?
(d) What does Philostratos think of pork?
(e) What is Philostratos criticizing strongly?

45. Bribery in Modern Athletics

This luxurious way of living stimulated the sex urge, and the athletes began to engage in illegal transactions of money, buying and selling victories. The sellers, I suppose, dispose of their chances for fame because they need the money; the buyers, because they lead such a soft life, purchase victory without the customary expenditure of effort. Those who steal or destroy a gold or silver votive offering feel the anger of the laws enacted to prevent robbing temples, but it is safe to buy and safe to sell the wreath of Apollo or the wreath of Poseidon, for which the very gods strove mightily. The wild olive of Elis is still unsullied because of its fame since early times, but as for the other games! Let me tell this one story out of many, by which you may learn the history of them all. A boy won the Isthmian crown in wrestling by agreeing to pay one of his competitors 3000 drachmas for the victory. When they came to the gymnasium the day after the competition, the boy who had agreed to lose asked for his money, but the other said, "I owe you nothing, since you tried to keep me from winning." When they could not reach an agreement, they each took an oath and went to the temple of the Isthmian god [=Poseidon], where the one who had given away his victory swore publicly that he had sold the contest of the god and that the price agreed upon had been 3000 drachmas. He spoke clearly when he made the confession, not using the tones of one who was ashamed to utter such impious words. The fact that it occurred before witnesses makes the story more believable, just as it also makes the act more wicked and unspeakable: he took this oath at Isthmia before the eyes of all Greece. What might not be happening in Ionia and in Asia Minor to bring shame to the contests? I do not excuse the trainers for this corrupt state of affairs. They take on the task of coaching with cash available, and they make loans to their athletes at a higher rate of interest than merchants who have to pay who are sailing across the sea. They pay no attention to the glory an athlete might win but advise him in buying and selling victories, keeping in mind what profit they themselves can make out of the transaction, either by lending money at interest to those who are buying victories or abandoning those who have sold them. This is all I need to say about this type of business activity, for thinking only of their own welfare, they are in the business of selling the noble qualities of their athletes.

46. Proper Training of Boys

But the gymnastes also err in this respect. They take a boy athlete, make him strip, and then exercise him as if he were a mature man; they tell him to load his stomach before he practices, to stalk off the field in the middle of practice, and to bring up a loud belch from the bottom of his stomach. By these actions, just like poor teachers, they take away from the boy his youthful enthusiasm and train him to be lazy, to postpone everything, to be dull, and to be less bold than he should be at this age. The boy should use movements as in a wrestling school. But by "movements" I mean having a soft massage of the legs and a vigorous one of the arms. The youth should keep time by clapping, since this makes their exercises more exhilarating. Helix the Phoenician underwent this type of training, not only as a boy but also when he entered men's competition, and he was more marvelous than words can tell, surpassing the athletes I know who follow the soft system of training.

47. The Tetrad System

No attention should be paid to the tetrad system, a theory which has virtually destroyed the whole field of athletics. By the tetrad system we mean a cycle of four days, each one of which is devoted to a different activity. The first day prepares the athlete; the second is an all-out trial; the third is relaxation; and the fourth is a medium-hard workout. The exercise of the first day, the one that prepares him, is made up of short, intense movements which stir up the athlete and prepare him for the hard workout to follow on the next day. The strenuous day (the second) is an all-out test of his potential. The third, the day of relaxation, so to speak, employs his energy in a moderate way, while on the day of the medium workout (the last day), the athlete practices breaking holds himself and preventing his opponent from breaking away. While the gymnastes are following this fixed routine of the tetrad, they pay no attention to the condition of the athlete they are training, even though he is being harmed by his food, his wine, the secret snacks he eats, mental strain and fatigue, as well as much else, part planned, part accidental. How will we cure this athlete by a schedule of tetrads?

48. Physical Signs of Poor Condition

You can recognize an athlete who overeats by his thick eyebrows, gasping breath, and prominent collarbones, as well as rolls of fat around his waist. Those who drink too much wine have an excessive paunch; too much drinking is also discovered by a fast pulse and by dampness at the waist and the knee. Many signs point to the athletes who indulge in sex. Their strength has been weakened; they are short of breath and no longer display initiative on offense. When they exert themselves they grow pale, and they are also detected in the following ways. When they strip, their collarbones are hollow, their hips do not fit properly, their ribs stick out, and their blood is cold. If you should get involved in training an athlete like that, he would never win a crown for you. Athletes like this have flabby cheeks, weak pulse, insufficient perspiration, restless sleep when they are digesting their food; their gaze wanders and indicates their preoccupation with sex.

49. Nocturnal Emissions

Those who have nocturnal emissions of semen (which cleanses the body of excess vigor) can be identified by their pale complexions, moist skin, and deficiency in strength, but those who have a good digestion because they get plenty of sleep are not to blame for what happens in the region of their hips and do not get out of breath easily. They are not to be compared with the athletes who indulge in sex. In the first group, their system is cleansed; in the second, it is weakened. It is a clear sign of weakness if the surface of the body seems to be more tender than usual, the veins swell, the arms are listless, and the muscles are shrunken.

50. Treatment for Athletes Who Have Overeaten

Those who have eaten too much, whether they are competitors in the light or heavy events, should be massaged in a downward direction, so that the excess weight may be removed from the important parts of the body. Pentathletes in this situation should practice one of the light events; runners should not push themselves too much but should take an easy workout, striding out with only a suggestion of hard effort; boxers should spar at arm's length and should dance lightly about as if on air. Wrestlers and pankratiasts should practice upright wrestling, but they should also practice falling and rolling. Let them practice this rolling, but if they have eaten too much they should be on top of their opponent more than underneath him and should not tumble headfirst, so that they will not incur any injury. The light athletes as well as the heavy should be massaged, particularly in the upper body, with a little oil, and the parts which have been oiled should be well kneaded.

(a) How do the suggestions of Philostratos differ from the tetrad system?
(b) Why should wrestlers practice falling? Does the reference to having someone else on top or underneath refer to the wrestlers or just to the pankratiasts?
(c) Does it seem as if the boxers practice footwork?
(d) What are the "light events" in the pentathlon?

51. Treatment for Athletes
Who Have Drunk Too Much

An excess of wine in the athletes' bodies requires moderate exercise to bring on sweating. We should not make people in this condition take hard exercise but we should not excuse them from their workout entirely, for it is better to draw off the contaminated humor so that the blood receives no injury. To do this, the gymnastes should rub the athlete dry and scrape him with a strigil, using a moderate amount of oil, so that the pores from which the perspiration comes do not become clogged.

(a) How would a coach who followed the tetrad system treat an athlete with a hangover?
(b) Evaluate the treatment which Philostratos suggests.

52. Treatment for Athletes
Who Have Had Intercourse

It is better for athletes who have just had intercourse not to take a workout. For how can they be men if they have exchanged crowns of victory and the herald's announcement for a shameful pleasure? If they do work out, they should exercise only after being warned to watch out for their endurance and their breath, because sexual pleasures cause the most harm in these areas. A nocturnal emission is the same as sexual intercourse, but as we have said, it is involuntary. Those who had had nocturnal emissions should take exercise carefully and should build up their strength more than usual, since they now have a deficit in their system, and they must get rid of the excess of perspiration which they have. Their workouts should be easy to do but spread out over a longer period of time than usual, so that their lungs may be exercised. They need a normal amount of oil thickened with dust. For this medicine preserves and refreshes the body.

(a) Why does Philostratos object to sex?
(b) What is the "medicine" Philostratos mentions in the last line of section 52?

53. Treatment for Apprehensive Athletes

Athletes who are apprehensive can be encouraged and put back on the right track by talk which raises their spirits, but they should also work out with those who do not eat or sleep well. Systematic training is good for these athletes; timid personalities are eager to learn, and this helps protect them. Fatigue without any visible cause is the beginning of sickness, and it is sufficient exercise for those who have tired themselves by wrestling in the mud[10] of the palestra to relax in the way I have described. On the next day after they have had an all-out workout in the dust, they should exercise in the mud with only slight effort. For a hard workout after a day in the dust is a poor cure for exhaustion; it does not restore the strength but lessens it. The type I have described is a wise type of training and one directed at the individual athlete.

(a) How sound is the suggested treatment of apprehensive athletes?
(b) Explain when the athlete should be pushed and when he should not, according to Philostratos.
(c) What do the phrases "workout in the mud" and "workout in the dust" mean as far as intensity of training is concerned?
(d) How does this type of training fit with the tetrad system?
(e) To what events is Philostratos applying his system? Can we make a guess about what he would suggest for other events?
(f) Do we believe today that mud is good for the skin?

54. Evils of the Tetrad System

An example of the tetrad system, which I have rejected, is the blunder made in the case of the wrestler Gerenos, whose gravestone in Athens is on the right as one goes to Eleusis. He was a native of Naukratis and a first-class performer, as the victories which he won in competition show. He happened to win at Olympia; and for two days afterward he celebrated his victory by drinking, entertaining his friends, and eating fancy food. As a consequence of this unaccustomed way of life, he was short on sleep. On the third day after his victory he came to the gymnasium and told his gymnastes that his stomach was upset and that he felt terrible in other ways. The gymnastes lost his temper, listened to him angrily, and was indignant that in breaking training he had upset the tetrad schedule. Finally through his ignorance he brought about his pupil's death in the middle of the work-out, by assigning the kind of exercise which he should have had sense enough to avoid even if his pupil had not told him of his condition. With the tetrad system being what it is and the gymnastes so poorly trained and so ignorant, bad accidents do happen. Is it not a misfortune for the world of sports to lose an athlete like the one I just described? How will those who have embraced the tetrad system use it when they come to Olympia where there is dust, just as I have described it, and traditional exercises? The Hellanodikai do not train according to a fixed schedule but devise every-thing on the spot, according to the situation, and the whip awaits a gym-nastes who does not follow their instructions. The commands they give cannot be changed, to the extent that they are ready to remove from the Olympic Games anyone who objects. This is the way it is with the tetrad system, and if you follow my ideas instead of it, we will show you a true science of athletics; we will improve the athletes; and the whole sport will be rejuvenated through a wise system of exercise.

(a) Describe what happened to the wrestler Gerenos. Was his gymnastes at fault? Should the athlete be blamed? What seems to have motivated the gymnastes to act as he did?

(b) Describe the relationship of the gymnastes and the Hellanodikai at Olympia. How does this compare with modern practice? How would an enthusiast for the tetrad system have made out at Olympia if he had tried to stick to his schedule? Was the Olympic training haphazard?

55. Equipment and Supplies: The Halteres

The halter is an invention of the pentathletes and was invented for jump-ing, from which it gets its name.[11] Since the jump is one of the most difficult events in competition, the rules permit encouragement of the jumper by means of a flute and assist him even more with the halter. For it guides the hands unfailingly, the jump is steady, and the landing is in good form. The rules show how important this is, for the officials refuse to have the jump measured if the mark of the feet is not correct.[12] Large sizes of halteres are used to exercise the arms and shoulders and round ones to exercise the fingers. They should be used by the athletes in the light as well as heavy events in all exercises except those designed to relax the athlete.

(a) This chapter is one of the chief sources of information about the use of weights in jumping. How could weights help the athlete land properly? Experiments might be interesting, but one should remember that the technique is probably complicated.

56. Equipment and Supplies: Dust

Dust which comes from clay is good for cleansing and for restoring a normal skin condition in those who suffer from an excess of oily secretions. Dust made from bricks opens up the sweat pores if they are clogged; dust made from asphalt warms any part of the body which has become chilled. Then there is black dust and yellow dust, both resembling earth and both useful for massage and building up the body. But yellow dust makes the body glisten and is quite handsome to observe when it is on the well-developed body of an athlete from a good family. The dust should be scattered on the body with wrist relaxed and fingers spread apart, sprinkling it more than pouring it on, and if it is done this way, a light film of powder will cover the athlete.

(a) Is it possible that dust can clean? How about dogs, birds, horses, and other animals?

(b) What are the alleged values of the different types of dust? Are they credible?

57. Equipment and Supplies: Punching Bags

A punching bag should be hung up for the use of boxers, but it is actually more important for there to be another one for the use of the pankratiasts. The bag for the boxers should be light, since the hands of the boxers are trained only for striking punishing blows, but the bag for the pankratiasts should be larger and heavier, so that they may practice keeping their feet as the bag swings back against them and so that they may also exercise their arms and fingers by striking something that resists a little. The athlete should also butt his head against the bag and submit himself to all aspects of the upright part of the pankration.

(a) Comment upon the difference in work between the two types of bags. How effective would these exercises be?

(b) In what sport or sports was butting permitted?

58. Sunbathing

Some people take sun baths without giving any thought to the kind of sun or to their own condition; those with experience and good sense do not sunbathe at all times but only when it will be helpful. When the wind comes from the north or when the day is still, the rays of the sun are clean and sunny, since they pass through the bright upper air.[13] When the wind comes from the south or the sky is slightly overcast, the sun's rays are damp and excessively hot, such as to enervate those who are training rather than strengthen them. That is what I have to say about the times when the sun is beneficial. Those who are sluggish should sunbathe more than others so that they can get rid of their excessive secretions. Those who are bilious should refrain from sunbathing so that fire may not be added to fire. Those of advanced years should bask in the warm sun without moving, just as if they were being toasted, but those who are young and bursting with energy should take their sun while active and should do all the exercises the Eleans practice. As for steam baths and dry rubs with olive oil, since these belong to an unscientific type of athletics, we will leave them to the Spartans, whose training has nothing like boxing or wrestling. The Spartans themselves say that they train in these two events, not to enter competition but only to strengthen themselves, and this fits in with their whipping, where their custom is to be torn to shreds at the altar.

(a) Comment on the result of sunbathing when there is a light overcast.
(b) Philostratos is proud of his scientific approach to athletics; there are two main theories he presents, neither of which seems to us to be particularly valid. One of them appears in this chapter. What is it? The second theory has to do with choosing the proper event for athletes. Some of this we believe today, but some ideas of Philostratos appear ridiculous. Give examples of each type.
(c) What city practiced steam baths and dry oil rubs?

31

Pausanias

The next author, Pausanias, is perhaps our most important single source for Greek athletics. Born in Asia Minor, he wrote his *Guide to Greece* in the period approximately 150–175 AD. His work is plain and readable. In many cases his descriptions have been verified by archeological remains. Without his help, many of the sites would be undecipherable.

It may be that Pausanias has written the best guidebook of all time. He was fortunate to live in the Golden Age of Rome, when most of the famous buildings of Greece (with a few exceptions) were still standing, and the 1700 years of neglect had not yet begun.

1

Archery

1.23.2–4   Near the entrance ⟨to the Acropolis⟩ is a bronze image of Diitrephes pierced with arrows. It was a great surprise to me to see this statue of Diitrephes, that is, the fact that he had been pierced with arrows, because no region of Greece uses the bow except Crete. For we know that the Lokrians of Opuntia whom Homer described as coming to Ilios [= Troy] with bows and sling, were hoplites in the Persian Wars. Skill in archery did not last even among the Malians. My opinion is that the Malians knew nothing about bows until Philoktetes, and they gave it up not long after.

(a) What does this tell about the drawings of Greek archers on vase paintings?
(b) How accurate would a description of modern archery be if one depended on drawings, cartoons, and the like?

Orsippos, First to Run Naked

1.44.1   Orsippos is buried near the hero Koroibos. He ran naked at Olympia when his competitors in accordance with ancient custom wore loincloths, and he won the stade (720 BC). They say that as a general he later acquired some territory from people on the border. I think he took off his loincloth at Olympia deliberately, knowing that a naked man can run faster than one in a loincloth.

(a) Compare this with other statements about nudity at the Olympic Games, Thucydides, for example. In particular, consider the dates.

Origin of Isthmian Games

There are stories about the rocks which stick up where the road is narrow. The story about the Molourian Rock is that Ino threw herself into the sea from it, holding the younger of her sons, named Melikertes; her husband had killed her older son Learchus. They say that the body of Melikertes was carried to the Isthmus of Corinth by a dolphin. Among the other honors which were given to Melikertes, whose name was changed to Palaimon, was the establishment of the Isthmian Games in his honor.

1.44.11

(a) The god to whom the Isthmian Games were sacred was Poseidon. Who then was Palaimon? To whom did he correspond at Olympia?

Description of Isthmia

The theater and the stadium of white stone are worth seeing. As you go into the sanctuary of the god there are statues of athletes who won victories in the Isthmian Games, and pine trees growing in a line.

2.1.7

(a) Contrast the detail of this description of Isthmia with that of Olympia in Books 5 and 6.
(b) Does Isthmia have as many physical remains as Olympia and Delphi?
(c) To what god were the Isthmian Games sacred? In whose memory were they supposedly begun? (See Pausanias 1.44.11 if necessary).

Description of Nemea

In these hills the natives still point out the cave of the lion, and the district of Nemea is some 15 stades away. Here there is a temple of Nemean Zeus, worth looking at except that the whole roof has fallen in, and there are no statues left. There is a grove of cypresses around the temple, and they say that Opheltes was killed there by a snake when his nurse put him down into the grass.[1] The Argives [= citizens of Argos] sacrifice to Zeus at Nemea, elect the priest of Nemean Zeus, and hold a race for men in armor at the winter festival.

2.15.2–3

And here there is the tomb of Opheltes, and around it is a border of stones, and within the sacred precinct are altars. There is a mound of earth, a memorial to Lykourgos, the father of Opheltes. They call the spring Adrasteia, either for some other reason or because Adrastos [= king of Argos] found it. They say that the name Nemea for this region came from the daughter of Asopos. And above Nemea is Mt. Apesa, where they say Perseus was the first to sacrifice to Apesantian Zeus.

Argos

Here is the Stadium, where they hold the games for Nemean Zeus and for the festival of Heraia.[2]

2.24.2

(a) Who was the local hero or demigod in whose honor the Nemean Games were held?

References to swimming suggest that the skill was almost universally acquired in Greece and Italy. There are very few references, however, to any competition in the sport. Here is one, describing games at Hermione, a seaside town in the Peloponnesos:

Swimming Contest at Hermione

2.35.1   Nearby is the temple of Dionysos of the Black Goat; they have annual contests here in music and offer prizes for competition in diving and/or swimming and in a boat race.

(a) There is a reasoning known as the *argumentum ex silentio* (= an argument from silence), in which one concludes that a given subject did not exist at a certain time because it is not mentioned. Why is such an argument dangerous?

(b) Discuss Pausanias' description of Isthmia and Nemea. Were they important games?

Kyniska, Daughter of King of Sparta, Won Chariot Race at Olympia

3.8.1   Archidamos [= king of Sparta] had a daughter named Kyniska, who had great ambitions for the Olympic Games, and was the first woman to raise horses and the first to win an Olympic victory. After Kyniska's time, other women, and particularly Spartan women, won Olympic victories, but no one is as famous for her victories as she is.

(a) Did Kyniska drive the chariot herself in the games?

Tisamenos, Olympic Pentathlete

3.11.6   It was prophesied that Tisamenos ⟨of Sparta⟩ would win five outstanding contests, so he trained for the pentathlon in the Olympics but he lost, although he was first in two events. For he beat Hieronymos of Andros in the run and long jump but was beaten by him in wrestling. And when he lost his victory he understood the oracle: when he sought his prophecy, the god said he would grant him five victories in war.

(a) Tisamenos got two firsts and a second out of five events, but lost. How does this information fit in with the scoring system of the pentathlon proposed in this book in Chapter 8?

Olympic Games Reinstituted by Iphitos

5.4.6   Because Greece at this time (776 BC) was tormented by civil strife and by pestilence, it came about that Iphitos asked the god at Delphi what could remove these evils. They say it was announced by the Pythian priestess that Iphitos and the Eleans should hold the Olympic Games again. Iphitos persuaded the Eleans to make sacrifices to Herakles too, for earlier they had thought that Herakles was hostile to them.

(a) What was the purpose of the Olympic Games restored in 776 BC?

(b) Which Herakles is meant? (See below, 5.7.6–8.)

Kallipateira, Mother of Athlete, Discovered at Olympic Games

From Mt. Typaion the Eleans, according to their laws, throw off any woman   5.6.7–8
who is found to have come into the Olympic Games or even to have crossed
the Alpheios River on the days that are taboo. But they say they never
caught anyone except Kallipateira. There are some, however, who call her
Pherenike, not Kallipateira. When her husband died, she disguised herself
as a coach and brought her son to Olympia to fight, but when her son
Peisirodos won, Kallipateira jumped over the fence by which they enclosed
the coaches and in doing so uncovered herself. Although they saw that she
was a woman, they let her off without punishment, thinking that punishment
would be a disgrace for her father, brothers, and son, all of whom had won
Olympic victories, but they passed a law that for the future all the coaches
should come to the competition naked.

(a) How often was punishment exacted on women who saw the Olympic Games?
(b) How good is the identification of those involved in breaking the rule?
(c) In mythology we speak of "etiological" myths, those that try to explain the
     cause for some custom or phenomenon. What does this study try to explain?

Early History of Olympic Games before Renewal by Iphitos

Those who are interested in the earliest history of Eleia say in regard to   5.7.6
the Olympic Games that Kronos first ruled in heaven and that a temple to
Kronos was built at Olympia by the people of that time, who were called
men of the Golden Age. After Zeus was born, Rhea[3] gave him to the Dak-
tylians on Mt. Ida to guard. They were also called the Kouretes and came
from Mt. Ida in Crete. Their names were Herakles,[4] Paionaios, Epimedes,
Iasios, and Idas.

Herakles, who was the oldest, arranged a race for his brothers in fun and   5.7.7
gave the winner a branch from a wild olive. They had so much of this wild
olive that they piled up fresh leaves to sleep on. The wild olive was said to
have been brought to the Greeks from the Hyperboreans, who are people
living beyond [= *hyper*] the North Wind [= Boreas].

This Idaean Herakles has the credit of being the first to set up games at   5.7.8
that time and to call them Olympic. He decided that they should be held in
every fifth year because he and his brothers were five in number.[5]

Some say that Zeus wrestled there with Kronos for the kingship, others   5.7.10
that he set up the games because of what he had accomplished in depos-
ing Kronos. Other victors are listed; Apollo contested with Hermes in a footrace and beat him and also defeated Ares in boxing. This is why, so they
say, the Pythian aulos song was introduced into the long-jump part of the
pentathlon, because it was sacred to Apollo, and Apollo had won Olympic
prizes.

After this, we are told, Klymenos, son of Kardys, came from Crete in the   5.8.1
50th year after Greece was covered by the Flood in Deukalion's time. He
was descended from the Idaean Herakles, and he put on games in Olympia

and built an altar to his ancestor Herakles and the other Kouretes and gave Herakles the additional name of The Helper.[6] Endymion, son of Aethlios, deposed Klymenos and put up the office of king as a prize for his sons for a race at Olympia.

5.8.2   In the next generation after Endymion, Pelops held the games in the most remarkable fashion of any up to that time. The sons of Pelops had gone from Elis all over the Peloponnesos, and Amythaon son of Kretheus held the Olympics, and after him Pelias and Neleus jointly held them.

5.8.3   Augeas also held the Games, and Herakles son of Amphitryon did too, when he captured Elis. And among the victors whom he crowned was Iolaos, who was driving the mares of Herakles. It was an established custom in ancient times to compete using someone else's horses. Homer at any rate has Menelaos driving Aethe at the funeral games for Patroklos, although the other horse was his own.

5.8.4   Iolaos on other occasions drove Herakles' mares. He won the chariot race, and Iasios, an Arcadian, won the horse race riding on a horse, and the sons of Tyndareos won, Kastor in running and Polydeukes in boxing. And it is said that Herakles himself won the wrestling and the pankration.

(a) How would you evaluate the contents of this section? Are they based on reliable information?

(b) How much does this section tell us about the Olympics in "historical times," that is, after 776 BC?

(c) What is the chief importance of this section? What are the arguments for including it? What are those for omitting it?

We will now leave the mythological era and move into the historical era, where we have both literary and archeological evidence. This is one of the most informative parts of Pausanias for athletics. You will find that modern authorities refer again and again to these sections.

Restoration of Games
by Iphitos in 776 BC

5.8.5   After King Oxylos, who also held the games, the Olympic Games were not held until the time of Iphitos (776 BC). When Iphitos, as I explained above, restored the games, the people of that time had forgotten the ancient customs, but they began gradually to remember, and when they remembered anything they made an addition to the games.

5.8.6   This much is obvious: from the time when there was a tradition of the Olympics Games, the first event was the stade, and Koroibos of Elis was the winner. There is no statue of Koroibos at Olympia, but his grave is on the boundaries of Eleia. For the 14th Olympics (724 BC), the officials put in the diaulos. A man from Pisa,[7] Hypenos, won the wild olive in the diaulos, and in the next games (720 BC) Akanthos ⟨won the dolichos[8]⟩.

5.8.7   For the 18th Olympics (708 BC) the officials remembered the pentathlon and wrestling. Victory in the first of these events fell to Lampis and that in the wrestling to Eurybatos; both were Spartans. In the 23rd Olympics (688

BC), they gave prizes for boxing, which Onomastos won, a citizen of Smyrna, which by this time was part of Ionia. In the 25th (680 BC) they put in a race for fully grown horses, and Pagondas of Thebes won with his chariot.

Seven Olympiads later (648 BC) they introduced the pankration for men   5.8.8
and a race for horses with riders. The horse of Krauxidas of Krannon was first, and Lygdamis from Syracuse defeated his opponents in the pankration. His monument is located near the quarries in Syracuse. And whether this Lygdamis equaled Herakles in size I do not know, but that is what the people of Syracuse say.

Traditions of boys' events do not seem to have been transmitted from   5.8.9
antiquity, but the Eleans introduced these events as they wished. Prizes were offered in running and wrestling in the 37th Olympics (632 BC); Hipposthenes the Spartan won the wrestling, Polyneikes of Elis the running. The 41st Olympics (616 BC) were the first in which boys were entered in boxing; Philytas of Sybaris defeated the other competitors.

The hoplite race was put in for the 65th Olympics (520 BC) for the pur-   5.8.10
pose, it seems to me, of military training. The first victor in this running with shields was Damaretos of Heraia. The chariot race for two fully grown horses called paired horses was put in for the 93rd Olympics (408 BC), and the winner was Euagoras of Elis. For the 99th Olympics (384 BC) they decided to have the chariot contest for colts, and the Spartan Sybariades won the crown with his chariot and foals.

Later they put in a race for a chariot drawn by a pair of colts and a colt   5.8.11
with rider. They say that Belistiche, a woman from the coast of Macedonia, won the race for a pair, and Tlepolemos the Lykian was announced winner for a colt with rider. He won in the 131st Olympics (256 BC) and the pair of Belistiche was victor in the two Olympics before this (that is, in 264 BC). In the 145th games (200 BC) a pankration for boys was offered, and the winner was Phaidimos, an Aiolian from the region of Troas.

Events at Olympia have also been eliminated, when the Eleans decided   5.9.1
not to have them. For example, in the 38th Olympics (628 BC) there was a pentathlon for boys, in which Eutelidas the Spartan got the wild olive. The Eleans then decided that boys should not compete in the pentathlon. A race for carts with four mules and the *kalpē* (see below) were put in, the first in the 70th Olympics (500 BC), the second in the next games. In the 84th Olympics (444 BC) they had a herald announce that in the future there would be no kalpē and no four-mule cart races. When these events were first put in, Thersios of Thessaly won the four-mule cart race, and Pataikus, an Achaian from Dyme, won the kalpē. In this kalpē, the animals were mares, and at the start of the last lap the *anabatai* [= drivers] leaped off and ran beside the mares, holding the bridle, just as those who are called anabatai still do in my time.

The order of events in our time, namely sacrificing first to the god after   5.9.3
the pentathlon and horse racing and having the other events later, was fixed in the 77th Olympics (472 BC). Before this, the contests for men and horses all took place on the same day. But during these Olympic Games

the pankratiasts fought until dark, because they had not been called early enough. The horse races were the cause of this but still more the contest in the pankration. Kallias the Athenian won the pankration, and in the future the pentathlon and the horse races would not delay the pankration.

5.9.4   The regulations about the officials which are in effect in our time are not the same as those set up in antiquity; Iphitos, for example, put on the games all by himself (776 BC), as did the other kings of Elis after Oxylos. But in the 50th Olympics (580 BC) the two men chosen by lot from all the Eleans were given the responsibility of the Games, and this number of officials (two) lasted a long time.

5.9.5–6   In the 95th Olympics (400 BC) nine Hellanodikai were appointed: three supervised the horse races, the same number oversaw the pentathlon, and the rest watched over the other contests. At the next Olympic Games a tenth official was added. After several changes in the number of Hellanodi- kai the number was stabilized at ten in 348 BC.

(a) What is Pausanias' explanation of how events were added?
(b) What was the date in years BC when the horse race was put in?
(c) Would you say that the reorganization of the games in 776 BC by Iphitos is a historical fact? Do we know the name of the first runner?
(d) Be able to convert Olympic Games to our BC dates.

Description of Altis (Olympic Sanctuary)

5.13.1   Inside the Altis [= sacred part of precinct] there is also a section reserved for Pelops. For the Eleans honored Pelops the most among the heroes,[9] just as they do Zeus among all the other gods.

5.13.8   The altar of Olympian Zeus is almost exactly midway between the Tem- ple of Pelops and the Temple of Hera, but ahead of them both. Some say that it was built by Herakles from Mt. Ida and some that it was built by local heroes two generations after this Herakles. It is made of ashes from the thighs of animals sacrificed to Zeus, just as at Pergamon. There is also an ash altar to Hera of Samos, no more impressive than the hearths in the region of Attika, which the Athenians call "improvised altars."

5.13.9   The first step of the altar in Olympia is 125 feet in circumference and is called the "Outer Circle." The step above the Outer Circle is 32 feet in circumference. The total height of the altar is 22 feet. The rule is to kill the animals in the lower part of the Outer Circle and then to carry the thighs to the top of the altar and burn them there as a sacrifice.

5.13.10   There are steps made of stone which go up into the Outer Circle from both sides. Unmarried girls are permitted to go up as far as the Outer Circle and so are married women at times when they are not barred from Olympia.

Games for Women

5.16.2   Every five years [= four years by our system] 16 women weave a robe for Hera and they also put on the Heraia [= Games of Hera]. This contest is a running event for unmarried girls. They are not all the same age, but the first to run are the youngest, after them the next older, and the last to run are the oldest of the girls. Here is their method of running. They let down their hair, gird the tunic a little above the knee, and uncover the right shoulder as far as the breast. They use the stadium for this event, although the length of the track is reduced by a sixth. To the victors they give crowns of olive leaves and a share of the cow which they sacrifice to Hera, and they may set up statues with their names inscribed. Those who assist the 16 who put on the games are also women.

They also trace these games for girls back into antiquity, saying that Hippodameia gathered these 16 women together to do honor to Hera for her marriage to Pelops and at the same time first put on the Heraian Games. 5.16.4

(a) What is the name of the sacred precinct at Olympia?
(b) According to legend, in whose honor were the Olympic Games established?
(c) Describe the altar of Olympian Zeus.
(d) Why does Pelops seem to us to be a poor choice for a hero?
(e) What restrictions were placed upon those who visited the altar of Olympian Zeus?
(f) Describe the Heraian Games. How many events were there?
(g) Where did the Peloponnesos get its name?

The Zanes

As one goes to the stadium by taking the route from the *Metroon* 5.21.2 [= Mother's Shrine], on the left along the base of Mt. Kronion, there is a course of stone built into the hill and steps through it at intervals. Against this course of stone have been set up bronze statues of Zeus. These were paid for by fines from athletes who defiled the games, and they are called "Zanes" by the locals.

The first six statues were erected after the 98th Olympics (438 BC), when 5.21.3 Eupolos the Thessalian bribed the contestants in boxing, Agetor of Arkadia and Prytanis of Kyziokos, and with them Phormion of the family from Halikarnassos who had won the boxing in the previous Olympics. They say that this was the first scandal involving athletes in the Olympics, and Eupolos and those who took the bribes were the first to be fined by the Eleans. Two statues are by Kleon of Sicyon, but we do not know who made the next four.

Except for numbers three and four, these six statues all have inscriptions. 5.21.4 The first of these two-line verses wants to show that the way to win at Olympia is not through money but by swiftness of foot and strength of body. The one on the base of the second statue says that the statue was set up in honor of religion and because of the piety of the Eleans and to frighten dishonest athletes. As for five and six, the sense of the first is to praise the Eleans in general and in particular for fining the boxers, and of the last that these statues are an object lesson to all Greece not to give bribes for an Olympic victory.

Pausanias goes on to describe ten other Zanes in much the same way. The bases of these statues are still extant, one inscribed with the signature of the sculptor Kleon. The offenses were all for bribery, with the following exceptions:

5.21.12   Apollonios of Egypt was the first Egyptian [= Greek from Egypt] to be found guilty; he was not fined for giving or accepting a bribe but for bringing disgrace upon the games in the following way.

5.21.13   He did not arrive at the games on time, and the Eleans, in accordance with the rules, kept him out of the contest. His excuse was that he had been delayed by adverse winds in the Kyklades Islands. Herakleides, who was of the same nationality, an Alexandrian, proved that this excuse was a deception, for in fact Apollonios had been delayed by getting money from games in Ionia.

5.21.14   So the Eleans kept Apollonios out of the contest as well as any other boxer who might show up late, and they crowned Herakleides *akoniti* [= without his having to fight]. Thereupon Apollonios wrapped his hands with the thongs as if for a fight, rushed in and hit Herakleides, who was already wearing the wild olive and had sought protection among the Hellanodikai. Apollonios' lack of restraint proved very expensive to him.

5.21.18   They say that a pankratiast from Alexandria, whose name was Sarapion, in the 201st Olympics (25 AD), was so afraid of his competitors that he ran off on the day before the pankration was scheduled. They say he was the only Egyptian, in fact the only Olympic competitor, to be fined for cowardice.

Zeus of the Oaths

5.24.9   The statue of Zeus which strikes the most terror into dishonest men is in the Bouleterion. Its name is Zeus of the Oaths, and it is the rule for the athletes and their fathers and brothers, and their trainers as well to swear over the flesh of a cut-up boar to break none of the rules of the Olympic Games. The adult athletes have to swear as well that they have been in strenuous training for ten months in a row.

5.24.10   Those who pass judgment on the boys and the colts[10] swear to make their decisions justly and without accepting gifts, and to keep secret who was approved and who was not.

Memorials to Athletes and Others

6.1.1   At this point in my discussion of dedicated objects I will describe the memorials to contestants in the horse races and athletes and noncontestants as well. Not all those who won in the Olympic Games have statues[11]; many who were famous for their accomplishments in the games and for other reasons as well still did not get a statue. My plan of writing compels me to leave them out, since this is not a record book of all the Olympic victors but a description of statues and other dedications. I shall not even describe all the statues which have been set up since I know which ones got the wild olive branch not by strength but by the luck of the draw.[12] I shall therefore list either persons of renown or the statues which are artistically superior.

Queen of Sparta

I have already explained about Kyniska, daughter of Archidamos, about   6.1.6
her family, and about her Olympic victories in the section about the Spartan
kings. At Olympia, beside the statue of Troilos, is a pedestal with a team of
horses and driver and also a figure of Kyniska herself, the work of Apelles,
and there are carved inscriptions about Kyniska.

Theagenes of Thasos

Theagenes (also spelled Theogenes) of Thasos wanted to win both the   6.6.5
boxing and the pankration in the same Olympics (480 BC). He defeated his
opponent Euthymos (the defending champion), but not even the great
Theagenes could get the wild olive crown in the pankration, since he was
exhausted by his fight with Euthymos. As a result, the Hellanodikai made
Theagenes pay a sacred fine of a talent[13] to the god and another talent to
Euthymos for damages, because it seemed to them that he had taken the
boxing crown from Euthymos through spite. Therefore they condemned him
to pay this private sum to Euthymos. Theagenes paid the god part of the
fine in the 76th Olympics (476 BC) and in a change from his previous plan
did not enter the boxing.

Dromeus, Long-Distance Runner

There was a man from Stymphalos, named Dromeus, whose record as a   6.7.10
long-distance runner was exceptional: he won two victories in the dolichos
at Olympia, the same number in the Pythian Games, three at the Isthmian
and five at the Nemean. He is said to have first thought of eating meat (as
part of his training diet). Until then the food for athletes was cheese fresh
out of the basket.

Timanthes, Who Committed Suicide
When His Strength Failed

The statue of Timanthes of Kleonai, who won the wreath for the pankra-   6.8.4
tion, was done by Myron of Athens and that of Baukis of Troizen, winner of
the men's wrestling, by Naukydes. They say that Timanthes came to his
end for the following reasons. Although he had given up competition, he still
tested his strength every day by drawing a heavy bow. He went on a trip,
the story goes, during which he neglected the exercise with the bow; when
he returned and was not able to draw his bow, he built a large fire and
threw himself into it alive. All such deeds as this which have occurred in the
human race, or will occur, should be considered insanity rather than manliness. At least that is my opinion.

Glaukos, "Plow Stroke"

After all these which I have mentioned comes the statue of Glaukos from   6.10.1–3
Karystos. They say that originally he was a farmer. And when his plowshare
fell out of the plow, he drove it back in place by using his fist as a hammer.
And when his father Demylos saw what his son had done, he brought him

to Olympia to compete in boxing. In these games Glaukos, who was without experience in competition, was badly cut up, and when he was fighting with his last opponent, people thought he should concede because of his numerous injuries. And, as the story goes, his father shouted, "Son, hit him one from the plow!" And hitting his opponent a harder blow, he suddenly won the match. They say that he won other crowns too, two at Pythia, and at Nemea and Isthmia, eight in each. His statue was set up by his son, and the artist was Glaukias of Aigina. The statue was a representation of a man shadowboxing because Glaukos was considered to have the most graceful motions of any of his contemporaries.

Damaretos

6.10.4   Damaretos won in the 65th Olympics (516 BC), when the hoplitodromos was first run, and a second time in the next Olympics. His statue was made showing a shield just like the ones in use in the games today but with a helmet on the head and greaves on the legs; these last two pieces of equipment over the years have been dropped by the Eleans and the other Greeks.

Theagenes of Thasos

6.11.2   Not far from the statues of the kings which I mentioned stands the statue of Theagenes of Thasos, son of Timosthenes. The Thasians, however, say that Theagenes was not the son of Timosthenes but that Timosthenes was a priest of Herakles of Thasos and that the spirit of Herakles, taking on the appearance of Timosthenes, slept with the mother of Theagenes. They also say that when the boy was nine years old, while he was going home from school, he was attracted by the bronze statue of one of the gods dedicated in the agora and picked it up and carried it off on one shoulder.

6.11.3   The citizens were outraged by his action but one gentleman of distinction and advanced years kept them from killing the boy, and ordered him to carry the statue back to the agora from his house. When he carried it back, his reputation for strength at once became widespread, and his deed was talked about all over Greece.

6.11.4   Those deeds of Theagenes which took place in the Olympic Games my account has already discussed (6.6.5), how he beat the boxer Euthymos and how Theagenes was fined by the Eleans. At those games a man named Dromeus from Mantineia was said to have been the first we know of to have won the pankration by default [= akoniti], but Theagenes prevailed in the pankration in the next Olympics.

6.11.5   He also had three Pythian victories, and these were in boxing; nine victories at Nemea; and ten at Isthmia, divided between boxing and wrestling. At the games at Pythia in Thessaly he gave up his specialties of boxing and wrestling and decided to make his mark among the Greeks as a runner, and he defeated his competitors in the dolichos run. His reason, I believe, was a desire to emulate Achilleus, by winning a victory in the home city of the man who was called the fastest of the heroes. His total number of victories was 1400.

When he passed away, somebody who hated him when he was alive came   6.11.6
up every night to the statue and whipped the bronze just as if he were beating Theagenes. The statue fell on him and ended his malicious actions and
because he was killed, his sons brought an accusation of murder against
the statue. The Thasians, depending on the opinion of Drakon, who in writing the Athenian laws on murder banished even lifeless objects, if it happened that they fell on a human being and killed him, sank his statue in the
sea.

As time passed, when the earth yielded no crops, the Thasians sent am-   6.11.7
bassadors to Delphi, and the god announced that they should restore those
they had exiled. But the men whom the Thasians restored in accordance
with this command brought no relief from the barrenness of the earth. And
so they sent a second time to Pythia [=priestess who gave the oracle at
Delphi], saying that although they had fulfilled the commands of the oracle
the anger of the gods persisted.

And the Pythian priestess answered them, "You have left your great   6.11.8
Theagenes unremembered." While they were at a loss to restore the statue
of Theagenes, some fishermen, so they say, letting down nets into the sea
to catch fish, brought up the statue in their net and brought it back to land.
The Thasians set it up where it had formerly stood and they offered the kind
of sacrifices which they give to a god.

I know of statues of Theagenes set up in many places, among both Greeks   6.11.9
and barbarians, and he cures diseases and receives honors from the local
inhabitants. The statue of Theagenes at Olympia is in the Altis, the work of
Glaukias of Aigina.

Three Famous Runners

The statue of Astylos of Kroton is by Pythagoras. Astylos won the stade   6.13.1
and the diaulos in three successive Olympics. In the last two games, he
announced that he was a Syracusan, to please Hieron [=ruler of Syra-
cuse], son of Deinomenes. Because of this, the people of Kroton voted to
turn his house into a prison and removed his statue.

A man of Lykia named Hermogenes from Xanthos won the wild olive in   6.13.2–3
eight events during three Olympics, and the Greeks called him "The Horse."
Polites was another man to marvel at. This Polites was from Keramos in
Karia, and he showed excellence at the Olympics in every kind of running,
for he changed from the longest and most taxing to the shortest and fastest
in a short time; and on the same day he gained victories in the dolichos
and the stade and won the diaulos as well.

Polites ⟨came in second in four races so that they changed the system[14]⟩   6.13.4
so that each of the runners is put ⟨into a heat⟩ by lot, and all do not compete
in the stade at the same time. They compete in separate heats and then
run again ⟨in the final⟩ for first place. And so the man who wins the stade
wins two races. The most distinguished feats of running were performed by
Leonidas of Rhodes. He was at his peak for four Olympics and won twelve
victories.

The Mare Named Breezy

6.13.9   A mare belonging to the Corinthian Pheidolas was called Breezy by the Corinthians. Just as her race began she happened to throw her rider. Nevertheless she ran the correct course and made the turns around the post. And when she heard the trumpet,[15] she sprinted and beat the other horses to the finish line. There she knew she had won and stopped running. The Eleans proclaimed Pheidolas the winner and allowed him to set up a statue of the mare.

Milo of Kroton

6.14.5   Dameas made the statue of Milo son of Diotimos; both artist and athlete were from Kroton. Milo gained six Olympic victories in wrestling, one of them in the boys' class. He also won six victories at the Pythian Games in the men's class and one in the boys'. He came to Olympia for a try at a seventh victory, but he was not able to throw his fellow citizen Timasitheos, who was young and not willing to close with him.

6.14.6   Milo is said to have carried his own statue into the Altis. Stories are also told about Milo and the pomegranate and Milo and the diskos. He used to hold a pomegranate in such a way that no one could make him release it, but he did not squeeze the fruit hard enough to hurt it. He also would stand on a diskos covered with oil and laugh at those who charged into him and tried to knock him off.

6.14.7   He performed other demonstrations too. He used to tie a cord around his forehead like a headband or a crown; then holding his breath and filling the veins of his head with blood, he would break the cord with the pressure of his veins. He is also said to have held out his right hand with his elbow pressed to his side. He had his thumb up and the other fingers close together: no one, no matter how hard he worked, could move his little finger.

6.14.8   They say he was killed by wild beasts. For somewhere near Kroton he came upon a dead tree, and there were wedges in the tree to split it. Milo had the idea of putting his hand in the crack of the tree. The wedges fell out and Milo, held fast by the tree, was found and eaten by wolves.

Kleitomachos, Wrestler, Boxer, and Pankratiast

6.15.3   The statue of Kleitomachos of Thebes was dedicated by his father, Hermokrates. He is known for the following. At the Isthmian Games he won the men's wrestling, and on the same day he defeated those competing in boxing and the pankration. His victories in the Pythian Games, three in number, were all in the pankration. At Olympia he was the first man after Theagenes of Thasos to win both pankration and boxing.

6.15.4   In the 141st Olympics (216 BC) he walked off with the prize in the pankration. The next Olympics saw this same Kleitomachos present himself as contestant in the pankration and boxing. Kapros of Elis wanted to wrestle and do the pankration on the same day.

6.15.5   When Kapros won the wrestling, Kleitomachos persuaded the Hellanodikai that it would be fair to them both if they were to move up the pankration so that he could compete before getting injured in the boxing. What he said seemed reasonable, so the pankration was moved up. Although he was beaten by Kapros in the boxing, he showed courage and an unwearied body.

Boys' Events

Eutelidas the Spartan won two victories in the 38th Olympics (628 BC) in the boys' wrestling and boys' pentathlon. This was the first and last time a boys' pentathlon was held. There is an archaic statue of Eutelidas, and the lettering on the base is hard to see because it is so old. 6.15.8

Earliest Statues

The first statues of athletes set up in Olympia were those of Praxidamas of Aigina, who won the boxing at the 59th Olympics (544 BC) and Rexibios of Opous, who won the pankration in the 61st (536 BC). These statues are not far from the pillar of Oinomaos. They are both made of wood; that of Rexibios of fig wood and that of the citizen of Aigina of cypress, not as well made as the other. 6.18.7

(a) How did Pausanias limit his book?
(b) What fines did Theagenes have to pay? Were these fines fair, in your judgment?
(c) Does the story of Timanthes and his bow sound probable? What kind of exercise did the bow provide? What did Timanthes shoot at?
(d) If Glaukos followed his father's instructions literally, what kind of blow did he strike?
(e) What change in equipment took place in the hoplitodromos?
(f) Name several ways in which the winning record of Theagenes was distinguished.
(g) Athletes today achieve great fame. In what way did some Greek athletes, Theagenes for example, get even greater honor?
(h) What does the anecdote about Astylos, who competed first for Kroton and then for Syracuse, show?
(i) From the story of Breezy, what can we learn about the number of laps in the horse-with-rider race?
(j) What kinds of control did Milo exhibit in his demonstrations?
(k) What is the typically Greek message in the story of the death of Milo?
(l) From the story of Kleitomachos, what do we learn about the physical demands of the pankration and boxing? What do we learn about the order of the events?

The Olympic Stadium

At the end of the Zanes which were built from the fines of the athletes is the entrance to the stadium called the Hidden Entrance. Through this the Hellanodikai come into the stadium, and the competitors too. The stadium is surrounded by a mound of earth in which seats have been built for the presiding officers of the games. Opposite these Hellanodikai is an altar built of white stone. 6.20.8

On this altar sits a woman who watches the Olympic Games, the priest- 6.20.9

ess of Demeter of the Earth; this is the honor which different women receive at different times from the Eleans. Girls are not forbidden to watch. At the end of the stadium where the start for the stade run is located[16] is the memorial to Endymion according to the Elean story.

The Hippodrome

6.20.10   If you climb up out of the stadium to the south where the Hellanodikai sit, you come to the place where the earth has been cleared for horse racing, and here is the starting gate for the horses. This starting gate is shaped like the prow of a ship, with its beak pointed into the track. Where the prow touches the Stoa of Agnaptos it broadens out. On the end of the prow is a bronze statue of a dolphin on a pole.[17]

6.20.11   Each of the sides of this starting gate measures more than 400 feet and there are stalls built into them. Those who participate in the horse races draw lots for these stalls. In front of the chariots or horses with riders stretches a cord in place of the usual husplex. For each Olympics they build an altar of unbaked brick, plastered on the outside, right in the middle of the prow.

6.20.12   On this altar is set a bronze eagle, with its wings fully extended. The official in charge of the race works the machinery on the altar. When he does so, he makes the eagle fly up, so that those who have come to the games can see it, and the dolphin falls down.

6.20.13   The first husplexes to be released on both sides are those toward the Stoa of Agnaptos, and the horses stationed in them are the first to run out. The horses which are running come abreast of those which have drawn the second position, and then the husplexes in the second row are released. This happens in the same way to all the horses, until at the beak of the prow they are all even. From this point it is a question of drivers showing their skill and horses their speed.

6.20.14   The original designer of this starting gate was Kleoitas; he was proud of his invention, as an inscription on his statue in Athens says, "Kleoitas, son of Aristokles, inventor of the horses' start at Olympia, made me." They say that after Kleoitas, Aristeides introduced some improvements in the mechanism.

6.20.15   One side of the track is longer than the other. On the longer side there is a mound, through which the racetrack cuts, a feature which frightens horses and is called Taraxippos [= terror of horses]. The shape is that of a round altar, and as the horses go racing past, from no apparent cause they are seized by extreme terror, and from this fear arises chaos; the chariots are smashed to pieces and the drivers are injured. Because of this the drivers make sacrifices and beg Taraxippos to spare them.

6.20.19   On one of the turning posts is a bronze statue of Hippodameia holding a ribbon and about to tie it around Pelops for his victory.

Gymnasium, Palestra, Quarters for Athletes

6.21.2   The runners and pentathletes train in the Gymnasium at Olympia. There is a base in the open air made of stone, and a memorial of a victory of the

Eleans over the Arkadians used to stand on this base. There is another smaller enclosed space, on the left of the entrance to the gymnasium, and here is the palestra for the athletes. Quarters for the athletes are by the wall of the eastern portico of the gymnasium and face southwest.

In the city of Elis[18] the ancient gymnasium is worth seeing. It was a rule that whatever was done with the athletes before they went to Olympia should be done in this gymnasium. There are tall plane trees growing inside the walls between the racetracks. The whole area is called the Xystos [= Smooth Ground] because Herakles son of Amphitryon, as part of his training, had to smooth the field every day and remove the thistles which had grown.   6.23.1

A separate track is set aside for the competition which the locals call the Sacred Track, and another track is used by runners and pentathletes for practice. In this gymnasium is the Plethrion[19]; here the Hellanodikai match the contestants by age and by their past performances. They also match them for wrestling.   6.23.2

There is another smaller gymnasium area, which is next to the big one, and they call it the Square because of its shape. The wrestlers hold their workouts here, and here they also match wrestlers who do not intend to wrestle any more, to box with the himantes. One of the two statues to Zeus, made from the fines paid by Sosander of Smyrna and Polyktor of Elis, is set up here.   6.23.4

There is also a third gymnasium called the Soft Ground because of the softness of the surface, and it is available for ephebes for the duration of the games.[20]   6.23.5

An alternate route leads out of the gymnasium, into the agora and to the place called the Council of the Hellanodikai; it is beyond the grave of Achilleus. It has been the custom for the Hellanodikai to go to the gymnasium by this route. They come before sunrise to arrange heats for the races, and about noon they move on to arrangements for the pentathlon and the events they call heavy.   6.24.1

The agora of Elis is not like those in Ionia, or the Greek cities around Ionia. It is built in the ancient style, with colonnades separated from each other and streets between them. The name today for this agora is the Hippodrome, and the local people do train their horses there.   6.24.2

(a) Did any women view the games?

(b) What functions did Elis serve in the Olympic Games?

Pausanias next describes a town in Arkadia, which is in the center of the Peloponnesos and is still wild and remote today. Guidebooks are full of such statements as, ''The road is not practical except on foot; the mountain track is easier but requires a guide''[21]:

Statue to Arrichion, the Pankratiast

In the agora of the Phigalians is a statue of Arrichion the pankratiast, archaic in all respects and not least in its stance. The feet are not far apart and the arms hang down the sides so that the tips of the hands are level   8.40.1

with the buttocks. The statue is made of stone, and they say that there was an inscription written on it, but this has disappeared over the years. This Arrichion won victories in the two Olympics before the 54th and won again in the 54th (564 BC) through the justice of the Hellanodikai and Arrichion's own courage.

8.40.2   For as he was fighting for the crown of wild olive with the one remaining contestant, the opponent, whatever his name was, seized Arrichion and squeezed him around the middle with his legs and at the same time choked him with his hands. Arrichion broke one of the toes on the foot of his opponent. Arrichion died from strangulation, and the one who was choking him, because of the pain in his toe, let him go at the same time. The Eleans crowned the dead body of Arrichion and declared him the winner.

(a) What information does this give about the pankration?
(b) What decided the winner?
(c) Why did the Spartans not permit their athletes to compete in the pankration?

Pausanias now turns to Phokis, a region of central Greece in which the famous oracle of Delphi was located:

Early History of Pythian Games at Delphi

10.7.2   Tradition says that the oldest contest ⟨at Delphi⟩ and the one for which prizes were first given was for singing a hymn to the god. Chrysothemis of Crete sang and won the singing; his father Karmanor is said to have purified Apollo.[22] Tradition also says that after Chrysothemis, Philammon won the singing contest and after him, his son Thamyris. They say that because of the air of solemnity which Orpheus gave his mystic rites and his conceit in other matters, he and Mousaios, who imitated Orpheus in everything, refused to enter the musical contest. They also say that Eleuther won a Pythian victory by the timbre and volume of his voice, for the song he sang was not his own composition. They also say that Hesiodos was dismissed from the contest because he had not learned to accompany himself on the harp as he sang. Homer came to Delphi to ask about matters he did not know, but even if he had intended to learn to play the harp, the skill would have been useless because of his trouble with his eyes.[23]

10.7.3   In the third year after the 48th Olympics, in which Glaukias of Kroton won the stade race, the Amphiktyonic League[24] had a prize for singing with the harp as before but added contests in singing accompanied by the aulos and in playing the aulos. The winners were proclaimed: Melampous the Kephalenian, who shone in singing with the harp, Echembrotos the Arkadian in singing with the aulos, and Sakadas the Argive in playing the aulos. This same Sakadas won the next two Pythian contests. At this time they offered prizes for the first time for athletes, with the full Olympic program except the four-horse chariot, and they introduced in addition a boys' race in the dolichos and the diaulos. In the second Pythian Games they did not summon the contestants to compete for prizes, but from this time on the contest was for a crown. They also dropped the singing with the aulos because the sound was unlucky. For singing with the aulos was the most

melancholy form of music. Therefore they stopped the competition in singing accompanied by aulos. They also put in a horse race, and Kleisthenes,
tyrant of Sicyon, was declared winner through his chariot. In the 8th Pythian
Games they set up rules for a contest for harpists who played songs without
singing: Agelaos of Tegea was crowned. In the 23rd games they put in a
race in armor: Timainetos of Phlious won the laurel wreath, five Olympiads
after Damaretos of Heraia had won the first race in armor at Olympia.

In the 48th Pythian Games they instituted a two-horse chariot race, which
the chariot of Exekestides of Phokis won. Four games later they had chariots with colts; the four-colt chariot of Orphondas of Thebes won. Many
years later they brought in from the Eleans the boys' pankration, two-colt
chariot racing, and races for a colt with rider. The first of these events, the
boys' pankration, was won by Iolaidas of Thebes in the 61st Pythian Games;
the race for a colt with rider was begun in the next set of games, and the
race for the two-colt chariot in the 69th games. In the race for a colt with
rider, Lykormas of Larisa was announced the winner, and Ptolemy the Macedonian was the winner with his two-colt chariot. The Macedonians in Egypt
liked to be called kings, which of course they were.

The crown for victory in the Pythian Games is made of laurel[25] for no   10.7.4
other reason, it seems to me, than because there is a story that Apollo
loved the daughter of Ladon.[26]

(a) In 10.7.2, Pausanias does not identify the god to whom the hymns were sung.
    Who was it?
(b) Did the singers at Delphi usually sing their own compositions? Did they ac-
    company themselves?
(c) Did the musicians sing their own compositions? Was there any accompani-
    ment for the singing?
(d) In what ways are the Pythian Games like the other three Panhellenic Games?
    In what ways are they different?
(e) Pausanias says near the end of this quotation that certain events, like the boys'
    pankration, were "brought in from the Eleans." Explain. What would the
    approximate date of these events be?

Description of Sacred Precinct and Stadium

The city of Delphi is on a steep slope and so is the Sacred Precinct of   10.8.5
Apollo. This large precinct is located in the highest part of the city, and is
penetrated by connecting alleys.

I shall list the dedications which seem to me to be most worthy of men-   10.9.1
tion, but I shall not bother with athletes or competitors in musical events
who accomplished nothing noteworthy. I have already discussed in my description of Elis whatever athletes have left a distinguished record. But take
Phaÿllos of Kroton, who never won in the Olympics but took the pentathlon
twice in the Pythian Games and won a third victory in the stade: he fought
against the Persians,[27] furnishing his own ship and using citizens of Kroton
as crew; he has a statue at Delphi.

From the Sacred Precinct you go into the theater, which is worth seeing.   10.32.1

As you climb out of the precinct [here there is a gap in the text] a statue of Dionysos set up by the Knidians. The stadium is the highest part of the city. It was constructed of the kind of stone which is found in most of Mt. Parnassos, until Herodes Atticus[28] improved it with marble from Mt. Pentelikos.

(a) There are several notable things about Phaÿllos; what are they?

Further Readings

Levi, P., *Pausanias: Guide to Greece* (Penguin 1971), 2 volumes, paperback. Excellent translation with copious notes.

32

Lucian

Lucian was born about 120 AD in Syria. His native language was not Greek, but he wrote some eighty works in Greek, mostly in dialogues. The dialect in which he wrote was an imitation of the literary language of V BC Athens. It is difficult to tell sometimes whether he is drawing his material from life or from the libraries. His *Anacharsis* is an imaginary dialogue between Solon, an Athenian statesman and poet of VI BC, and Anacharsis, a historical traveler from Scythia (=southern Russia), who visited Greece in search of wisdom. Harris (SpGR, p 103) says of this dialogue, ''The Greek sporting life depicted in the work is that of Lucian's own day.'' Judge for yourself as you read the dialogue.

1

Anacharsis

Anacharsis: And another thing, my dear Solon, why are those young men 1
acting in this way? Look, some of them are grappling and tripping each other, others are choking their friends and twisting their limbs, rolling about in the mud and wallowing like pigs. But before they began to do this, I noticed they first took off their clothes, then put oil on themselves, and in a peaceful fashion took turns in rubbing each other. But now, experiencing some emotion I do not understand, they have lowered their heads and are crashing into each other, and butting their heads together like rams! And look! There is one who has just seized the other by the legs and thrown him down; then he flopped on him and did not allow him to get up, but shoved him down into the mud. And now he is finally twisting his legs around the other person's waist and choking him with his arm under his throat. The other is slapping him on the shoulder, trying to ask him, I suppose, not to choke him to death. They do not avoid getting covered with dirt even to save the oil, but on the contrary wipe it off, and smearing themselves with mud and rivers of perspiration they make themselves ridiculous, in my opinion, by sliding in and out of each other's hands like eels.

2   Others are acting in the same way in the open part of the courtyard. However, these are not in the mud, but they have this deep sand in the pit which they sprinkle on themselves and each other, just like roosters, so that they cannot break out of their grasp, I imagine, since the sand decreases the slipperiness and offers a surer grip on a dry skin.

3   Others also covered with dust are standing up straight and striking and kicking each other. See that one there! Poor fellow, he seems to be ready to spit out a mouthful of teeth considering how full of blood and sand his mouth is; he has got a blow to the jaw, as you can see for yourself. But the official there does not separate them and stop the fight—at least I assume he is an official from his scarlet cloak. On the contrary he encourages them and cheers the one who struck that blow.

4   All around different people are all exercising: some raise their knees as if running, although they remain in the same place, and as they jump up they kick the air.

5   What I want to know is, what reason do they have for doing this? It seems to me these actions are almost insane, and there is no one who can easily persuade me that people who act like this have not lost all their senses.

[In 6 and 7, Solon explains that customs differ from one land to another. He then explains to Anacharsis what is happening.]

8   *Solon:* This place, dear Anacharsis, is what we call a gymnasium and it is sacred to Lykeian Apollo. You can see his statue, leaning against a stele, holding his bow in his left hand. His right arm is bent above his head as if the artist were showing the god resting, as if he had completed some laborious task. As for those exercises in the nude, the one done in the mud is called wrestling. Those in the dust are also wrestling. Those who strike each other standing upright we call pankratiasts. We have other athletic events: we have contests in boxing, diskos, and the long jump, and the winner is considered superior to his fellows and takes the prize.

9   *Anacharsis:* These prizes of yours now; what are they?

Solon: At Olympia there is a crown of wild olive; at Isthmia, one of pine; at Nemea, one woven of celery; at the Pythian Games, laurel berries sacred to the god, and here at home at the Panathenaic Games, oil from olive trees which grow in the sacred precincts. What are you laughing at, Anacharsis? Do these prizes seem valueless to you?

[In 10–14, Solon explains the symbolic value of the prizes, justifies the pursuit of athletics, and the education of the citizens. Then Anacharsis asks Solon to explain the government of Athens.]

15   *Solon:* It is not easy, my friend, to explain everything at once in concise form, but if you will take one thing at a time you will learn everything about our belief in the gods, as well as our attitude toward parents, marriage, or anything else. I will now explain our theory about young men and how we treat them from the time when they begin to know the difference between right and wrong and are entering manhood and sustaining hardships, so that you may learn why we require them to undergo these exercises and

force them to subject their bodies to toil, not just because of the athletic games and the prizes they may win there, for few of them have the ability to do that, but so that they may try to gain a greater good for the entire city and for themselves. For there is another contest set up for all good citizens and the crown is not made of pine nor of wild olive nor of celery, but is one which includes all of man's happiness, that is to say, freedom for each person individually and for the state in general: wealth, glory, pleasure in our traditional feast days, having the entire family safe from harm, and in a word, to have the best of all the blessings one could have from the gods. All this happiness is woven into the crown to which I referred and is acquired in the contest to which these exhausting exercises lead.

[In 16–23, Solon goes into more detail about the training of young men and about the responsibility of the citizens.]

Solon: As for physical training, which you particularly wanted to hear about,   24
we proceed as follows. When the boys reach an age when they are no longer soft and uncoordinated, we strip them naked. We do this because first, we think they should get used to the weather, learning to live with different seasons, so they are not bothered by the heat nor do they yield to the cold. Then we massage them with olive oil and condition the skin. For since we see that leather which is softened by olive oil does not easily crack and is much stronger, even though it is not alive, why should we not think that live bodies would benefit from oil? Next we have thought up different kinds of athletics and have appointed coaches for each type. We teach one how to box, another how to compete in the pankration, so that they can become used to hard work, to stand up to blows face to face, and not to yield through fear of injury. This creates two valuable traits in our young men: it makes them brave in the face of danger and unsparing of their bodies, and it also makes them strong and vigorous. Those who wrestle and push against each other learn how to fall safely and spring up nimbly, to endure pushing, grappling, twisting, and choking, and to be able to lift their opponent off the ground. They are not learning useless skills but they get the one thing which is the first and most important thing in life: through this training their bodies become stronger and capable of enduring pain. There is another thing too which is not unimportant. From this training they acquire skills which they may need some day in war. For it is clear that if a man so trained grapples with an enemy, he will trip and throw him more quickly and if he is thrown he will know how to regain his feet as easily as possible. For we prepare our men, Anacharsis, for the supreme contest, war, and we expect to have much better soldiers out of young men who have had this training, that is, the previous conditioning and training of naked bodies, which makes them not only stronger and healthier, more agile and fit, but also causes them to outweigh their opponents.

You can see, I should think, the results of this, what they are like when   25
armed, or even without weapons how they would strike terror in their enemies. Our troops are not fat, pale, and useless nor are they white and

scrawny, with bodies like women, enervated by lying in the shade, simultaneously shivering and streaming with rivers of sweat, gasping beneath their helmets, particularly if the sun, as now, is burning with noontime heat. What use could people be who get thirsty and cannot endure dust; soldiers who panic if they see blood, who die of terror before they come close enough to throw their spears or to close with the enemy? But our troops have skin of high color, darkened by the sun, and faces like real men; they display great vigor, fire, and virility. They glow with good health, and are neither shriveled skeletons nor excessively heavy, but they have been carved to perfect symmetry; they have used up and sweated off useless and excess flesh, and that which is left is strong, supple, and free, and they vigorously keep this healthy condition. For just as the winnowers do with wheat, so our athletes do with their bodies, removing the chaff and the husks and leaving the grain in a clean pile.

26   Through training like this a man can't avoid being healthy and can stand up indefinitely under stress. Such a man would sweat only after some time, and he would seldom be seen to be ill. Suppose someone were to take two torches and throw one into the grain and the other into the straw and chaff—you see, I am returning to the figure of the winnower. The straw, I think, would burst into flames much more quickly, but the grain would burn slowly with no large flames blazing up nor would it burn all at once, but it would smoulder slowly and eventually it too would be burned.

Neither disease nor fatigue could easily attack and overcome such a body or easily defeat it. For it has good inner resources which defend it against attacks from outside, so as not to let them in, neither does it admit the sun or the cold to its hurt. To avoid yielding to hardships, great vigor springs up within, something prepared long in advance and held in reserve for time of need. This vigor fills up at once and waters the body in a crisis and makes it strong for a long time. For the previous training in bearing strain and hardship does not weaken their strength but increases it, and when you fan it the fire burns stronger.

27   We train them to run, getting them to endure long distances as well as speeding them up for swiftness in the sprints. This running is not done on a firm springy surface but in deep sand, where it is not easy to place one's foot forcefully and not to push off from it, since the foot slips against the yielding sand. We train them to jump over ditches, if they have to, or any other obstacles, and in addition we train them to do this even when they carry lead weights as large as they can hold. They also compete in the javelin throw for distance. In the gymnasium you also saw another athletic implement, bronze, circular, like a tiny shield with no bar or straps. You handled it as it lay there and expressed the view that it was heavy and hard to hold on to because it was so smooth. Well, they throw this up in the air both high and out, competing to see who can throw the longest and pass beyond the others. This exercise strengthens the shoulders and builds up the arms and legs.

28   As for this mud and dust, which originally seemed so amusing to you, my

friend, listen while I tell you why it is used. First, their fall will not be on unyielding dirt but they will fall safely on soft ground. Next, their slipperiness has to be greater when they sweat in the mud. You likened them to eels, but the facts are neither useless nor humorous: it adds not a little to strength of the sinews when they are forced to hold firmly to people in this condition when they are trying to slip away. Do not think it is easy to pick up a sweaty man in the mud, covered with oil and trying to get out of your arms. All these skills, as I said earlier, are useful in combat, if it were necessary to pick up a wounded friend and carry him easily to safety or to seize an enemy and bring him back in your arms. And for this reason we train them beyond what is necessary, so that when they have practiced hard tasks they may do smaller ones with much greater facility.

We believe the dust is used for the opposite reason than the oil is, that   29
is, so that a competitor may not slip out of his opponent's grasp. For after they have been trained in the mud to hold fast to something which is escaping from them because of its slipperiness, they then practice escaping out of the arms of their opponent, no matter how impossibly firm they may be held. Furthermore when this dust is used liberally it checks the perspiration and makes their strength last longer and furnishes protection against harm from drafts which otherwise attack the body when the pores are open. Besides, the dust rubs off the accumulation of dirt and makes the skin gleam. I should dearly like to stand one of those white-skinned fellows who live in the shade beside one of our boys who work out in the Lykeion, and after I had washed off the dust and the mud, ask you which one you would like to resemble. For I know that you would choose at first glance, without hesitation, even without putting either through any tests, the one which is solid and hard rather than soft, weak, and pale, because what little blood he has has been withdrawn into the interior of his body.

[In 30–35, Anacharsis ridicules the idea that athletic training could be useful in war. Why not save your strength, he asks. Solon explains that strength cannot be saved like a bottle of wine; it must be constantly used.]

Anarcharsis: I just don't understand what you said, Solon. It is too intel-   36
lectual for me and requires a sharp mind and keen insight. But above all, tell me this, why, in the Olympic Games and at Isthmia and Delphi and elsewhere, where so many competitors, you say, assemble to see these young men compete, you never have a contest with weapons but you bring them before the spectators all naked and exhibit them getting kicked and punched, and then, if they have won, give them berries and wild olives? It would be worth knowing why you do this.

Solon: My dear Anacharsis, we do this because we think that their enthusiasm for athletics will increase if they see that those who excel at them are honored and are presented to crowds of Greeks by heralds. Because they are to appear stripped before so many people, they try to get into good condition, so that when they are naked they will not be ashamed, and each one works to make himself capable of winning. As for the prizes, as I said earlier, they are not insignificant: to be praised by the spectators, to be a recognized celebrity, and to be pointed out as the best of one's group. As a result of these prizes, many of the spectators who are of the right age for competition go away completely in love with courage and struggle. If someone should remove love of glory from our lives, what good would we ever achieve, Anacharsis, or who would strive to accomplish some shining deed? But now it is possible for you to imagine from these games what sort of men these would be under arms, fighting for fatherland and children and wives and temples, when they show so much desire for victory in competing for laurel berries and wild olives.

37   Furthermore, how would you feel if you should observe fights between quails and between roosters here among us, and see the great interest which is shown in them? Wouldn't you laugh, particularly if you should learn that we do this in accordance with our laws and all men of military age are instructed to be present and to see these birds fight until they are exhausted? But it is no laughing matter, for eagerness for danger creeps insensibly into their souls so that they try not to seem less courageous and bold than the roosters nor to give in too soon because of injury or fatigue or any other distress.

As for trying them in armed combat and seeing them receive wounds—never! It is brutal and dreadfully wrong, and in addition it is economically unfeasible to destroy the bravest, whom we could better use against our enemies.

38   Since you tell me, Anacharsis, that you expect to travel to the rest of Greece, if you get to Sparta, remember not to laugh at them nor think that they have no purpose when they compete in a theater, rushing together and striking each other, fighting over a ball, or when they go into a place surrounded by water, choose up sides, and fight as if in actual war, although as naked as we Athenians are, until one team drives the other out of the enclosure into the water, the Sons of Herakles beating the Sons of Lykurgos or vice versa; after this contest there is peace and no one would strike another. In particular, do not laugh if you see them being whipped at the altar, streaming with blood, with mothers and fathers standing by, not at all bothered by what is happening but on the contrary threatening them if they do not hold up under the blows, urging them to bear up under the pain as long as possible, and to be strong under this hideous treatment. To tell the truth, many have died in these contests, not thinking it manly to yield before the eyes of their friends and relatives while they are still alive, no, not even to flinch. You will see honors paid to statues of people like this erected at public expense by the state of Sparta.

[In 39 and in 40, Solon explains that he instituted the contests to improve courage. When Anacharsis asks why the Athenians do not introduce flogging, Solon replies that they do not care for foreign ways. Anacharsis says he thinks the people in Sparta are crazy, and he promises to tell Solon the next day how people in Scythia train their youth.]

(a)   In 1, 2, and 3, distinguish the different forms of athletics.
(b)   In 1, what seems to be one form of surrender? What contests were decided by surrender of one competitor?

(c) In 4, what do we call this form of calisthenics?

(d) In 8, what is meant by a "gymnasium"? How does it differ from a modern "gym"?

(e) List the kinds of crowns awarded at the Panhellenic Games.

(f) Do our athletes spend as much time on skin conditioning as the Greeks?

(g) What does Solon say repeatedly is the end purpose of athletics? Has this view ever been held in modern times? Do we have any strictly "military" games? American troops found the hand grenade a useful weapon. Why? Which of the common Greek athletic events had no military application?

(h) How much of Solon's view of conditioning is still held today? How about enduring thirst ("water discipline") in the army? With reference to 26, does a good athlete start to sweat early or late?

(i) In 27, is there evidence for any hurdle races? Was the javelin throw for distance, or accuracy, or both? Does Lucian think the *halteres* helped or hindered in the long jump? How sound is the technique of practicing running in sand? Does throwing the diskos develop the body as Lucian says?

(j) Consider the advantages and disadvantages of the use of dust, oil, and mud, as explained in 28 and 29. Try to think of practical reasons rather than such reasons as "clean" or "dirty."

(k) Does Lucian's idea of a good athlete seem similar to ours?

(l) In this dialogue is there any evidence for team sports?

(m) What arguments does Lucian have Solon give to justify the flogging at Sparta? How do these compare with his arguments for the Athenian style of training?

(n) Legislators are sometimes called "solons" by the press. What is the reference?

33

Greek Anthology

The *Greek Anthology* is a collection of epigrams (=short poems) in sixteen books, written in Greek. We have included only those written between V BC and V AD. Even so, this is a wide time span, 1000 years, and we must be cautious about our conclusions. A poem written in III AD may be poor evidence to support a statement in a poem written in V BC. The collection in its present form was collected in X AD, based mainly on three older anthologies. There is doubt about the authorship of some of the epigrams.

1

Three brothers dedicate to Pan these implements of their trade: Damis gives the net he uses for animals of the mountains; Kleitor gives this fishing net, and Pigres offers this net which does not tear and which entangles birds by their necks. Their home never saw them returning with empty nets, one hunting in the woods, the second in the air, and the third in the sea.

6.14, Antipater of Sidon

2

Visitor: "Who dedicated you, beardless Hermes, beside the husplexes?"
Hermes: Hermogenes did."
Visitor: "Whose son is he?"
Hermes: "Son of Daimenes."
Visitor: "Where did he come from?"
Hermes: "From Antioch."
Visitor: "Why did he pay you this honor?"
Hermes: "Because I helped him in the stade."
Visitor: "At what games?"
Hermes: "At Isthmia and Nemea."
Visitor: "He ran in those games?"
Hermes: "And came in first."

Visitor: "Whom did he defeat?"
Hermes: "Nine other boys, and he flew as if he had my feet."[1]

6.259, Philippos

(a) Where is the archeological evidence for the husplex?
(b) The stadium at Olympia had room for twenty runners. How many actually competed in the race mentioned above?

3

Nikis the African, son of Lysimachos, has dedicated his Cretan quiver and curved bow to you, Artemis. The arrows which filled the belly of the quiver he spent shooting at deer and spotted does.

6.326, Leonidas of Alexandria

(a) Is there any significance in the fact that the quiver is called "Cretan"?
(b) Where was Nikis' home?

4

When the great fleet of King Xerxes was routing all Greece,[2] Skyllis invented underwater warfare. Diving into the secret waters of Nereus he cut the anchor lines of Xerxes' ships. The Persian ships with all their crews drifted silently ashore and perished. This was the first deed of Themistokles.

9.296, Apollonides

(a) What kind of endurance should a swimmer have to cut underwater the cables of a significant number of ships?

5

Tlepolemos from Myra, son of Polykrites, set up a herm of Hermes as a starting point for the sacred races, a contest of 20 stades. Labor on, runners, get that soft laziness out of your legs!

9.319, Philoxenos

(a) For what specific race or races was this herm intended?
(b) How far is 20 stades?

6

The courage which you see, O stranger, in this bronze image of Kleitomachos is equal to the strength which all Greece saw. For as soon as he stripped the bloody boxing gloves from his hands, he fought in the fierce pankration. In the third event he did not get his shoulders in the dust but, wrestling without incurring a fall, won the triple victory at Isthmia. He was the only Greek to achieve this prize, and Thebes of the seven gates and his father Hermokrates were crowned with glory.

9.588, Alkaios (III BC)

(a) What was the order of the heavy events at Olympia before 212 BC? (See Pausanias 6.15.4–5.) What was the order changed to in 212 BC? What was the order in the Isthmian Games?

(b) What prizes did Hermokrates win?

(c) What was noteworthy about his win in the wrestling?

7

With a face like yours, Olympikos, do not go to a pool or look into reflecting water. For if you see your face clearly like Narcissos,[3] you will perish, and you will hate yourself until your death.

11.76, Lucillius

(a) Narcissos died because the image he saw in the water was so beautiful. How about Olympikos?

8

When Odysseus returned safely to his home after 20 years, only his dog Argos recognized him when he saw him. But you, Stratophon, after you have boxed for four hours, neither dogs nor your fellow citizens can recognize. If you will be so kind as to view your face in a mirror, you will affirm with an oath, "I am not Stratophon."

11.77, Lucillius

(a) Allowing for exaggeration, what do we learn from this epigram about the length of a boxing contest? About the physical damage?

9

This statue of the boxer Apis was set up in gratitude by his competitors. For he never injured any of them.

11.80, Lucillius

(a) In the *Victor List* of Julius Africanus, it is noted under the year 240 BC that a boxer completed the circuit games *atraumatistos*, "without being injured." What did he have in common with Apis?

(b) This comic epigram imitates serious ones. Where is the difference? What reason do we think will be given for this honor to Apis?

10

Charmes, competing in the dolichos in Arkadia with five others, finished seventh, strange to say, but true. "Since there were six runners," you will perhaps say, "how could he finish seventh?" A friend of his came by wrapped in his cloak and shouted, "Go, Charmes, go!" And so Charmes finished seventh. If he had five friends more, Zoilus, he would have been number twelve.

11.82, Nikarchos

11

Whether Perikles ran the stade or sat out the stade, no one knows. He was a miracle of slowness. While the noise of the husplex was still in our ears, a competitor was receiving the crown, and Perikles had not advanced a finger's breadth to the goal.

11.86, Anonymous

(a) What information does this give us about the construction of the husplex?

12

Onesimos the wrestler, Hylas the pentathlete, and Menekles the sprinter came to the soothsayer Olympos, wanting to know which of them would win their event. The fortune teller, after inspecting the animal which had been sacrificed, replied, "You are all going to win, unless someone surpasses *you,* or throws *you,* or runs past *you.*

11.163, Lucillius

(a) The fortune-teller says that these three will all win, unless what happens?

13

Yesterday I dined with Demetrios the trainer,[4] most blessed of all mortals. One athlete lay in his lap, another hung over his shoulder, the third brought him his supper, and the last served him with his drink, a handsome set of four. Jokingly I said to him, "And do you, my friend, massage the boys at night?"

12.34, Automedon

14

I am not a wrestler from Messene or Argos. Sparta, land of men, Sparta is my home. The others know the tricks of wrestling, but I, as is fitting for Spartan boys, win by strength.

16.1, Damagetos

(a) What does this show us about the "Spartan mentality"?

15

Diophon son of Philon won at Isthmia and Delphi in jumping, speed of foot, javelin, diskos, and wrestling.

16.3, Semonides

(a) What information does this give us about the order of the pentathlon events? Before answering, reflect that these epigrams are written in verse.

16

This is a beautiful statue of beautiful Milo, who won seven times at Olympia and never fell to his knees.

16.24, Semonides

(a) This is sometimes quoted to show that to have one knee touch the ground constituted a fall. Comment. (Note that the plural "knees" is used.)

17

If you ever heard of Demostratos from Sinope, you are looking at him now, the man who six times won the wreath of pine at Isthmia. His back never left its print in the sand from a fall in the twisting and turning wrestling match. Look at his face as full of desire to attack as a wild animal's; see how he maintains his old desire for victory. The bronze statue says, "If I

could be freed from my base, I would dust myself like a living man for
victory number seven."

16.25, Philippos

(a) What type of fall is referred to here?

Further Readings

The Greek Anthology is available in translation in five volumes in the *Loeb Classical
Library*.

Notes

Chapter 1

1. We thus omit the questions of athletics in earlier periods, such as ancient Egypt, Crete, and the Minoan civilization, and their possible influence on Greek athletes.
2. For an evaluation of Coubertin, see *The Olympic Games* by Lord Killanin and John Rodda, particularly the chapter "The Founder of the Modern Games," and *The Myth of Greek Amateur Athletics* by David C. Young.

Chapter 2

1. An unknown weight.
2. Meaning not clear.
3. "Solid hoofed," said of horses to contrast them with oxen, which are cloven hoofed.
4. The immediate purpose of the Trojan War was to recover Helen, wife of Menelaos.
5. This implement, called the *solos,* is described as "formless," which does not suggest a flat diskos. However, the act of hurling seems to be like throwing the diskos and not like putting the shot.

Chapter 3

1. *Bulletin de correspondance hellenique,* Suppl IV (1977).
2. Stephen G. Miller, "Turns and Lanes in the Ancient Stadium," *American Journal of Archaeology* 84 (1980), pp 159–166.

Chapter 8

1. *Akoniti* means "without dust," but in Greek sport it has several meanings, as will be explained in Chapter 9. We can be sure, since Akmatides put it in the inscription, that it was creditable to him.

Chapter 11

1. But apparently not in the Olympic Games, since an Olympic victory would surely be mentioned.

2. All slain at Troy.
3. He and his brother were sons of Zeus.
4. Polydeukes is here called by his patronymic, "son of Tyndaris," although he was actually the son of Zeus.
5. One of the giants who fought with the gods.

Chapter 12

1. From Franz Mezö, *Geschichte der Olympischen Spiele* (Munich 1930), pp 100–101; translation by Ludwig Drees, *Olympia: Gods, Artists, and Athletes* (New York 1968), p 83.
2. The brutish adversary of Theagenes is black, but this does not mean that color prejudice is present in this novel. The black king Hydaspes is treated sympathetically, and Theagenes has fallen in love with the king's daughter Charikleia.
3. Hydaspes says here specifically that Theagenes will wrestle, but the match that follows is rather different from classic wrestling. It is in fact more like the pankration.
4. According to Ethiopian custom, Hydaspes is required, much against his will, to sacrifice the stranger.
5. That is, experienced in sports.

Chapter 13

1. See W.S. Ferguson, *Hellenistic Athens* (London 1911), p 293.

Chapter 17

1. An open space surrounded by a colonnade.
2. Porticoes with curved benches. The letters refer to the accompanying diagram.
3. Sweating room like a modern sauna.
4. In a portion of *Vitruvius* not given here.
5. See the diagram. The fourth side is the stadium.
6. In ancient Greece marriages were arranged by the parents. There were no boy–girl romantic relationships, at least not in the upper classes. There was a class of women called *hetairai*, which means "companions." These girls were given an education, particularly in singing and dancing. Although sex was usually included in the activities they were expected to perform, it would be a mistake to equate hetairai with prostitutes. Some of them became quite wealthy.

Chapter 19

1. In Athens a year was dated by the name of the archon (= official) of that year.

Chapter 20

1. Lightly armed soldiers, less heavily armed than the hoplites, having sword, spear, and a light shield, whereas the hoplites had helmet, breastplate, greaves, and a heavy shield plus sword and spear.

Chapter 21

1. Probably these terms have technical meanings.
2. Meaning not clear.

3. Evidence that the rulers occasionally interfered with the contest, as did Achilleus in the chariot race in the *Iliad*.
4. This may mean that the officials had the power to stop a fight in case of a foul, and start it again.
5. Does this mean some competitors were excused?
6. "Stopped" seems to have been a technical term meaning that his opponents all withdrew from the contest because they knew they could not defeat him.
7. Not the Olympic Games held at Olympia.
8. Games at which the prizes were money.
9. A puzzling bit of information. Why does he say "in the same year," since the games only took a few days? One suggestion (Moretti IAG, p 153) is that while the stade and diaulos were part of the standard Nemean Games, the hoplitodromos was run in a separate contest during the winter. Supporting this view is Pausanias 2.15.3: "The people from Argos hold a contest for armed men during the winter festival at Nemea."
10. The inscription is badly damaged, and the meaning is not certain.
11. The emperor is believed by some scholars to have been the notorious Caracalla, and the date is thought to have been 215 AD.
12. The meaning of the favor is not clear; perhaps they had not qualified.
13. The Greek idiom is remarkably similar to this English expression, if the reading is correct.
14. The *aureus* was a Roman gold coin worth 25 *denarii*. The denarius, about the size of a dime, was a minimum day's wage. This prize of 100 aurei was therefore equivalent to 2500 working days.
15. This may be a slang term for "showed them up."
16. Choiak was the Egyptian month that fell on 27 November to 25 December. The month of Mechir, when Dios hoped to see his sister, was 26 January to 24 February.

Chapter 22

1. The distance from Athens to Olympia is 213 miles on a flat route along the shore of the Gulf of Corinth. A shorter route through the mountains appears to be about 190 miles.
2. A talent was a weight of gold worth 3000 darics; a daric was a coin containing $100 worth of gold. A talent contained $300,000 worth of gold. The prize for the first man to reach the top was therefore $3,600,000, but the purchasing power of gold then was much higher than today.

Chapter 24

1. Made from the berries of the mistletoe.
2. Xenophon explains elsewhere that the trap was fastened to a wooden clog about 2 feet long and 3 inches thick.
3. This refers to the use of flint for lighting lanterns.
4. The slinger grasped the free end of a 4-foot-long staff with both hands, in order to swing the missile in the pouch at the other end.

Chapter 29

1. Date 476 BC. The city of Western Lokroi was in southern Italy. It was a Greek city, not Roman or Italian. We are told this poem was unusual in being composed at Olympia immediately after the victory.
2. Date 486 BC. Like the preceding ode, this is much shorter than most Epinikian odes,

which are usually about 100 lines long. The typical ode, furthermore, usually has a myth at its center.

3. The Alkmanidai were a famous Athenian family. The man for whom this ode was written, Megakles, was the great-grandson of Alkmaeon, from whom the family took its name. In 548 BC the family agreed to repair the temple of Apollo at Delphi and acquired great renown by doing it in a much more lavish manner than promised.
4. The port that served as entrance to Delphi.
5. Megakles had been ostracized (=exiled) by the Athenians only a few months before his victory.

Chapter 30

1. If you make a fist, you will see that the thumb projects beyond the knuckles. With the sharp glove, however, the fingers are inserted into a band of leather, which causes the fingers to move ahead of the thumb. The thickness of the leather means that the thumb cannot now be used as a poking weapon in a "thumb stab."
2. Gaining victory by luck of the draw or by default. The Greek word is *akoniti* (see Chapters 8 and 9). Contrary to Philostratos, it was considered honorable if one's opponents forfeited because they were sure of being beaten.
3. The Olympic Games were held at the time of the full moon, and the date varied from August 6 to September 19.
4. According to Pausanias 6.24.1, the training was carried on in the city of Elis; the coaches worked with the runners in the morning, and with the pentathletes and heavy athletes in the afternoon.
5. Philostratos seems to have made an error here. Pausanias 5.8.9 and the *Victor List* of Julius Africanus say that the boys' stade was introduced in the 37th Olympics (632 BC) and that Polyneikes of Elis won.
6. Ancient medicine taught that ill health was often the result of a wrong proportion of four liquids or "humors," namely blood, phlegm, black bile, and yellow bile.
7. Prometheus was a mythological figure said to have fashioned men out of mud and then stolen fire from heaven to give them.
8. A curved implement used by ancient Greeks and Romans to scrape off oil, perspiration, and dust.
9. An unknown tree similar to the olive.
10. The pankratiasts often practice in mud; because the combatants could not get a firm stance in mud, the chance of injury was small. Mud was also supposed to have a beneficial effect on the skin. See also the discussion in Chapter 32.
11. The Greek word for "jump" is *halma*.
12. The most reasonable interpretation is that if the contestant falls back or sideways, the jump is not measured.
13. Through the *aether,* from which we get the word "ether." The Greeks believed that the *aether* was a rarified form of air, quite different from the air we breathe, possessing various desirable qualities.

Chapter 31

1. An oracle had said that the child Opheltes should have to learn to walk before he touched the ground.
2. The Nemean Games were not always held at Nemea. The city of Argos moved them to their own city. It is possible that by the word *Heraia* (=festival of Hera) Pausanias meant games for women, since this is the name for the girls' games at Olympia.

3. Mother of Zeus; she had to protect Zeus because her husband Kronos devoured all their children as soon as they were born, because an oracle had warned that he would be deposed by his son.

4. Not the Herakles who performed the twelve labors and was the son of Zeus and Alkmena.

5. The Greek (and Roman) way of counting sequences of numbers was different from ours. In our way of counting, if the Olympic Games are held in 1960 and then again in 1964, we describe this as "every fourth year." The Greeks and Romans on the other hand would have described it as "every fifth year," because they counted both ends of the sequence (1960, 1961, 1962, 1963, and 1964).

6. Because the famous Herakles supposedly lived a hundred years or so before the Trojan War, this account is an attempt to reconcile the antiquity of the games with the name of Herakles.

7. A district in Eleia, not to be confused with the Italian city with the leaning tower.

8. The manuscripts lack the words in angular brackets, but the sense is clear.

9. A "hero" was a demigod. Pelops came to Pisa (the district in which the Olympic Sanctuary was located) to marry Hippodameia, daughter of King Oinomaos. This king had said that he would give his daughter only to the man who could defeat him in a chariot race. If a suitor lost the race he would be put to death. Thirteen young men had already lost their lives in the attempt. Pelops bribed Myrtilos, the armorbearer of Oinomaos, to remove the linchpin from the king's chariot. In the race the chariot broke, Oinomaos was killed, and Pelops gained the victory.

10. To certify that they will compete in the right age group and meet other requirements.

11. Few victors could afford full-sized inscribed statues such as Pausanias is going to describe. Most offerings were small and inexpensive statuettes.

12. The system of elimination permitted a person to win without fighting, because all his competitors had eliminated each other or had withdrawn.

13. A "talent" is a sum of money varying in value in different areas, but always a large amount.

14. There is a gap in the manuscript; words in angular brackets are a guess but the sense is clear.

15. Marking the last lap.

16. If the stade run started at the east end, it would therefore finish at the west end. Since Pausanias speaks of a special start for the stade, we must assume that the other races started at the west end. The diaulos and the dolichos (if an even number of laps) would end at the line from which they started.

17. This whole hippodrome area has been so devastated by floods that not a trace remains. Furthermore, the account by Pausanias does not seem clear.

18. About 34 miles west of the Sanctuary of Olympia.

19. The Plethrion was so named because it was one *plethron* (= 100 feet) in length.

20. It is not clear whether these ephebes were competitors in the boy's events or not. It may be that the ephebes (that is, young men of military age) who were not competitors in the games were given a place to work out and keep in shape.

21. Quoted from Peter Levi's *Pausanias* (vol 2, p 471, footnote) about the town mentioned in the following selection.

22. After Apollo killed the Python, the snake god.

23. Perhaps people with physical defects were disqualified from competition.

24. A loose federation of small neighboring Greek states who usually met twice a year at Delphi.

25. The ancient laurel was a tree, whereas the modern American laurel is a shrub.

26. Pausanias leaves out an essential part of the story that all his contemporaries would

know: Apollo pursued Daphne (= laurel tree), who in answer to her prayers was turned by the gods into a laurel tree to escape his attention. Apollo then declared the laurel to be sacred to him.

27. At the battle of Salamis in 480 BC.
28. Herodes Atticus lived from 101 to 177 AD, and was a liberal benefactor of many Greek cities.

Chapter 33

1. Hermes, messenger of the gods, had winged sandals.
2. In his invasion of 480 BC.
3. A young man who fell in love with his reflection in the water and killed himself in frustration because he could not embrace the reflection.
4. The Greek word *paidotribes,* translated as "trainer," means "one who massages boy athletes"; in this poem it is used in a double sense.

Bibliography

Anderson, J.K., *Ancient Greek Horsemanship* (Berkeley 1961).

Arieti, A.J., "Nudity in Greek Athletics," *Classical World* 68 (1975), pp 431–436.

Bean, G.E., "Victory in the Pentathlon," *American Journal of Philology* 60 (1956), pp 361–368.

Broneer, O., "Balbis, Husplex, Kampter," *Isthmia* II (1973), pp 137–142.

────── "Starting Devices in Greek Stadia," *American Journal of Archaeology* 76 (1972), pp 205–206.

Brophy, R.H., "Deaths in the Panhellenic Games, Arrichion and Creugas," *American Journal of Philology* 99 (1978), pp 363–390.

Butler, A.J., *Sport in Classic Times* (Los Altos CA 1975), pp 34–35; 195–198.

Casson, L., *The Ancient Mariner* (New York 1959).

────── *Travel in the Ancient World* (Toronto 1974), pp 65–94.

Corpus Inscriptionum Graecarum (CIG) (Berlin 1828–1877).

Crowther, N.B., "Studies in Greek Athletics, Part I," *Classical World* 78 (1985), pp 498–558; "Part II," *Classical World* 79 (1985), pp 73–136.

────── "Weightlifting in Antiquity: Achievement and Training," *Greece and Rome* 24 (1977), pp 111–120.

Dittenberger, W., *Sylloge Inscriptionum Graecarum*, 3rd edition (Syll³) (Leipzig 1924).

Drees, L., *Olympia: Gods, Artists, and Athletes* (New York 1968).

Ebert, J., "Zum Pentathlon der Antike," *Saxon Academy* 56.1 (1963), pp 2–34. (In German)

Finley, M.I., and Pleket, H.W., *The Olympic Games: The First Thousand Years* (New York 1976).

Forbes, C.A., "Accidents and Fatalities in Greek Athletics," *Classical Studies in Honor of William Abbott Oldfather* (Urbana 1943), pp 50–59.

────── *Greek Physical Education* (New York and London 1929; reprinted 1970).

Forbes, R.J., *Studies in Ancient Technology* II (Leiden 1965).

Frost, K.T., "Greek Boxing," *Journal of Hellenic Studies* 26 (1906), pp 213–225.

Gardiner, E.N., *Athletics of the Ancient World* (AAW) (Oxford 1930; reprinted by Ares Press, Chicago).

────── *Greek Athletic Sports and Festivals* (GASF) (London 1910).

—————— "The Method of Deciding the Pentathlon," *Journal of Hellenic Studies* 23 (1903), pp 54–70.

—————— "Phaÿllos and his Record Jump," *Journal of Hellenic Studies* 24 (1904), pp 70–80.

Gardiner, E.N., and Pihkala, L., "The System of the Pentathlon," *Journal of Hellenic Studies* 45 (1925), pp 132–134.

The Greek Anthology (Loeb Classical Library), 5 volumes (London 1918).

Harper's Dictionary of Classical Literature and Antiquities (New York 1923).

Harris, H.A., *Greek Athletes and Athletics* (GAA) Indiana 1966).

—————— *Greek Athletics and the Jews* (Cardiff 1976).

—————— "An Olympic Epigram," *Greece and Rome* 7 (1960), pp 7–8.

—————— *Sport in Greece and Rome* (SpGR) (Ithaca 1972).

Inscriptiones Graecae (IG) (Berlin 1913–1940).

Killanin, Lord M. and Rodda, J., *The Olympic Games* (New York 1976).

Kyle, D., "Directions in Ancient Sport History," *Journal of Sport History* 10, no 1 (1983).

Lattimore, R., *Odes of Pindar* (Chicago 1947).

Lawler, L.B., *Dance in Ancient Greece* (London 1964).

Lee, H.M., "Modern Ultra-long Distance Running and Philippides' Run from Athens to Sparta," *Ancient World* 9 (1984), pp 107–113.

—————— "The TEPMA and the Javelin in Pindar," *Journal of Hellenic Studies* 96 (1976), pp 70–79.

Lefkowitz, M.R., and Fant, M.B., *Women's Life in Greece and Rome* (Baltimore 1982).

Lesky, A., *A History of Greek Literature* (New York 1966).

Levi, P., *Pausanias: Guide to Greece* (Penguin 1971).

Matthews, V.J., "The Hemerodromoi," *Classical World* 68 (1974), 161–167.

McLeod, W., "The Range of the Ancient Bow," *Phoenix* 19 (1965), pp 1–14.

Merkelbach, R., "Der Sieg im Pentathlon," *Zeitschrift für Papyrologie und Epigraphik* 11 (1973), pp 261–269.

Miller, S.G., *Arete* (Chicago 1979).

—————— "Turns and Lanes in the Ancient Stadium," *American Journal of Archaeology* 84 (1980), pp 159–166.

—————— "Tunnel Vision: The Nemean Games," *Archaeology* 33 (1980), pp 54–56.

Moretti, L., *Iscrizioni Agonistiche Greche* (IAG) (Rome 1953).

—————— *Olympionikai* (Mem. Scienze Morali 1957 ser. 8, vol 8, 2).

Morgan, M.H., *Vitruvius* (Cambridge 1926).

The Oxford Classical Dictionary (OCD) (Oxford 1970), 2nd edition.

Papalas, A., "The Development of Greek Boxing," *Ancient World* 9 (1984), pp 67–76.

Pease, A.S., "Notes on Mountain Climbing in Antiquity," *Appalachia* 132 (1961), pp 289–297.

Perlman, P., "Plato 833C–834D and the Bears of Brauron," *Greek, Roman, and Byzantine Studies* 24 (1983), pp 115–130.

Pleket, H.W., "Games, Prizes, Athletes and Ideology," *Arena* (=Stadion) 1.1, pp 49–89.

Poliakoff, M., "Jacob, Job, and Other Wrestlers," *Journal of Sport History* 11, no 2 (1984), pp 48–55.

—————— *Studies in the Terminology of the Greek Combat Sports* (Königstein 1982).

Pomeroy, S.B., *Goddesses, Whores, Wives, and Slaves* (New York 1975).

Robinson, R.S., *Sources for the History of Greek Athletics* (Urbana 1955; reprinted by Ares Press, Chicago).

Romano, D.G., "The Ancient Stadium: Athletes and Arete," *Ancient World* 7 (1983), pp 9–16.

Rousing, G., *The Bow* (Bonn, Lund 1967).

Sanders H.A., "Swimming among the Greeks and Romans," *Classical Journal* 20 (1924), pp 566–568.

Scanlon, T.F., *Greek and Roman Athletics: A Bibliography* (Chicago 1984).

Segal, E., " 'To Win or Die': A Taxonomy of Sporting Attitudes," *Journal of Sport History* 11 (1984), pp 25–31.

Smallwood, E.M., "The Legislation of Hadrian and Antoninus Pius against Circumcision," *Latomus* 18 (1959), pp 334–347.

Snodgrass, A.M., *Arms and Armour of the Greeks* (Ithaca 1967).

Spears, B., "A Perspective of the History of Women's Sport in Ancient Greece," *Journal of Sport History* 11 (1984), pp 32–47.

Sweet, W.E., "A New Proposal for Scoring the Greek Pentathlon," *Zeitschrift für Papyrologie und Epigraphik* 50 (1983) pp 287–290.

———— "Protection of the Genitals in Greek Athletics" *Ancient World* 11, nos 1 & 2 (1985), pp 43–52.

Todd, T., "A Legend in the Making," *Sports Illustrated,* 5 November 1979, pp 414–454.

Vicker, M., *Greek Symposia* (London n.d.), published by Joint Association of Classical Teachers, 31–34 Gordon Square, London.

Wace, A.J.B., and Stubbings, F.H., *A Companion to Homer* (London 1963).

Whibley, L., editor, *A Companion to Greek Studies* 4th edition (Cambridge 1931).

Willcock, M.M., "The Funeral Games of Patroclus," *Bulletin of the Institute of Classical Studies* 20 (1973), pp 1–11.

Yalouris, N., editor, *The Eternal Olympics* (Athens 1979).

Young, D.C., *The Myth of Greek Amateur Athletics* (Chicago 1984).

———— "Professionalism in Archaic and Classical Greek Athletics," *Ancient World* 7 (1983), pp 45–51.

Index of Testimonia

The testimonia are all by Greek writers except where noted. Following the author's name and dates, the Arabic numerals indicate the chapter numbers and the testimonia within each chapter. After the entry for Alkaios, for example, 12.7 means "Chapter 12, Testimonium 7."

Africanus, Sextus Julius (II–III AD, historian), 1.1, 1.2, 6.6, 11.8, 11.9, 19.3
Alkaios (VII–VI BC, poet), 12.7
Ammonius (I–II AD, grammarian), 5.7
Anecdota Graeca, ed. I. Bekker (1814–1821), 3.12, 6.1
Anonymous, 2.1, 19.8, 33.11
Aristophanes (V–IV) BC, comic playwright), 19.15
Aristotle (IV BC, philosopher), 4.7, 6.5
Arrian (II AD, historian), 3.13, 22.7, 23.10
Artemidoros (II AD, writer on dreams), 12.2
Athenaeus (II–III AD, literary scholar), 18.8, 18.9, 20.11, 20.12, 27.2, 28.6, 28.7, 28.9

Bacchylides (V BC, poet), 7.1

Cicero (I BC, Latin writer and politician), 5.9
Cornelius Nepos (I BC, historian), 3.18, 28.12

Demosthenes (IV BC, orator), 28.11
didaskalia (brief comment on a play, author and date unknown), 27.5–27.7
Dikaiarchos (IV BC, geographer), 22.11
Dio Cassius (II–III AD, historian), 10.4
Dio Chrysostomos (I–II AD, orator), 11.13

Diogenes Laertius (III AD, biographer), 17.7, 17.8
Diogenianos (date unknown, collector of proverbs), 23.1
Dionysius of Halicarnassus (I BC, historian), 19.6

Epictetus (I–II AD, philosopher), 17.5, 18.4
Euripides (V BC, tragic playwright), 18.9, 20.9
Eustathius (XII AD, scholar), 3.2, 5.5, 11.5

Fronto (II AD, Latin philosopher), 5.10

Galen (II AD, physician), 14.1, 14.2, 17.9–17.12
Greek Anthology, 4.4, 5.12, 6.7, 10.1, 11.6, 12.7, 13.2, 24.8, 24.14, 24.25, 33.1–33.17

Heliodoros (III AD, novelist), 12.8
Herodotus (V BC, historian), 3.5, 8.3, 23.3
Historiae Augustae Scriptores, 19.16, 22.14
Homer (VIII BC?, epic poet and singer?), 2.2–2.4, 22.13, 24.7, 24.17–24.19, 25.1, 28.1–28.5
Horace (I BC, Latin poet), 27.3, 27.4

Illustration Credits

Cover Athlete with diskos. Museum of Fine Arts, Boston, H.L. Pierce Fund (00.338).

1. Stadium at Olympia. Photograph by author.
2. Stadium at Delphi. Photograph by author.
3. Panathenaic amphora. Metropolitan Museum of Art, New York, Rogers Fund 1914 (14.130.12).
4. Turning post. Martin von Wagner Museum, University of Wuerzburg, L328. Photograph by author.
5. Starting line. Photograph by author.
6. Starting gate. Photograph by author.
7. Race in armor. British Museum, London, K66551.
8. Relay race. Musée du Louvre, Paris, N3357.
9. Athletes with diskos and javelin. Staatliche Antikensammlungen und Glyptothek, Munich, 2637WAF.
10. Diskos-shaped gong. Daremberg-Saglio, *Dictionnaire des Antiquités.*
11. Diskos thrower. Staatliche Antikensammlungen und Glyptothek, Munich, 3012.
12. Long jump, takeoff. Museum of Fine Arts, Boston, H.L. Pierce Fund (01.8033). Photograph by author.
13. Long jump, "float." Museum of Fine Arts, Boston, H.L. Pierce Fund (01.8020).
14. Long jump, landing. Metropolitan Museum of Art, New York, Rogers Fund 1908 (08.258.30).
15. Athletes holding javelins. British Museum, London, B1346.
16. Javelin throw, cross step. Museo Archeologico Nazionale, Naples, 81516. Photograph by author.
17. Wrestlers starting bout. Staatliche Antikensammiungen und Glyptothek, Munich, 1455WAF. Photograph by author.
18. Wrestlers, side body lock. Fitzwilliam Museum, Cambridge, GR4-1954.
19. Wrestlers, flying mare. British Museum, London, E94b.
20. Dusting opponent before match. Museo di Villa Giulia, Rome, 50438. Photograph by author.
21. Officials marking ring. Museo Nazionale, Taranto, 115472. Photograph by author.
22. Boxer adjusting gloves. Ashmolean Museum, Oxford, 1914.729.
23. "Sharp gloves," detail. Museo delle Terme, Rome. Photograph by author.
24. Signal of surrender. British Museum, London, B271a.
25. Boxers' stance, artistic convention. Ashmolean Museum, Oxford 1914.729.
26. Boxer's stance, artistic convention. Vatican Museums, 9502-3 (H1016). Photograph by author.
27. Tripping in pankration. Staatiche Antikensammiungen und Glyptothek, Munich, 1541 WAF.
28. Foul in pankration. British Museum, London, E78.
29. Foul in pankration. British Museum, London, B610.
30. Horseback riders. British Museum, London, B133b.
31. Four-horse chariot. British Museum, London, B606.
32. Two-horse chariot. British Museum, London, 1928 15-19-1.
33. Piggyback ball game. British Museum, London, B182a.
34. Dribbling a ball. Ashmolean Museum, Oxford, 1970.6.
35. Field hockey. National Museum, Athens. Photograph by author.
36. Team ball game. National Museum, Athens. Photograph by author.

37. Weight training. Martin von Wagner Museum, University of Wuerzburg, L.476. Photograph by K. Oehrlein.
38. Hoop rolling. Ashmolean Museum, Oxford, 1886.587.
39. Juggling. Metropolitan Museum of Art, New York, Rogers Fund 1941 (41.162.147).
40. Yo-yo. Antikenmuseum Staatliche Museen, Preussischer Kulturbesitz, Berlin, F2539.
41. Palestra scene. Antikenmuseum Staatliche Museen, Preussischer Kulturbesitz, Berlin, F2180.
42. Use of athletic supporter. Martin von Wagner Museum, University of Wuerzburg, L.328. Photograph by author.
43. Palestra scene. Reverse side of vase shown in Plate 41.
44. Revelers. British Museum, London, E54.
45. Man and woman wrestling. Antikenmuseum Staatliche Museen, Preussischer Kulturbesitz, Berlin, F1837.
46. Girl runner. British Museum, London, 208.
47. Male and female athletes. Museo di Villa Giulia, Rome, 48239. Photograph by author.
48. Girl in track clothes. Musée du Louvre, Paris, CA2259.
49. Girls swimming and diving. Musée du Louvre, Paris, F203.
50. Youth diving. Staatliche Antikensammlungen und Glyptothek, Munich, 10.
51. Girls swimming and diving. Museo di Villa Giulia, Rome, 38. Photograph by author.
52. Sailing vessel. Staatliche Antikensammlungen und Glyptothek, Munich, 8729.
53. Beaching boat. British Museum, London, B508.
54. Victorious rowers. Museo della Città Romana, Rome; original in National Museum, Athens. Photograph by author.
55. Accident in harbor. Museo della Città Romana, Rome; original in Ny-Carlsberg Glyptothek, Copenhagen. Photograph by author.
56. Successful hunter. British Museum, London, B421.
57. Fishing from rock. Museum of Fine Arts, Boston, H. L. Pierce Fund (01.8024).
58. Fishing from boat. Tomb of Hunting and Fishing, Tarquinia.
59. Scythian bow. Musei Capitolini, Rome, Photograph by Barbara Malter.
60. Doubly convex bow. Musée du Louvre, Paris, G341.
61. Strolling musician. British Museum, London, E315.
62. Youth playing cithara. Metropolitan Museum of Art, New York, Fletcher Fund 1956 (56.171.38).
63. Young man playing diaulos. British Museum, London, E38.
64. Dancer in long gown. British Museum, London, D11.
65. Topless dancer. Staatliche Museen zu Berlin, Antiken-Sammlung, Berlin, 7092.
66. Women running or dancing. Vatican Museums, 14959 (H4887). Photograph by author.
67. Wild dance. Musée du Louvre, Paris, G58.
68. Bird dance. British Museum, London, 97 7-27-2.
69. Dancing lesson. Staatliche Museen zu Berlin, Antiken-Sammlung, Berlin, F2400.
70. Theater at Athens. Photograph by author.
71. Theater at Delphi. Photograph by author.
72. Theater at Epidauros. Photograph by author.
73. Comic and tragic masks. Museo delle Terme, Rome.
74. Comic actor wearing mask. British Museum, London, B226.
75. Symposium. Museo Archeologico Nazionale, Naples, 281. Photograph by author.
76. Wild party. British Museum, London, E71a.
77. Preparing game of kottabos. British Museum, London, F275a.
78. Guest playing kottabos. Metropolitan Museum of Art, New York. Gift of Ernest Brummer, 1957 (57.12.21).
79. Hetaira at symposium. British Museum, London, E68a.
80. Sacrifice to Herakles. British Museum, London, E505a.

Index and Glossary

Achaians: synonym for Greeks, 16

Achilleus: outstanding Greek warrior in *Iliad*, 11, 13

Aias: Greek warrior and participant in funeral games for Patroklos, 22

Akoniti: technical term meaning "without dust," 56 *n,* 62, 216 *n*

Altis: sacred precinct at Olympia, 238

Amphora: common storage vase for oil, wine, or grain, 8, Plates 45, 49. *See also* Panathenaic Games

Antilochos: contestant in Homeric chariot race, 13–21

Aphrodite: goddess of love and beauty, 187

Apollo: patron god of archery, Plate 60; of athletics, 252

Archery: in Homer, 25; types of bows and techniques of shooting, 175–81, Plates 58–60, 232

Archon: one of ten officials governing Athens, 128 *n*

Aretē: excellence, 135

Argives: synonym for Greeks, 16

Argos. *See* Nemean Games

Arkadia: synonym for Olympia, 217

Armor, 6; in Homer, 24

Arrichion: *pankratiast,* 84–85, 221, 247–48

Artemis: virgin goddess of hunt, and sister of Apollo, 177, Plate 60

Asclepiades: *pankratiast,* 146–47

Atalanta: mythological girl known for athletic prowess, 134, Plates 45, 48

Athene: goddess of arts and science, and patron goddess of Athens, 15

Athletics: attitudes toward, 118–23; desire to win, 118–19; moderation, 119; professionalism, 119–21; adverse criticism, 121–22

Atraumatistos: "without injury," said of boxers, 71, 260

Aulos: wind instrument, 184–85, Plates 61, 63; used with long jump, 50–51, Plate 14

Balbis: starting line in race, 28, Plate 5; area from which *diskos* was thrown, 41

Balkline: line over which *diskos* thrower may not step, 52–53

Ball playing, 96–103, Plates 33–36; evaluation by Galen, 96–100, 102

Bater: takeoff board in long jump, 46, Plate 12

Biga: two-horse racing chariot, 91, Plate 32

Black figure vase: style in which figures were represented by black paint, and background by red clay of vase, Plates 14, 45, 52

Boating, 163–64, 166–68, Plates 52–55

Boxing: combat sport, 4; in Homer, 21–22, 68–80, Plates 21–26; gloves, 68–71, 216; injuries, 69, 71; surrender, 72; visit of Dio Chrysostomos to games, 73–77; bout of Polydeukes, 77–80; punching bag, 229

Bribery, 223–24, 239–40

Chariot racing: in Homer, 13–21; in Sophocles, 92–94. *See also Biga;* Damonon of Sparta; Horse racing; *Quadriga*

Cheating. *See* Bribery

Choregos: producer of plays, 195

STEPHEN J. CHAMBERS M.A.
15 BEACONSFIELD AVENUE
COLCHESTER
ESSEX CO3 3DH
TELEPHONE: (0206) 41796